Dads
for
Daughters

Dads *for* Daughters

How Fathers Can Give Their Daughters a Better, Brighter, Fairer Future

MICHELLE TRAVIS

CORAL GABLES

Dads for Daughters: How Fathers Can Give Their Daughters a Better, Brighter, Fairer Future

Published by Mango Publishing,
a division of Mango Media Inc.

Cover and Layout Design: Jermaine Lau

For permission requests, please contact the publisher at:

Mango Publishing Group
2850 Douglas Road, 2nd Floor
Coral Gables, FL 33134 USA
info@mango.bz

For special orders, quantity sales, course adoptions and corporate sales, please email the publisher at sales@mango.bz. For trade and wholesale sales, please contact Ingram Publisher Services at customer.service@ingramcontent.com or +1.800.509.4887.

Library of Congress Cataloging
ISBN: (p) 978-1-64250-132-2 (e) 978-1-64250-133-9

BISAC: FAM020000—FAMILY & RELATIONSHIPS / Parenting / Fatherhood

LCCN: 2019948622

Printed in the United States of America

For my husband **Richard**
and for my daughters, **Jordan** and **Alex**,
who inspire me every day.

Table of Contents

INTRODUCTION

Calling Dads of Daughters to Step Up for Gender Equality

For decades, women have been breaking down barriers, cracking the glass ceiling, and proving and reproving themselves. Women have heeded expert advice to negotiate harder, be more confident, and take greater risks. Most recently, women have embraced Facebook COO Sheryl Sandberg's call to "lean in" to their careers with ambition and fearlessness. But despite all of this effort and tenacity, our next generation of girls is still growing up in a profoundly unequal world.

Standing on the shoulders of so many women who have leaned in before them, today's women have made remarkable progress, so it's easy to believe that gender inequality is a thing of the past. In the US, women have entered the workforce in record numbers and are the sole or primary earners in forty-two percent of families. Women have become CEOs, Supreme Court Justices, political leaders, military commanders, astronauts, sports stars, and entrepreneurs. We even came close to having our first woman president.

But behind the success stories are numbers that reveal the barriers that women still face. At Fortune 1000 companies, women fill less than seven percent of CEO positions and less than twenty-one percent of all board seats. Only a quarter of all colleges and universities are headed by women, although more women hold college degrees than men. Even with the unprecedented success of women candidates in the 2018 midterm elections, women fill just twenty-three percent of all Congressional seats. Only four women have ever sat on the Supreme Court, and women make up only a third of all federal court judges. Women also remain under-represented in STEM education and jobs, particularly in computer science and engineering. To top it off, more than fifty years after the Equal Pay Act became law, women still earn about eighty cents per dollar compared to men in virtually every domain.

As bad as things are for women at the top, it's even worse for women and girls at the bottom. In the wealthiest country in the world, one in eight women live in poverty, a rate that's thirty-five percent higher than for men. While women make up nearly half of the American workforce, they account for sixty percent of the nation's lowest-paid workers. Single mothers, women with disabilities, and elderly women disproportionately fill the ranks of America's poorest citizens. On every measure of economic and social wellbeing, women and girls of color are even farther behind. Around a quarter of African American and Latina women are poor, and girls of color are more likely to live in poverty than any other children.

The depth of gender inequality from top to bottom became even clearer with the advent of #MeToo revelations. As thousands of brave women and men shared their experiences of sexual harassment and abuse, we realized how much further we still need to travel to achieve gender equality. While the movement appeared to spring from the Hollywood peaks, #MeToo actually started years ago when activist Tarana Burke coined the phrase to support women and girls of color, who face particularly high rates of sexual assault. At the same time that this seismic shift has strengthened women's voices, it has also raised challenging questions about future strategies for achieving equality. Many of us are asking, "What's next?"

While there's obviously no single response, there is an obvious fact that should inform our path forward: men still hold most of the positions of power within businesses, governments, and communities. That means that men still have a high degree of control over the resources that dictate the pace of women's progress. It took researchers at the World Bank writing a 458-page World Development Report to reach this unsurprising conclusion: achieving women's equality will ultimately require the commitment of men. "If you're going to change things," says Supreme Court Justice Ruth Bader Ginsburg, "you have to be with the people who hold the levers."

But how do we engage more men in gender equality efforts? And how do men who want to support girls and women get started? In response to these questions, researchers are discovering some heartening news. There is already a group of men who are becoming particularly interested in women's equality and showing a willingness to join the battle. These men are uniquely positioned to recognize their stake in the ultimate outcome. These men are dads of daughters.

Researchers have found that having a daughter tends to decrease men's support of traditional gender roles and increase their support for antidiscrimination laws, equal pay policies, and reproductive rights. As a result, dads of daughters are more likely than other male leaders to champion gender diversity in their companies and communities. A recent study of male CEOs, for example, found that the majority were just "bystanders" on gender equality issues—men who didn't actively support or resist women's advancement initiatives. The few CEOs who stood out as vocal women's advocates, however, were more likely to have a daughter who had faced sex discrimination herself.

This research points the way forward to a new stage in the gender revolution. In the wake of the *Lean In* and #MeToo movements, women have an opportunity to find ready, willing, and able male allies, and dads of daughters have an opportunity to step up and engage fully in the quest for women's rights. As we all seek greater equality for our daughters, dedicated dads have the power to help make that world a reality.

For many men, having a daughter is a profoundly life-changing event. The father-daughter relationship can make men stronger and more vulnerable at the same time. Having a daughter can make men more compassionate, more protective, and more committed to being good partners, parents, and providers. There is something about the father-daughter bond that can unite men from all backgrounds and all walks of life.

This bond has inspired many dads to become more engaged parents to support their daughters' dreams. Dads want their daughters to be safe, happy, and successful. They want their daughters to be treated with respect, dignity, and fairness. Increasingly, they're encouraging their daughters to be outspoken, competitive, and ambitious. In a recent survey, dads rated strength and independence among the top qualities they hoped to instill in their daughters.

The investment that dads are making in their daughters is paying huge dividends. Involved dads raise girls who are more confident, have higher self-esteem, and have better mental health. Girls with supportive dads have stronger cognitive abilities, are more likely to stay in school, and achieve greater financial success. Involved dads also help daughters become more socially adept and enter healthier relationships with other men.

But what happens when a dad raises his daughter to believe she can do anything and then sends her into a world with unequal career opportunities, workplaces built by and for men, a massive gender pay gap, few female mentors in leadership positions, and deeply ingrained gender stereotypes? At a 2018 Women's Summit, Michelle Obama asked dads of daughters this very question. She asked them to think about their own workplaces, and about "the times you turn your head, you look the other way, the times you're sitting at a table where there are no people of color, no women." "If you're tolerating that," she said, "that's the workplace that is going to be waiting for your little girl. You've sold her a bill of goods! You told her she could be anything, but you're not working to make sure that can be actualized."

Dads who are committed to seeing their daughters achieve their dreams have an opportunity to change the world that their daughters enter. If men want that world to be safe, fair, and welcoming, they can use their voices and influence to make a difference. Even without a conscious revolution, dads of daughters in leadership positions tend to exercise their power in ways that advance women's equality—often without being aware of it. CEOs who are dads of daughters, for example, have a smaller gender pay gap in their companies than in firms run by other men. Legislators who are dads of daughters are more supportive of laws protecting reproductive rights than are other male lawmakers. And judges who are dads of daughters have a more feminist voting pattern than other male judges in cases involving sex discrimination.

Imagine the impact that dads of daughters could have by actively joining the cause of making the world better for women and girls. Imagine the progress women could make by inviting all dads to participate. This book is a call to action to move beyond just imagining. It's a call for dads of daughters to come together and fuel the revolution, and it's a call for women to engage these dedicated men in the fight for women's rights. At the same time, this book is a celebration—it shows why dads of daughters are key leaders in moving gender equality forward. It's also a "how-to" by offering concrete ways that more dads of daughters can become dads *for* daughters, and by revealing what a difference that would make.

As a woman who's been asked to "lean in"—while juggling a full-time job and raising two daughters—I understand that this is no small request. Men are feeling the stress of work/family conflicts in increasing numbers, rivaling the experiences of women. Finding the time and the resources to become part of a gender equality revolution is easier said than done. While the #MeToo movement has grabbed our attention, it's also made men more afraid to mentor women out of concerns about possible missteps or misperceptions. Some men think that it's not their place to get involved, while others want to support women but lack role models for doing it effectively. It's hard to know where to start or what one individual can achieve when facing such a daunting task.

That's where *Dads for Daughters* can help. This book is written to encourage, inspire, and connect men who are ready to step up despite the challenges. The stories, research, and resources in this book provide strategies for supporting men to engage in gender equality efforts both big and small.

In this book, men will find a range of arenas where they can focus their energy and make a difference—from mentoring women to equalizing pay, from sports fields to science labs, from building empathy to combatting gender bias, from boardrooms to ballot boxes. To help men get started—and to help women recruit men to support gender equality efforts—this book shares advice and resources for taking action. In addition, this book shares the stories of dads of daughters who've already joined the fight. Their stories provide role models and reveal what even the most unlikely of male activists can achieve.

All of the men highlighted in this book share the common bond of being a dad to at least one daughter, and they've all credited their daughters for motivating them to focus on gender equality. A CEO who invested in female entrepreneurs within his company's supply chain. A lawyer who created part-time positions at his firm that still keep women on partnership track. A head coach who hired the NBA's first female assistant coach. A governor who broke from his party line to sign a bill expanding rights for sexual assault victims. A conservative Supreme Court Justice who left work early to pick up his daughter's kids from daycare so she could launch her career and who supported family leave laws as a result. A manager who got girls interested in technology by creating a comic book series featuring a female tech superhero. An engineer who provided computer skills training to support girls who've been victims of India's sex trafficking trade. A teacher, an Army colonel, a pipefitter, a firefighter, and a construction contractor who joined forces to battle for parity in girls' high school sports. All of these dads, and many others, were inspired to support gender equality because of their daughters.

But these dads can't do it on their own. They've shown what's possible, but they need other men to share the responsibility. Each dad has a different platform, a unique community to influence, and an individual impact to make. This book offers a path forward for other men who want to flex their empathy muscles on their daughters' behalf.

Of course, many men are powerful women's allies without having daughters in their lives, and *all* men have a stake in a gender-equal world. Gender equality isn't just good for women; it's also good for men. According to The World Bank's World Development Report, gender equality enhances national productivity, promotes the physical health and mental wellbeing of both women and men, and improves policy decision-making. Simply put, "gender equality is smart economics." John Gerezema, the CEO of a data analytics firm, has found that every type of organization—"from families to business to communities"—functions better when women have equal respect and responsibility. "As human beings, and as fathers of daughters, we believe that gender equality is a moral good in and of itself," says John.

So this book isn't intended to lessen the need for all men to understand the importance of gender equality. Nor does it assume that having a daughter is either a necessary or sufficient step toward that end. Not all girls and women have fathers in their lives, and not all men are in positions of power. This means that not every part of this book will speak to everyone. Some chapters are geared toward men seated in uniquely influential roles in their companies and communities. And some of the book's areas of focus, such as corporate leadership, workplace mentoring, and entrepreneurship, are unlikely to get at the most intractable inequalities for girls and women who live in poverty, who lack access to education and healthcare, and who face multiple sources of inequality including race or disability. But there are parts of this book that should speak to everyone, including chapters on building empathy, combating gender stereotypes, rethinking masculinity, and leveraging political power to advance women's health and economic security.

The magnitude of the task, however, doesn't mean that we shouldn't begin somewhere. *Dads for Daughters* is a starting point. It offers support and guidance for engaging a group of men who are uniquely motivated—and uniquely well-positioned—to pick up the baton and start running. Dads of daughters are strong recruits to support gender equality for several reasons. First, there is significant evidence that the father-daughter relationship is a powerful way for building men's empathy skills, increasing men's awareness of gender inequality, and motivating men to act. Many dads of daughters already want to get involved, but they're not sure what to do. Second, researchers have found that dads of daughters often have more credibility with other men when advocating for gender equality. Because men tend to listen to dads of daughters who talk about the importance of women's rights, that makes fathers particularly strong recruiters as well.

Inspiring dads of daughters to support women's equality doesn't diminish the monumental efforts that so many women have made to advance women's rights. To the contrary, it reveals a hidden contribution that girls and women can make in their role as daughters, and it charts a promising path forward for women to accelerate progress. In calling dads of daughters to step up and launch a new phase in the gender equality revolution, this book advances the larger goal of getting everyone to see their stake in a world that's just as committed to the lives of girls and women as it is to boys and men. Women and men are stronger working together. Together, we can support a happier, fairer, more successful future for all of our daughters to thrive.

CHAPTER 1

Building Pipelines to the Top

Despite rumors of its demise, the glass ceiling is alive and well. We're all familiar with Sheryl Sandberg, the COO of Facebook, who authored the bestselling book, *Lean In: Women, Work, and the Will to Lead*. And we can all name other impressive women who've leaned in all the way to the C-suite. Carly Fiorina was the first woman to lead a top-twenty company as the CEO of Hewlett-Packard. Meg Whitman served as the CEO of both Hewlett-Packard and eBay. Marissa Mayer even had a baby while she was the CEO of Yahoo! So how bad could things really be?

The leadership landscape is actually pretty bleak for women in the corporate world. Women make up almost half of the American workforce, but very few are making it into positions of power and influence. At Fortune 1000 companies, women fill fewer than seven percent of CEO positions, fewer than eight percent of COO positions, and fewer than nine percent of CFO positions. So for every Sheryl, Carly, Meg, and Marissa, there are hundreds of men filling the C-suites of America. At the current rate of change, it will take another hundred years to achieve gender equality in the executive echelons. Things aren't much different in Britain, where there are twice as many CEOs named John than all the women CEOs combined in the top hundred companies on the London Stock Exchange.

Even at the top, women are at the bottom. Higher ranked companies tend to be the least likely to hire women CEOs. In the Fortune 1000, women-led companies have an average ranking that's 480 places below the average ranking for companies lead by men. None of this can be blamed on lesser education. Although women run only a quarter of all colleges and universities in the US, women hold more college degrees than men and earn sixty percent of all master's degrees. Yet women's voices are still not being heard at the top.

This means that dads are sending their daughters into a business world with vastly unequal opportunities in leadership roles. At the same time, dads who are already leaders in the corporate world are far better positioned than women outsiders to change this reality. So as women continue to lean into their careers with skill and ambition, dads of daughters could accelerate progress by becoming inside allies and advocates. It's far more efficient for male leaders to build pipelines for women into leadership roles than it is for women to keep banging their heads on the glass ceiling until it finally shatters for good.

Dads of daughters have more to gain by advocating for women at their jobs than just increasing opportunities for their daughters, although that's a nice pay-off by itself. Gender diversity is also good for a company's bottom line. Having women well-represented in decision-making roles increases innovation and responsiveness to a diverse customer base. Research and development teams that include women are more creative and identify more novel solutions to technical problems. Gender diverse companies are also a less volatile stock investment, according to a study of 1,600 firms by Morgan Stanley.

Having women on a company's board of directors is particularly important for a company's long-term success. Directors are the elected representatives of the stockholders. Although we often hear about individuals in the C-suite, it's the directors who set management policy and make strategic decisions. This influential role is dominated by men. Currently, women fill less than twenty-one percent of all board seats at Fortune 1000 companies.

Dads of daughters who have taken a risk to support more women directors have discovered that it isn't a risk at all. Promoting women onto board seats benefits companies in a variety of ways. Boards of directors with women are better at problem-solving and decision-making. As a result, companies with the most women board members significantly outperform other companies on a range of financial measures, including return on equity, return on sales, and return on invested capital. A study by Credit Suisse Research Institute of nearly 2,400 large companies found that those with at least one woman board member outperformed those with all-male boards by twenty-six percent over a six-year period. Female board representation also helps companies be more responsive to customers. Women directors understand that women control about twenty trillion dollars of consumer spending worldwide, and they're often more focused on innovative ways to sell products and services to women.

According to executive coach Susan Bloch, having more women on a board of directors also makes a company more attractive to investors. Gender-diverse boards produce lower corporate debt and tend to avoid risky corporate decisions. Fortune 500 companies with the highest percentage of women on their boards are more likely to appear on Ethisphere Institute's list of the World's Most Ethical Companies. Having more women board members also translates into higher corporate social responsibility ratings, which boosts a company's reputation. But despite all of this evidence, many male board members still don't prioritize adding women to their team. "In the twenty-five years I've worked as an international business coach," says Susan, "I've witnessed business leaders suffer from the same blind spot—not enough women on their boards."

In addition to improving their companies' performance, men who advocate for more women on their boards of directors can also pay benefits forward to other women. A forty-three country study found that companies with a higher proportion of women board members also have more women in senior management positions and a smaller gender pay gap. The more women a company has on its board, the more likely the company is to hire women corporate officers in the future.

Even armed with this compelling data, building pipelines for women into leadership positions is challenging. Motivated by their daughters to take action, several dads have been experimenting with gender diversity initiatives in various industries, and their stories are a good place to start.

Women's Rise at Coca-Cola

Muhtar Kent arrived in the US from Turkey in 1978 with no job and a thousand dollars to his name. What he lacked in possessions, he made up with ambition. He had an uncle in New York City who kindly shared his home until Muhtar figured out how to build his own American dream. At the time, Muhtar's main objectives were paying rent, making his dad proud, and becoming a successful businessman. It took a few decades to add "become an outspoken feminist" to his list of life goals. But once he had a daughter, that became Muhtar's top priority.

Growing up the son of Necdet Kent, Muhtar had big shoes to fill. Necdet was born in Istanbul, and he became one of Turkey's most respected diplomats. During World War II, he risked his life to save dozens of Turkish Jews from the Nazis while he was stationed in France. Although he was awarded Turkey's Supreme Service Medal for his bravery, he never thought of himself as a hero. He believed in tolerance and hard work, and he was fiercely committed to his family.

Muhtar was born after the war in 1952, while Necdet was serving as the Turkish Consulate General in New York. Muhtar spent his youth abroad, attending high school in Turkey and studying economics and business administration in London. After returning to Turkey for required military service, Muhtar finally headed back to New York to start a business career.

It took only a few weeks working at a big city bank before Muhtar became bored and restless. He started scanning newspapers for something more exciting, and he came across an ad for jobs at the Coca-

Cola Company. Muhtar sent in his resume and was disappointed when he was only offered a position driving trucks. That still beat pushing papers in a bank cubicle, so he jumped at the opportunity. Muhtar spent the next nine months hauling Coca-Cola products around the country in a bright red truck. He'd wake up at 4:00 a.m. to arrive at supermarkets before they opened so he could stock shelves and build displays. It wasn't glamorous work, but Muhtar loved being on the front lines of a national retail market. He soaked in knowledge about distribution and marketing strategies, and he was an incredibly quick study.

Muhtar's work ethic was rewarded with a rapid string of promotions. By the early 1990s, he was overseeing operations in twenty-three countries as a Senior VP of Coca-Cola International. In 1999, he left Coca-Cola to become an executive at one of Europe's largest international beverage companies. He was so successful that Coca-Cola recruited him back as the President and COO of its North Asia, Eurasia, and Middle East Group. In 2008, Muhtar reached the pinnacle of the international business world when he was named Coca-Cola's CEO and Chair of Coca-Cola's board of directors.

During most of Muhtar's meteoric rise, he wasn't focused on women's equality or the role of women in business. But around the time that he took the leadership helm at Coca-Cola, his daughter, Selin, was graduating from college and forging her own way in the business world. When Muhtar saw the challenges that Selin faced as a woman trying to launch a business career, he began thinking differently about his leadership role. "I would like to see my daughter flourish professionally in a world that is more just and equitable for women," he said.

Motivated by his daughter, Muhtar took a hard look around his company. He noticed that his workforce didn't mirror the world—or even his own customers. Women are responsible for seven out of every ten purchases of Coca-Cola products, but there were very few women in top positions at his firm. Women held only thirteen percent of all senior leadership roles, and only two of Coca-Cola's fifteen board members were women. Women were also in short supply in the jobs that fed into leadership positions. Only twenty-eight percent of the jobs that were one tier below leadership were filled by women, and the company had no plan to fix the problem. Muhtar was frankly a little embarrassed. He decided to roll up his sleeves.

Inspired to create a company where he would feel comfortable hiring his own daughter, Muhtar launched a Global Women's Initiative to develop female talent and promote gender equality. To get started, he established a Women's Leadership Council and tasked it with setting metrics for increasing the number of women leaders at Coca-Cola. The Council had four goals: recruitment, development, advancement, and retention of women.

Muhtar knew that he had to hold his leadership team accountable for results. He credits his daughter for giving him the sense of urgency he needed to make progress. He didn't want his company's program to just pay "lip service" to feminism. So he identified women's leadership as its own priority instead of burying it in a general diversity campaign. He also set explicit goals for moving women into leadership positions. Most importantly, he told his managers that their performance reviews and future pay would be tied to whether they met the goals. "When we did that," says Muhtar, "everything started to change."

In less than four years, Muhtar increased women in Coca-Cola's management ranks from twenty-two to forty percent. Since Muhtar began his initiative, women have held leadership positions in Coca-Cola's finance, science and regulatory, quality control, and human resources departments. The company's Controller, Head of Mergers and Acquisitions, and Internal Audit executive positions have all been held by women, who have also lead operations in Europe and Turkey.

Muhtar also figured out the importance of having women board members. Despite doubling the number of women on his board in his first four years, Muhtar decided he wasn't going to be satisfied until at least half of his board members were women. To speed up the process, he advocated for setting director term limits to increase turnover and create more openings for women.

Setting term limits for board members was controversial, but Muhtar was willing to ruffle feathers to make progress on women's equality. Muhtar shares this characteristic with other dads of daughters, who are more likely than other male business leaders to champion gender diversity in their companies. A study of forty male CEOs in Australia found that the strongest women's advocates were more likely to have a daughter who had faced sex discrimination herself. "I could see the struggle that my daughter was going through," said one outspoken CEO, "so there was an emotional resonance."

While Muhtar's mission to expand women in leadership began with a desire to see a better world for his daughter, he quickly recognized that women were an untapped resource that could make Coca-Cola even more successful. Having women in Coca-Cola's leadership ranks kept the company more connected to its customers. Women control enough of the global spending to have an economic impact that is larger than the economies of the US, China, and India combined. So Muhtar also talked with his daughter often to make sure he didn't lose touch.

When Selin was twenty-eight and deciding where to take her own business career, Muhtar gave her some advice. "Follow your heart," he told her. "It's all about being passionate about what you do." Selin listened to her dad and became a successful jewelry designer in New York City. She sells her brand in boutiques in Los Angeles, London, Paris, and Tokyo, and she's making a big splash in the fashion world. Her work has been highlighted in *Vogue*, *Elle*, and *Harper's Bazaar* magazines, and her jewelry has been spotted on Jennifer Lawrence, Emma Watson, and Angelina Jolie. But just like her dad, Selin stays committed to her values, like making sure that her jewelry uses responsibly-sourced materials to reduce environmental impact. Selin names pieces from her jewelry collections after powerful women who have left a mark on their communities.

Although Muhtar stepped down as Coca-Cola's CEO in 2017, he's still the chair of Coca-Cola's board of directors and is working hard to see the company meet its gender diversity goals. He also serves on the board of directors for Catalyst, a nonprofit that advances women's workplace equality. During the 2016 presidential election, Muhtar was mentioned as a possible running mate for Hillary Clinton, so perhaps politics will be in his future as well.

Given all that he has learned from his daughter, Muhtar now proudly self-identifies as a feminist. "If you're a male and you're at the top," says Muhtar, "you have to be a feminist." When asked why, Muhtar gives two reasons. One is that gender diversity is good for economic and social progress. The other is that advancing women's equality is simply the right thing to do for the sake of our daughters.

Empowering Wonder Women

Jason Kilar is the dad of three daughters, and he's never hesitated to take what he calls "considered risks." Jason has become a proponent of gender equality in the entertainment industry, where he's an innovator in digital media and television distribution. "Life is an exercise in living with the certainty of uncertainty," he recently told the graduating students at the University of North Carolina at Chapel Hill, where he applauded the characteristics of hutzpah and moxie. He urged them not to let fear of uncertainty hold them back from pursuing their dreams, which is advice he's heeded well in his own career.

After graduating from college and earning his MBA at Harvard Business School, Jason took a risk with a little-known start-up in Seattle that was dabbling in the online distribution of books, music, and videos. Despite raised eyebrows from friends and family, Jason trusted his instincts and spent the next nine years rising to an executive position at what has become the world's largest internet-based retailer and a household name in e-commerce: Amazon.

In 2007, Jason took an even bigger risk by becoming the co-founder and CEO of a video on demand service known as Hulu. Although Hulu was a joint venture with several industry giants, including The Walt Disney Company, 21st Century Fox, and Comcast, it was eagerly panned as a doomed endeavor in its early days. Tech industry leaders referred to Hulu as "ClownCo," and they ran a digital counter on a website to track the number of days until its predicted demise. But Jason forged ahead with his own brand of thoughtful stubbornness, intent on reimagining how television is delivered. "We are crazy," Jason readily admitted of his Hulu team. "All entrepreneurs need to be."

While Jason was building Hulu—which became a highly successful venture despite its critics—he was also helping his wife Jamie raise four small children, including three daughters. Sadie is now a high-schooler, and Ivy and Ruby are middle-schoolers. Jason admits that having three daughters made him more aware of situations where girls or women aren't getting equal opportunities. It's as if having daughters made his "antennae much more sensitive," and now he sees both the overt and the inadvertent barriers that create an uneven playing field—things that he didn't pay much attention to before he had three girls. "It's fascinating that it took in my case having daughters to become naturally aware of this," he remarks, "and I think that our challenge is to figure out how we can have that sensitivity and awareness even if we don't have daughters."

Having daughters not only increased Jason's focus on gender equality, but also affected how he approached his leadership role in the entertainment industry. He found himself seeing everyday situations at work through the lens of his daughters, who've become ever-present in his analysis of the world. He'd find himself in a business meeting where women's views were under-valued, and he'd start thinking, "Things should work a little bit differently because of Ivy, or Ruby, or Sadie."

Jason has become more willing to speak up when he sees gender bias, and he looks for opportunities to work with people who are committed to empowering women in his industry. Sometimes he still finds himself sitting in boardrooms of entertainment and media companies where women are largely absent from the table, but he remains optimistic. He is particularly hopeful about progress that's being made on the industry's creative side.

Jason can't contain his enthusiasm when he talks about the 2017 blockbuster movie *Wonder Woman* as an example of women's forward momentum. The film stars the indomitable Gal Gadot, and it was directed by Patty Jenkins, the first female director of a live-action superhero studio film. *Wonder Woman* is one of Jason's favorite movies, both for its entertainment value and as a dad. "I've run into so many fathers who have daughters who just high-five each other when they talk about it," says Jason. He says they all rave about one scene in particular, where Wonder Woman leads the charge across a battlefield, dodging bullets as the men huddle behind her in a bunker.

The movie is remarkable because Hollywood almost never allows female directors to tell a story through the lens of a strong female character. But Jason believes that *Wonder Woman*'s resonance—and more importantly, its commercial success—will change things. *Wonder Woman* is not only the top money-making film ever directed by a woman, but it's also one of the top thirty highest-grossing films of all time in the US. "Make no mistake," says Jason, "whether you're a male or female studio head, you're going to do what commercially is going to lead to the greatest return." So Jason is thrilled that Patty Jenkins got a lucrative deal directing a sequel, and Hollywood is figuring out that it's actually good business to invest in strong female characters.

Jason knows that the entertainment industry has a lot of leverage in our society. It's not just one of our country's biggest exports, but its product can inspire, shift conversations, provide role models, and shape kids' minds. That's one of the reasons Jason wants to see more women in the boardrooms of media and entertainment companies.

Jason left Hulu in 2013 to tackle new challenges. He has since served on the Board of Directors of DreamWorks Animation and co-founded a subscription video service called Vessel. In thinking back on his career choices, Jason has some advice for his three daughters. "I hope that they never accept the world at face value, and instead listen to their inner voices about the way the world should be," says Jason. "That's when real change happens."

Change has been notoriously slow in the male-dominated gaming industry where Bill Hornbuckle has worked for nearly forty years. Bill is the President of MGM Resorts International, a hospitality company with hotels and casinos around the world. It wasn't until Bill's two daughters, Lindsey and Sara, became young adults that he started thinking deeply about equal opportunities for women. "I think about them excelling," Bill says, "and it now more than ever focuses me."

When his daughters were seeking jobs, Bill told them to choose employers based on their track record for promoting women. That advice got Bill looking harder at his own company, which he wanted to be a place where he'd be proud to have his daughters work. "I wouldn't be truthful in telling you I was feeling that a decade ago," he admits. Once Bill prioritized gender equality, he increased the women in MGM's management ranks to forty-three percent, and MGM Resorts was named a Top Corporation for Women's Business Enterprises in 2016.

Fred Paglia is another executive who's made the connection between being the dad of a daughter and being a women's ally in his workplace. Fred works in the foodservice industry, which is the second largest employing industry in the US. When he became the president of the North American division of Foodservice at Kraft Foods Group, he realized that his company wasn't a place where his own daughters would have equal opportunities to rise. "My girls are fourteen and twelve," he said at the time, "and to be genuine with you, I wake up every day and look into their eyes before I leave for work and try to make the path a little easier for them. What father wouldn't want to do that?"

Fred was savvy enough to know that he didn't actually know how to accomplish his goals. So he approached Fritzi Woods, who was the CEO of the Women's Foodservice Forum, to get advice. The Forum is an organization dedicated to advancing women into executive roles in the foodservice industry. Fritzi was so impressed by Fred that she invited him to join the Forum's board, and they became partners in expanding opportunities for women in their industry. Fritzi said that most of the progress she saw in her industry had been the result of male leaders like Fred—dads who are "hoping to pave the way for their young daughters."

How Dads Can Get Started

If you're the dad of a daughter and you're in an influential position in the corporate world, it's time to make the connection between your role as a dad and your role as a business leader. As a father, you can begin this journey by asking yourself if your workplace is a place where you'd want your daughter to work. Is it a place where your daughter would be welcomed, valued, and taken seriously? Is it a place where your daughter could thrive professionally with the same opportunities as men? Is it a place where your daughter could become a leader? If the answers to these questions are "no," then there's work to be done.

After taking Jason Kilar's advice and watching *Wonder Woman* (alongside your teen daughter, if you have one), the next step is establishing a concrete strategy for advancing women into leadership roles at your company. In general, a successful strategy requires setting specific goals, making the goals public to increase accountability, and linking the goals to managers' performance reviews and compensation. More specific strategies often depend on the existing workplace culture and particular industry—a lesson that Fred Paglia learned at Kraft Foods—which means seeking expert advice on how to establish an individualized women's leadership initiative at your firm.

An excellent resource is Jeffery Tobias Halter's book, *Why Women: The Leadership Imperative to Advancing Women and Engaging Men*. This book makes the business case for gender diversity in leadership roles, which can arm dads with ammunition to convince colleagues why they should care. The book also describes best practices of Fortune 500 companies that have established successful women's leadership strategies, so you don't have to re-invent the wheel. The LeanIn.org's *Women in the Workplace Guide* also provides action checklists to help establish hiring, evaluation, and performance practices to reduce gender biases that create hurdles for advancing women into leadership positions.

Dads of daughters can also find a wealth of information from Catalyst, which consults with companies to build workplaces that advance women into leadership roles. Catalyst has worked with more than 800 organizations to diagnose barriers to women's advancement, engage men as women's advocates, and create more inclusive workplace cultures. Catalyst also networks business leaders to share information about successful strategies.

One focus of Catalyst's work is diversifying companies' boards of directors. Catalyst offers business leaders a database of experienced women candidates for board positions. Business leaders can also find or refer women candidates for board positions on theBoardList.com, which includes over 2,000 qualified businesswomen. Created by Silicon Valley executive Sukhinder Singh Cassidy, theBoardList.com has helped place more than 100 women on boards of directors. The Catalyst Women on Board program also links highly qualified business women with male board members for a two-year mentoring program that positions women for board membership and executive opportunities.

Dads of daughters can also take advantage of Catalyst's MARC initiative, which stands for "Men Advocating Real Change." Dads can become MARC Leaders by participating in workshops or executive dialogue sessions to become effective women's advocates and break down barriers to women's advancement. Catalyst also offers tools for dads to set up MARC Teams at their companies. MARC Teams meet regularly to discuss gender diversity, using Catalyst guides on various topics, such as tips for eliminating bias from performance reviews.

Men in corporate leadership positions can also join the Catalyst CEO Champions for Change initiative. Members take either a corporate or a personal pledge to support women's advancement. Leaders who take the corporate pledge agree to share their gender diversity data with Catalyst to support research and accelerate progress.

Another step that dads of daughters in corporate leadership roles can take is to implement some variation of the National Football League's "Rooney Rule." Named after former Pittsburgh Steelers owner Dan Rooney, the rule requires NFL teams to interview a minority candidate for all head coaching and senior operations positions. Although the rule doesn't force teams to hire minority candidates, merely opening the door helped double the number of minority head coaches in the league.

Jason Kilar supports having a similar rule for female candidates in high-level positions in the entertainment industry. "Just getting women in the room," he explains, "could go a long way toward disrupting the biased hiring practices that have historically favored men." Checkr, a leader in employee background screening services, recently adopted a "Rooney Rule Plus," which requires managers to include at least two women or minority candidates in final stage interviews for every position before making an offer. In 2017, forty-four prominent law firms partnered with the Diversity Lab to pilot a variation of the Rooney Rule called "the Mansfield Rule." Named after Arabella Mansfield, the first woman attorney in the US, the rule requires law firms to ensure that at least thirty percent of candidates for leadership positions are women or minorities.

In addition to setting specific gender diversity goals, dads of daughters can become more effective corporate leaders just by talking with their daughters to increase awareness and understanding of the challenges that women face in the corporate world. Gail Golden is the founder of an executive development company, and she's seen the power of the father-daughter relationship first-hand. As an executive trainer, Gail has learned that getting men to connect their role as dads to their role as business leaders can make them more effective diversity advocates. "Having a daughter changes a man's leadership style," says Gail, "making him more aware of discrimination and more likely to fight bias against female employees."

In Gail's experience, dads learn the most when they ask their daughters if they've ever faced sex discrimination themselves. When a dad's own daughter faces unequal treatment or limited opportunities, the experience can shift his priorities. At that point, it's no longer abstract statistics. It's a feeling of not being able to protect your daughter from harm. And while many dads are deeply invested in their daughters' success, there's often nothing they can do to directly fix their own daughter's unfair situation. That frustration can prompt dads to start advocating for gender equality in their own companies. "Although we like to pretend that we are 'all business,'" says Gail, "in fact we bring our whole selves to work, like it or not." For dads of daughters, that can be a very positive thing. As executive coach Susan Bloch explains, "Daughters are educating their fathers that they deserve a seat at the leadership table."

CHAPTER 2

Making Workplaces Work for Women

Two of the greatest barriers to women's corporate success are too few mentors and too little flexibility. This is the product of workplaces that were designed by men for other men, with men still largely at the helm. But common workplace structures don't work for many women (nor an increasing number of men). These workplace structures also don't help a company's bottom line.

In today's competitive environment, Wharton business school researchers are finding that mentors are more important than ever for both employees and organizations. Yet women still have a harder time securing senior mentors than men. KPMG surveyed over 3,000 professional and college-aged women, and a large majority said they didn't feel confident finding a mentor or approaching senior managers. As a result, women are twenty-four percent less likely than men to get advice from senior leaders. The barriers are often greater for women of color, with sixty-two percent reporting that the lack of an influential mentor holds them back. This concern is well-supported by research finding that people with mentors are indeed more likely to get promoted.

Leadership experts W. Brad Johnson and David Smith have researched why male mentors are in short supply for women in business. They've found that many men are uncomfortable mentoring women because it's an unfamiliar role. Some men are worried that they may make a mistake or say something that's perceived as sexist. Some are concerned that others may read something inappropriate into the relationship. Some are anxious that mentoring women will reduce their status in the workplace or trigger disapproval from other men. Add up all these concerns, and it's no wonder that when Catalyst surveyed men about their biggest barrier to supporting gender equality, seventy-four percent said "fear."

Unfortunately, at the same that #MeToo has exposed a pervasive culture of sexual harassment, the reckoning has also increased men's fears about mentoring female colleagues. The percentage of male managers who report feeling uncomfortable mentoring women has more than tripled from five to sixteen percent in the wake of #MeToo. That means that one out of every six male managers is hesitant to mentor a woman. The number of male managers who are hesitant to work alone with a woman has more than doubled. A stunning sixty-four percent of men in vice president positions and above are reluctant to meet alone with a junior woman.

Given these anxieties, it's not surprising that women are having a harder time than men securing influential mentors. Women also get less value out of the mentoring relationships that they have. To allay their anxieties when mentoring women, men sometimes fall into gender stereotype traps. Men are often overprotective instead of giving honest feedback and pushing their female mentees to take risks. This makes it harder for women to get growth opportunities and reach leadership positions.

No matter how hard it may be for men to mentor women, it's even harder for women leaders when the responsibility falls on them, particularly when performing the critical role of internal promotion. When a senior woman publicly sponsors junior women colleagues at her company, her performance evaluations take a hit. In contrast, when a senior man publicly promotes a female colleague, his performance evaluations go up. That's because women who mentor women are often seen as playing favorites, while men who mentor women are viewed as diversity champions. As frustrating as this double standard is, it should give men an added responsibility to sponsor women in their firms. Men who mentor women benefit personally as well. Male mentors build their interpersonal skills, expand their knowledge, and create more diverse networks, which makes them better leaders.

As important as mentoring is for achieving workplace equality, flexibility is even more critical. When women are asked whether they'd rather have a raise, a promotion, an extra week's vacation, or more flexibility in their day, the top response is more flexibility. In a study of over 1,500 white collar professionals, ninety-five percent of women said they needed some form of flexibility, but only thirty-four percent said they had access to the flexible work options that they needed.

Lack of flexibility isn't just one of the top reasons that women leave jobs, it's also a top reason why women leave the workforce altogether. In one survey, seventy percent of women who had left the workforce said they would still be working if they had more flexible work schedules. Another survey of career-oriented stay-at-home moms revealed that fifty-five percent would prefer to be working, but they needed more family-friendly workplace policies. That's an enormous loss of talent, innovation, and human capital. On the other hand, when employers commit to flexibility—including flexible schedules, reduced-hour or part-time options, telecommuting, or job-sharing arrangements—women are far more likely to stay and advance.

An increasing number of men are also seeking workplace flexibility, which provides even more incentive for employers to innovate. Employees who lack flexible work options are twice as likely to be dissatisfied with their jobs and move to other companies. The number of professional employees who quit their jobs because they lacked flexibility nearly doubled from 2014 to 2017, at which point nearly a third of those who quit their jobs cited lack of flexibility as the reason. This means that employers are paying enormous sums to hire and train new employees, not to mention the indirect costs from loss of continuity, reduced productivity, and decreased morale.

In addition to day-to-day flexibility, many women also leave the workforce because of inadequate maternity and family leave policies. Almost one in four working women in the US return to work within two weeks after giving birth. That's because out of 193 countries in the world, the US is one of only a handful that doesn't have a national law requiring maternity or paternity leave—an accolade that we share with Papua New Guinea, Suriname, and a few other South Pacific island nations. Over half of nations worldwide require at least fourteen weeks of paid maternity leave, and over forty percent require eighteen weeks or more. Over forty percent of countries also mandate some amount of paid leave for fathers. But because the US has no national paid family leave law, it's up to company leaders to take charge.

Currently, only thirty-five percent of US companies offer paid maternity leave, and only twenty-nine percent offer paid paternity leave. At the same time, half of employees report that if they had the choice, they'd pick more parental leave time over a pay raise. When women do have access to paid maternity leave, however, they're often afraid to use it. This is particularly the case in the male-dominated tech industry, where fifty-two percent of women said they returned early from maternity leave out of fear that spending time with their newborns was hurting their careers.

Men undoubtedly can relate to these concerns. Like women, most men don't have access to paid family leave. For men who do, most report even greater pressure than women not to use their time off because they'll be viewed as uncommitted to their jobs. When men do take family leave, they're often treated more harshly than women. In a large poll of employees who had access to parental leave benefits, fifty-four percent said that men are judged more negatively than women for taking the same amount of parental leave. One in three men reported that their jobs would be in jeopardy if they took their family leave time. As a result, men who have access to paternity leave typically use only a third of the time that's available. While sixty-six percent of women take all of their available parental leave, only thirty-six percent of men do the same.

Expanding paternity leave isn't just something that more men are seeking, it's also vital for advancing women's equality. When men take paternity leave, it reduces the stigma on all employees for being involved parents. Research also suggests that having dads involved with newborns reduces stress, depression, and illness for new moms. Men who take paternity leave also tend to share childcare more equally, which allows women more capacity to take Sheryl Sandberg's advice and "lean in" to their careers. In Iceland, where the majority of fathers take parental leave when they have children, companies have the smallest gender pay gap in the world.

So men have a critical role in making workplaces work for women. As in other areas, dads of daughters are leading the way. Large companies with male CEOs who have daughters tend to invest more in work/life employee benefits than companies lead by other men. Finance professors Henrik Cronqvist and Frank Yu discovered this while studying corporate social responsibility ratings at about four hundred large companies in the US. CSR ratings quantify a firm's investment in employees and the community. The ratings measure, among other things, whether a firm provides childcare benefits, flexible hours, and employee health programs.

The study found that companies run by a male CEO who has at least one daughter have CSR ratings that average 9.1 percent higher than the median rating for similar-sized firms. The biggest effect on a firm's CSR rating comes from a male CEO's first-born daughter, although later-born daughters also increase a firm's CSR rating incrementally. When a firm changes its CEO from a man who has one or more daughters to a man without daughters, the firm's CSR rating tends to quickly drop.

Imagine what dads of daughters could do for workplace flexibility and mentoring if they prioritized them at their workplaces. What if dads experimented with alternative work arrangements and set up formal mentoring programs to ensure that women don't fall through the cracks? What if dads publicly set concrete goals and regularly measured their progress? What if dads took all their paternity leave and encouraged other men to do the same? Four dads of daughters in Silicon Valley's tech industry have taken up this challenge to become role models for how to get started.

The Silicon Valley Coaches

When Richard Dickson became the Chair of Fenwick & West LLP, a Silicon Valley technology and life sciences law firm, his two daughters, Jordan and Alex, were seven and five years old. Even during elementary school, Jordan and Alex weren't just athletic, competitive, and opinionated. They were also budding feminists. Jordan could often be spotted in a "Girls Rule" tank-top, while Alex's favorite purple t-shirt displayed the Shakespeare quote: "Though she be but little, she is fierce." While saying grace before a meal at their grandparents' house, they once changed the word "amen" to "awomen," just to be fair. The phrase, "girl power," is invoked frequently around Richard's house, and his daughters aren't afraid to speak up and question his authority. Jordan and Alex have grown up truly believing that girls can do and become anything they want.

So when Richard stepped into his law firm's leadership role, he felt an obligation—and a fair amount of pressure—to meet his daughters' expectations about gender equality. "Your daughters are part of your identity," says Richard, "so the increased importance of a world that's fair and equal to them is something that has an impact."

Advancing women's equality in a corporate and technology-focused Silicon Valley law firm is no easy task. Nationwide, only eighteen percent of law firm equity partners are women, even though women have made up about half of all law students for the past twenty-five years. The numbers are even lower for women in corporate law, which is the largest part of Fenwick's practice. The gender pay gap in the legal profession is also staggering. The median compensation for partners at the two hundred largest law firms is about twenty percent less for women than men, even in the equity ranks. Women are also scarce in leadership positions at the technology, life sciences, and other Silicon Valley companies that make up most of Fenwick's client base. Women fill less than twenty-five percent of general counsel positions at Fortune 500 companies, and only seventeen percent of venture-backed start-ups have a woman founder—a percentage that hasn't changed since 2012.

Fortunately, Richard could build on a strong foundation set by the firm's prior Chair, Gordon Davidson, who's also the dad of a daughter. Business professor Isabel Metz studies diversity management and she's found that companies with the greatest gender diversity are ones with multiple generations of leaders who are committed to the cause. "We are talking here about cultural change, and we all know that cultural change doesn't happen in a few months or a year," she explains. "It takes one passionate leader, followed by another, that persistently has this issue in the spotlight, and it will have a snowball effect."

This effect is picking up speed at Fenwick & West because of the two dedicated dads of daughters who have led the firm back-to-back over the last several decades. Gordy joined the firm in the 1970s after getting bitten by Silicon Valley's start-up bug. With Stanford degrees in law, electrical engineering, and computer systems, Gordy quickly established himself as a leader in technology law. His clients range from start-ups to Fortune 1000 companies. He's worked on over fifty public offerings and lead more than a hundred mergers and acquisitions valued at more than $75 billion. Because of his visionary leadership, he was elected as the firm's Chair in 1995. Serving in that role for the next eighteen years, Gordy grew the firm from about 150 to 325 attorneys, and he nearly tripled the firm's revenue.

Despite his firm's financial success and his status as Silicon Valley's legal guru, Gordy dedicated himself to advancing women attorneys before that path had been forged by others in the male-dominated legal profession. Gordy recruited his firm's first woman attorney and mentored her throughout her career. He later helped craft a part-time schedule for her and was an outspoken advocate for electing her to become the firm's first reduced-hour partner. In 2001, Gordy was among the first to sign up for the San Francisco Bar Association's "No Glass Ceiling" initiative, which committed his firm to specific goals for increasing women partners.

In becoming an early Silicon Valley advocate for gender diversity, Gordy was nudged along the way by his high-achieving daughter, Laurie. While Gordy was leading his firm, his daughter finished high school, graduated from college, and began a teaching career. While watching her journey, Gordy became motivated to dig deeper into the barriers and biases that were pushing women out of the legal profession.

Gordy's firm was having a hard time retaining women attorneys, particularly women with children. So in 2006, he convened a task force to examine how law firm billable-hour requirements and scheduling practices affected women attorneys. Law firms demand notoriously long hours, in part because clients are typically billed based on the number of hours an attorney spends on a client's work, instead of based on projects or outcomes. So more attorney work hours means higher law firm profits. It also means that attorney salaries and promotions typically depend on the number of hours an attorney clocks. Gordy suspected that this was part of the retention issue for lawyer moms, so his firm hosted a forum to discuss how to keep women attorneys after they have kids.

Based on what he learned, Gordy established a formal part-time program that's open to all attorneys. Most importantly, attorneys who work part-time may still become partners, which was a groundbreaking shift from most firms' second-class mommy-tracks. Of the last thirty attorneys who've been elected to Fenwick's partnership, eight have been working reduced-hour schedules, which includes six women. Although the policies were triggered by the desire to retain women, they've also benefitted men who are seeking work/family balance.

Gordy stepped down as Fenwick's Chair in 2013, and the partners chose Richard to take his place. While helping raise two young daughters, Richard had built a successful practice advising high-tech, internet, telecommunications, software, and semiconductor companies. After leading many Silicon Valley start-ups through venture capital financing, mergers and acquisitions, and initial public offerings, Richard became the head of Fenwick's start-up group and the leader of the corporate department before replacing Gordy as the firm's Chair.

Richard built on Gordy's work by focusing on advancing women into leadership roles. As a dad of daughters, Richard saw this focus as both a moral responsibility and a business opportunity. Watching his daughters grow their talents reminded him that his firm is a talent organization. Law firms are service providers, and their assets are their people. So recruiting, keeping, and promoting the most talented individuals has been Richard's highest leadership goal. Having daughters made him more attuned to the importance of gender diversity for achieving that goal. "Our greatest opportunity is the retention and promotion of women because they're half of the talent pool," says Richard, "but that's something that the legal industry has not been very good at recognizing."

Richard became convinced that effective mentorship was the key for having more women attorneys rise to the partnership ranks. But mentorship takes skill, commitment, and most of all, empathy. Richard's capacity to be more empathetic was perhaps his most important gift from his daughters. "My daughters have made me more of a softie," he admits, "but in a good way." Richard believes that empathy is one of the most important leadership skills. "It's the ability to take the perspective of others and to put yourself in the shoes of different people who have different experiences," he explains.

The empathy that Richard gained from being the dad of daughters helped him see that his firm's informal mentoring process wasn't working for many women as well as it was for most men. He noticed that most male associates easily found mentors because the partners were mostly men with whom they could easily relate. But talented female associates were often falling through the mentorship cracks, which made it harder for them to achieve their full potential at his firm.

Starting as the leader of the corporate department, Richard created a mentorship program to support women's development. He identified the partners who were the most skilled at mentoring and the best positioned to provide valuable work experiences. He then asked all of the associates to submit requests for partners they might prefer as mentors. That was particularly useful for many women who faced greater barriers to seeking support directly from powerful male leaders. Richard then set about thoughtfully pairing the most effective male mentors with aspiring women associates. He also asked the partners to become proactive rather than reactive. In particular, he asked the male mentors to identify challenging, high-profile opportunities for their women mentees to hone their skills.

Richard also made sure that mentoring and diversity contributions are considered every year when setting each partner's pay. "It should be a badge of honor for men to sponsor women," says Facebook COO Sheryl Sandberg, and that's definitely becoming the case at Fenwick & West. One of the things that Richard is most proud of as the firm's Chair is that women corporate associates often request him as their mentor.

Research supports Richard's belief that strong mentoring is key to retaining women. Women who have valuable relationships with male mentors are more loyal to their organizations, in part because male mentoring creates a feeling of inclusion, which is in short supply for women in male-dominated industries. This is something that most men don't realize. At the same time that eighty-two percent of women report feeling excluded at work, ninety-two percent of men report that they don't exclude women at their jobs.

In addition to mentoring, Richard has also tackled some of the structural barriers to women's success. "We need to experiment," he says, and he's willing to challenge conventions when needed. He helped design his firm's first job-sharing arrangement, where two attorneys each worked part-time and shared the same clients, office, and email inbox. His goal was to support reduced-hour work in practice areas where full-time client demands had made part-time legal work challenging. His firm has also encouraged clients to switch from billable-hour fees to fixed fees, which lowers the pressure on attorneys to log extremely high working hours. "Billable hours have become less of a factor for partners over the years," says Richard, "and that has been very beneficial to the goal of recruiting and retaining women, not to mention the job satisfaction of many men."

Although Gordy and Richard know that more work is needed before the legal profession offers an inclusive work environment for women, they've established their firm as a leader. Fenwick & West has been ranked among the country's top ten law firms for diversity by *The American Lawyer* and *Law360*, and it's been recognized for ten years as one of the Best Places to Work by the *Silicon Valley Business Journal* and the *San Francisco Business Times*. In 2016, the Euromoney Legal Media Group Americas Women in Business Law Awards recognized Fenwick as the best national firm for women in business law in North America. The following year, Silicon Valley's legal newspaper, *The Recorder*, honored five women from Fenwick—more than any other firm—on its prestigious list of Women Leaders in Tech Law.

In 2016, Gordy was honored for his work expanding women's opportunities in the legal profession by receiving the first annual "Bill Campbell (Man Who Gets It) Award" from Watermark, a Bay Area group of women executives and entrepreneurs. Watermark CEO Marlene Williamson launched the award because she knows that women will break down leadership barriers more quickly with the buy-in of men.

The award is named after Bill Campbell—who's known as "Coach" throughout the Silicon Valley—because of Bill's long-time support of women. Like Richard, Bill is a proud dad of two daughters, Margaret and Kate. Bill began his career as the CEO of Go Corporation, the spectacularly well-funded Silicon Valley start-up that sought to mainstream pen-based computing. Bill later became the CEO of Intuit and served on Apple's board of directors.

Bill's most important role, however, has been as Silicon Valley's behind-the-scenes advocate for women. Throughout his career, Bill quietly dedicated himself to mentoring, supporting, and opening doors for many of the first female executives and entrepreneurs in the tech industry. "Bill was focused on diversity, especially gender diversity, before it was cool and even in the news," says Shellye Archambeau, one of Bill's mentees who became the CEO of MetricStream.

Other women who proudly count themselves as Bill's mentees include Caroline Donahue, the former CMO of Intuit; Donna Dubinsky, the former CEO of Palm and co-founder of Numenta; and Juliet de Baubigny, a partner at the venture capital firm Kleiner Perkins. "There is no doubt the opportunities he gave me vaulted me in my career," says Donna. "It gave me a seat at the table in a fundamental way."

Shellye wholeheartedly agrees. "He was definitely a strong figure in my career," she says. "We have a talent shortage in tech and we are not leveraging fifty percent of the population the way we should. But Bill has enabled more women's talent to be not just tapped, but given the opportunity to demonstrate the full talent that they have."

Mari Baker, a former Intuit Vice President, was on maternity leave in 1995 when Bill picked her for the VP role. She doubted whether she could do the job with a new infant, but Bill made the position work. Bill had a rule that all company meetings must take place between ten a.m. and five p.m., in part because he wanted to spend time with his own kids. Diane Greene also credits Bill for recruiting her to the Intuit board of directors and convincing her not to leave the tech industry when the challenges became overwhelming. "He made us feel empowered," she says. As a result, Bill's mentees often dedicate themselves to mentoring other women. "He's given women the sense that they belong," says Diane, "and then they go out and give other women the sense that they belong."

It was Bill's idea to launch a women's entrepreneurship conference, which is how he teamed up with Watermark. So it was fitting for Watermark to name its "Man Who Gets It" award after Bill. Fenwick's Gordy Davidson was honored to be the award's first recipient. "I have tried to be a vocal leader in recruiting and promoting women, with the simple argument that, otherwise, we will miss at least half of the talent that is available," says Gordy. "All women need is the mentorship and the opportunity to demonstrate their talents." He hopes to continue Bill's legacy in the Silicon Valley for years to come. Bill passed away at age seventy-five in 2016, but he left behind two proud daughters, many successful women executives and entrepreneurs, two inspired leaders of Fenwick & West, and a more gender-inclusive tech industry.

Another tech leader who also figured out the value of gender inclusive workplaces early in his career is Adam Bain, the former COO of Twitter. Adam became inspired when thinking about his own daughter's future. "I look forward to the day when both my daughter and my son can enter the workforce in an environment where women have just as much opportunity as their male counterparts," says Adam.

To make his workplace a place where he'd want his daughter to work, Adam partnered Twitter with the United Nations HeForShe IMPACT Initiative. IMPACT commits corporate executives to publicly report their progress on gender diversity. Adam pledged to increase the number of women in tech positions at Twitter to sixteen percent and raise the total number of women to thirty-five percent by 2016. Adam was particularly focused on increasing women in leadership roles, where he set a 2016 goal of twenty-five percent. "When you think about the future, you often think about your kids," Adam explained. "My first two bosses in business were both incredibly inspiring and powerful female executives and I learned everything from them. I want both my daughter and my son to have the same experience that I did, which is to have the opportunity to have female managers and mentors who inspire them to do things they never thought possible."

To achieve his goals, Adam made several policy changes at Twitter, including giving women up to twenty weeks of fully-paid maternity leave. Twitter also provides mentors and hosts roundtables for new moms and moms-to-be to learn how the company can support women's re-entry after having a baby. That led to other changes, like providing medical grade pumps in the company's nursing rooms and reimbursing women for supplies and shipping costs to send breast milk home when they're travelling for work. Twitter also gives its employees free premium memberships to Care.com, which helps employees find quality childcare.

Adam had done his research, so he knew that these investments would not only be good for women, but also good for Twitter. "The science here is pretty simple," says Adam. "When you look at the various business studies that look at company performance and inclusion numbers, it's just a fact, it's not even a theory, that companies that are more mindful around inclusion perform better." In thinking ahead to the corporate world he hopes will exist for our next generation of girls, Adam jokingly tweeted to the Twitter recruiting office that his daughter "will be graduating from college [fourteen years] from now with a computer science/ math double major." He asked them to "please keep an eye out" for her application.

How Dads Can Get Started

For dads of daughters who are in positions of corporate power, mentoring women colleagues can be an important and rewarding contribution to advancing women's equality. Just like other goals that you've set and achieved in your professional life, you don't have to go this one alone. There are excellent resources available for honing your mentoring skills.

A great first stop is *Athena Rising: How and Why Men Should Mentor Women* by W. Brad Johnson and David Smith. Brad and David are professors in the Department of Leadership, Ethics, and Law at the United States Naval Academy. They're also dads of daughters, so they understand both the motivation and the anxieties that may come with mentoring women. Their book shares a wealth of advice about how men can become successful, effective, and empathetic mentors for women.

One thing that Brad and David have discovered is that when men (including themselves) mentor women, they often reduce their anxieties by falling into so-called "man-scripts." They describe these man-scripts as "roles men have long been conditioned to play in stereotypical male-to-female relationships." While these roles can make the mentoring relationship more comfortable for men, they can also enable gender bias to undermine success.

One of the most common man-scripts is the "protective father." This is when a man replicates a father-daughter relationship when mentoring female colleagues. While this can ease men's discomfort about mentoring women, it often makes men unwilling to give negative feedback or push women to challenge themselves. Women often regret that male mentors aren't as tough or honest with them as they are with men, so they don't know how to improve, take risks, and grow. "A man who falls back on a father script with a woman at work believes in his heart of hearts that he's being helpful and he's being protective and shielding her," explains Brad. "But the problem is he's not allowing her to experience the same challenges and opportunities that a male mentee would get. He's not allowing her to go out and make mistakes and fail and to build up that immunity as she learns to overcome challenges." Acting like a father at work can also be patronizing, which undermines women's autonomy.

So while Brad and David definitely believe that dads should be motivated by their daughters to mentor women at work, they shouldn't act like dads when taking on a mentoring role. They should be inspired by their father-daughter relationship, but they shouldn't replicate it on the job. Brad knows from personal experience that this can be tricky, so he recommends that men talk about it openly with the women they mentor. When Brad is mentoring a woman, he tells her, "Look, occasionally, you're going to see me acting like a dad and I don't intend to do that, when I do it, will you promise to bring it to my attention and tell me to stop it?'"

Athena Rising offers men many other tips for improving mentoring skills. Perhaps the most important is to spend less time talking and more time listening, which is what mentees want most. What makes male mentors most effective for women, says David, is "listening with a purpose as opposed to thinking about what it is I'm going to tell you next." Additional advice is available from Sheryl Sandberg's LeanIn.org, which recently launched the #MentorHer campaign, which helps build men's mentoring skills. Research has found, for example, that women are more likely than men to get very vague feedback that they can't implement, so the #MentorHer campaign teaches men to give women precise, skills-specific feedback.

All of these mentoring tips work better if your firm has a formal mentoring program, which is something you can help establish if it doesn't already exist. Formal mentoring programs reduce the social barriers for women to find mentors in the first place. They can also reduce men's concerns about the relationship being misperceived. Establishing a common set of specific goals for the relationship also paves the way for greater success. Catalyst has found that this groundwork pays particular dividends for women, who receive about 50 percent more promotions when they have formal mentoring programs than when they find mentors on their own. But whether your firm has a formal mentoring program or not, the most important thing is to get started. "Powerful male mentors don't wait," explain Brad and David. "They purposefully identify promising women in their organization and reach out, initiating interaction and support without being asked."

Increasing flexibility at your workplace can be more challenging because it often requires both formal policies and cultural shifts in attitude. An excellent place for dads to start is by reading Josh Levs's book, *All In: How Our Work-First Culture Fails Dads, Families, and Businesses—And How We Can Fix It Together*. Josh is a journalist who wrote *All In* after his employer, Time Warner, denied him fair parental leave when he had his third child. While the company gave moms ten weeks of paid leave after giving birth, it gave dads like Josh only two. Josh was forced to file a discrimination complaint when Time Warner wouldn't reconsider, and he ultimately got the policy changed. Parents around the country supported Josh throughout the ordeal, knowing that shared parental leave not only supports involved fathers, but is also essential to advancing women's equality.

Since then, Josh has become an advocate for parental leave laws and workplace flexibility that offer both women and men a healthier work/family balance. Josh's book builds a compelling case for why paid parental leave—for both moms *and* dads—supports healthier kids, stronger families, and more successful companies. Share Josh's book with your male colleagues to start a conversation about the importance of work/family balance. Men's voices are often under the radar when it comes to paid family leave and workplace flexibility. "Dads can change that," says Josh, "by joining the public conversations on gender issues, sharing experiences, and amplifying the arguments women have been making. Women can help by making sure men are welcomed into these conversations with open arms and minds."

The stories of dedicated dads in Josh's book will also support fathers in taking perhaps the most important personal step to advance women's equality: proudly and visibly using your paternity leave if you have it available. Speak up in support of paid paternity leave. Applaud other men for seeking and using it. And never leave your parental leave benefits on the table. "Women have done a great job of speaking out about this," says Josh. "It's time for men to join in—in a big way."

If you do, Alexis Ohanian is one dad who will support you all the way. Alexis is the co-founder of Reddit and Initialized Capital, and he's also tennis superstar Serena Williams's husband. Alexis became an outspoken advocate for paid paternity leave after he used Reddit's sixteen weeks of paid leave to care for his daughter Olympia. Alexis acknowledges the reality of "career fear"—the concerns men have about stigma, retaliation, and career deceleration if they use their paternity leave. But he encourages dads to take their leave anyway because the payoffs for their families far exceed the costs. While he's advocating for a federal paid family leave law, he wants you to know that he's got your back. "[L]et me be your air cover," says Alexis. "I took my full sixteen weeks and I'm still ambitious and care about my career. Talk to your bosses and tell them I sent you."

On the policy side, company leaders can begin by filling out the Workplace Flexibility Scorecard created by New Agency Partners. The Scorecard is part of a Flexible Workplaces HR Toolkit, which is available for free online. The Scorecard helps leaders understand their current practices and existing level of commitment to workplace flexibility. Leaders can use the Toolkit's sample policies, procedures, and employee guidebooks to set up flextime, part-time, telecommuting, or compressed workweek options. The Champions of Change initiative also offers an online Flexible Workplaces Toolkit to help leaders establish and monitor flextime practices. For large companies, leaders might also team up with Werk, which offers an analytics software program to assess the specific flexibility needs and solutions in your workplace. The Werk platform helps companies create customized flexible work policies and measure their impact.

Because so many women leave the workplace after having kids, company leaders should also offer better support for women who are exiting and re-entering their jobs from maternity leave. Strong support comes from clear communication and thorough preparation.

One of the best resources to provide that support is Lori Mihalich-Levin's Mindful Return initiative. Lori is an attorney, a mom of two kids, and the author of *Back to Work after Baby: How to Plan and Navigate a Mindful Return from Maternity Leave*. Lori advises companies and offers online courses for both women and men who take parental leave. The course includes a "Leave Template" that allows employees to communicate their plans with their workplace teams before leaving. The course also assists women with the daunting logistics of returning to work, including plans for nursing and childcare, while helping men address the "career fear" that's often associated with taking leave.

When dads of daughters—or other men—become advocates for workplace flexibility or mentors for women, it's not just women who gain. Men benefit, too. So do businesses. The same study that found that only thirty-four percent of women had access to the workplace flexibility they needed found that fifty-one percent of men needed more flexibility as well. Flexibility gains for women are gains for everyone seeking a healthier work/life balance. Learning from mentoring relationships also goes in both directions. As Brad Johnson and David Smith explain, "[d]eliberately and skillfully mentoring women is an opportunity for us to open our minds, listen, and become better employees, colleagues, and men."

CHAPTER 3

Welcoming Girls into STEM

Even after three decades, Qusi Alquarqaz still adores being an electrical engineer. He always hoped that his two daughters would follow in his footsteps, but his plan was not to be. After his first daughter, Rawan, announced that she wanted to study fashion design and business, Qusi pinned his remaining hope on his younger daughter, Ryzan. She recently told her dad that she might go to law school to become an international lawyer. Qusi will support her no matter what career she chooses, but he still had a lingering desire to convince at least one daughter of the joys of being an engineer.

With almost thirty years of experience in the power industry, Qusi could make a persuasive case. "Wherever you look you will see engineering's positive impact on humanity," he told his daughter. He explained how engineers get to innovate, solve problems, and improve communities. He mentioned the prestige and good pay. He even played on her emotions. "Imagine how life would be like without engineers," he said. "Engineers avert disasters and protect the world. Be part of that and create a change!" But none of his encouragement worked. His daughter's answer was still no.

Qusi's desire for his daughters to become engineers is unusual, which is part of the problem. A recent survey asked 770 parents in 150 countries about the careers they wanted for their kids, who were eleven to sixteen years old. Parents of boys were twice as likely as parents of girls to say that science and technology were the fields they most wanted their child to pursue. The disparity was even bigger for engineering in particular. While eleven percent of parents would choose engineering for their son, only one percent would choose it for their daughter.

Even though Qusi is among the one percent of parents who want their daughters to become engineers, he still couldn't spark his daughters' interest. He asked them why they weren't drawn to engineering, and they said that none of their teachers ever talked about it as a career. That concerned Qusi, who thinks that schools should actively encourage students to become engineers. He also saw his daughters struggle to stay engaged with chemistry and math because the teachers weren't using real-life problems or examples. When they couldn't understand the theory, his daughters concluded that they weren't smart enough for a math or science career.

Qusi also blames the male-dominated reputation of the engineering profession. "When people think about engineering," he says, "they often think about hard hats, steel beams, winches, long hours, relocation every few years, and instability. There is a misunderstanding that engineering involves tedious or hard physical labor suitable for men only." Lurking behind those misperceptions is a lack of female role models, which makes it harder to get girls excited about becoming engineers.

The data bears out Qusi's concerns about the lack of educational pipelines for girls into STEM. Girls and boys perform similarly in math and science during primary school, but girls never participate in computer science and engineering at the same rate as boys. Although women are earning close to sixty percent of all bachelor's degrees, they earn only forty-three percent of math degrees, thirty-nine percent in physical sciences, nineteen percent in engineering, and eighteen percent in computer science.

These disparities carry over into the workforce. In the US, women fill only a quarter of all STEM jobs. Sometimes art-related jobs are added to this group—changing the acronym to STEAM—which may raise the percentage of women slightly. But overall numbers hide the extremely low participation rates of women in engineering and computer science. Most of these women head into the social, biological, and life sciences, filling only eleven percent of jobs in physics, astronomy, and engineering. Women are particularly scarce in mechanical engineering, where they make up only eight percent of the workforce. Even worse, the percentage of women in computing jobs has actually decreased from thirty-seven percent in 1995 to only twenty-two percent in 2017. This is likely linked to the massive gender pay gap in the field. For those holding an advanced degree and working full-time in science or engineering, women's median annual salary is over thirty-one percent less than men's.

Perhaps most disturbing is that many women who earn STEM degrees don't end up in STEM jobs. Thirty-eight percent of women who get engineering degrees stop being engineers or never take an engineering job in the first place. Almost half of women who enter the tech field eventually leave—a rate that's more than double that of men. The exit rate is particularly high for women after having their first child because of the minimal support for childcare and nursing and the lack of flexible hours. This loss doesn't just cost women, it also costs the tech industry itself. Silicon Valley tech companies spend more than $16 billion a year in turnover costs to replace and re-train workers to fill jobs that women and minorities leave.

Women's exodus from the field—and their reluctance to enter—also results from a pervasive culture of sexual harassment. Dubbed "The Elephant in the Silicon Valley," the full extent of sexual harassment in the tech industry is just coming to light as part of the #MeToo movement. In a recent survey of over 200 women who had been in the tech industry for at least ten years, a stunning sixty percent reported facing unwanted sexual advances at work. Ninety percent of the women had witnessed sexist behavior at conferences and company offsites, and one in three had feared for their personal safety in work-related situations. In another study of minority female scientists, every single respondent reported experiencing bias at work.

Not wanting to jeopardize their careers, thirty-nine percent of the women who experienced sexual harassment didn't report it. That's a rational decision in an industry where retaliation is rampant and women are viewed as outsiders. Sixty-six percent of the women said they were already excluded from social and networking events, and fifty-nine percent said they weren't given the same opportunities as their male colleagues. For women who did report sexual harassment, sixty percent felt unsatisfied by the response they received. Many women leave the tech industry altogether after facing sexual harassment.

The result of the hostile work environment, pay disparity, and gender stereotypes isn't just that women are being excluded from prestigious and satisfying jobs. It's also that society is missing out on a vast source of talent and creativity. Researchers have found that greater gender diversity in tech companies leads to more radical innovation. A study of over 4,000 tech companies in Spain found that mixed-gender research and development teams were more creative, identified more novel solutions to problems, and had better decision-making processes than all-male teams.

Having women involved in early product development also helps ensure that products are designed with women consumers in mind—smartphones sized for women's hands, artificial hearts that fit into women's chest cavities, health apps that track menstruation, and virtual assistants that direct questions about sexual assault to appropriate resources. Design failures in all of those areas have been linked to male-dominated development teams. So ensuring equal opportunities for women in STEM isn't just good for women, it's also good for business.

After hearing his daughters' explanations for their lack of interest in STEM careers, Qusi started thinking about how to create a better environment for female engineers. "It should be our goal and duty to make a place for women in engineering," he decided. Qusi sees the problem as a pipeline issue: change education and culture from an early age, and that could change girls' career paths. As a senior member of the Institute of Electrical and Electronics Engineers, Qusi has been increasing public awareness of how engineering, computing, and technology advance the public good, and of the importance of getting girls interested in science and technology to bring new contributors into the field. He's also become a women's mentor and an advocate for bringing women engineers into schools to share their experiences.

Several other dads of daughters have responded to Qusi's plea by focusing even earlier in the pipeline. These dads have realized that welcoming girls into STEM requires a gender-bending cultural shift that empowers young girls to imagine themselves as engineers, mathematicians, techies, and scientists—as well as opens young boys up to the idea that STEM classes and careers are for everyone. Two dads have found creative ways to pique girls' interest after learning from their daughters that nothing empowers girls quite like a girl superhero.

STEAMTeam 5

For Greg Helmstetter, becoming a dad was both a joyful and an unsettling event. When his daughter, Kamea, was born, Greg found himself wondering about the world she was facing. In imagining what she might grow up to be, he couldn't help but worry about the power of technology to dictate job requirements or eliminate jobs entirely. He decided that teaching Kamea STEM skills would be the best insurance against an uncertain future.

This was an impressive goal for a dad who's neither a scientist nor an engineer. Greg was a Silicon Valley entrepreneur who moved to Arizona to become a partner in Monsoon Strategy, a business consulting firm. But even as a businessman, Greg decided that it was critical to surround his daughter with math, science, and technology. "Not to try to force her into these fields," he explains, "but to give her the widest range of options possible." Greg felt personally responsible for doing this well because he and his wife were homeschooling their daughter. "It's on us if she's getting taught well," he says, which pushed him to think more creatively about how to get her interested in STEM skills.

Despite the best of intentions, Greg's plan hit a roadblock. As he looked around at toys, children's books, and TV programs, he found nothing depicting girls who were excited about using science, math, and technology. So Greg began inventing his own games and stories—often with his daughter's Barbie dolls—to inject STEM concepts into playtime. Suddenly, Kamea's Barbies weren't just changing outfits, they were devising plans to catch ninja spies or launching a company to manufacture electric cars. In one of Greg's stories, the Barbie dolls were the executives of a dog food factory and they used their profit from selling Mega Blok dog food to fund an animal shelter. Greg admits that at first, he was mostly just finding ways to make doll time more tolerable for himself, but he realized that he could use his stories to disrupt gender stereotypes and inject values.

Greg's stories initially focused on his own entrepreneurial skills, but doll time soon became STEM-training time. Before long, the Barbie dolls were using technology, science, and math skills like superpowers to solve problems, rescue animals, and invent new products. Word of Greg's girl-powered lessons soon spread through the playground network. Other parents of daughters started asking Greg where they could get copies of his stories. Greg saw a gaping hole that needed to be filled to enable young girls to see themselves as future scientists, engineers, mathematicians, and techies.

Greg enlisted the help of his business partner, Pamela Metivier, to co-found a publishing branch of their company to create children's books that empower girls to become the next generation of STEAM leaders. They expanded Greg's stories into an all-star cast of five girls, each with her own skillset and personality, with the goal of producing a five-book series. What young girl could resist a book series called *STEAMTeam 5*, in which ordinary girls use extraordinary STEAM skills to solve mysteries, fix problems, and make the world a better place?

The *STEAMTeam* girls are so hip—and so super-skilled—that they're sure to inspire. There's Sandia Scientist, who goes surfing with her dog Phyto, and who loves chemistry, biology, astronomy, quantum physics, and forensics. She's always asking questions, doing experiments, and solving mysteries. There's Treeka Technologist, who's been programming and taking things apart since she was four, and who enjoys cryptology, puzzles, lock picking, and meditation. When she was little, she reprogrammed her talking teddy bear to respond "good idea, Treeks" to everything she says. They're joined by Evelyn Engineer, who loves inventing and tinkering with cars, planes, and robots, and who can design a pretty impressive booby-trap. Ariana Artist is the team's creative force, who loves drawing, sculpting, 3D animation, and making electronic music. Mattie Mathematician rounds out the team with her passion for numbers and logic.

While all the team members have unique super-skills, Greg made sure that the girls aren't depicted as natural geniuses. The stories show how the girls developed their skills through hard work over time, and how it takes teamwork to solve problems. The books aren't filled with explicit math and science lessons, but with entertaining stories about female role models to get girls excited about using STEAM skills. "They go on adventures and do fun things," Greg explains, "and they happen to use STEAM skills because they're good at them, and they're good at them because they have passion."

While Greg definitely wants to reach young girls who need to see themselves reflected in tech-centered stories, he also wants his books in the hands of boys, who need to see girls in tech roles from an early age. Greg's all about promoting female empowerment, but he knows that men are still gatekeepers, so he wants just as many boys reading his books as girls.

Greg's daughter Kamea still serves as "a focus group of one" to give feedback on his stories. Greg hopes that *STEAMTeam 5* will inspire the next generation of girls to follow their passions in math, science, and technology. "*STEAMTeam 5* is much more than just a book," Greg explains, "it's a movement designed to get girls interested in STEM/STEAM from a very early age, and to keep them interested."

Ella the Engineer

Like Greg Helmstetter, New York native Anthony Onesto's inspiration for changing the male-dominated tech culture came from his two daughters, Ella and Nicolette. Anthony was the Director of Talent Development for the digital marketing and consulting company Razorfish. While watching his daughters, he discovered a gap in the interest level that girls and boys have in technology. That prompted him to look around his own tech company, and he was startled to realize that only ten of the eight hundred coders were women. "That was my 'what now' moment," he says. "How do we get more girls to get excited about coding?"

Anthony checked out the TV shows and media that his daughters watched, and just like Greg, he found an absence of role models depicting females in computer science and technology. This imbalance starts ingraining stereotypes at a very young age. When girls are asked to draw a scientist or someone who's good at math, they're more likely to draw a man than a woman. In talking with female engineers, Anthony heard the same message—no role models, no mentors, nobody to emulate. That's when he had his "Ally McBeal moment." He remembered that when Ally showed up as a clever and quirky attorney on the hit TV show in the late nineties, the number of girls who applied to law school skyrocketed. So Anthony decided it was time for a female tech-superhero to start changing the course of girls' futures.

While Anthony is a big supporter of coding organizations that reach girls at an older age, he thinks that starts too late. "By then," he says, "many young girls have completely written off the field, whether they realize it or not." To reach younger girls, Anthony focused instead on comics. He couldn't find a single female comics hero who solved problems using engineering, software, or technology, so it was time to invent one of his own.

Despite his success as an entrepreneur and executive, Anthony ran into some obstacles. For one thing, he's not a professional cartoonist. By his own admission, he can't draw and he doesn't know how to tell a story. For another, he had no funding. But with passionate recruiting, Anthony built a team to create his vision, which is how Ella the Engineer was born.

Ella the Engineer is a comic book hero who uses coding, hacking, and programming skills to solve problems that young girls can understand. Anthony's hope is that by creating a techie supergirl who other girls want to emulate, more girls will get interested in pursuing technology careers. "Imagine you give a young girl an opportunity that had not been presented to her before," he explains, "a path to a career that is both rewarding and successful. A place where it was rare for her to play. A place where the opportunities seem endless these days."

Ella the Engineer is named after Anthony's youngest daughter, who helped him pitch the idea at a TEDxYouth event. Both of his daughters, Ella and Nicolette, as well as Anthony's son, Frankie, serve as advisors for the comic books to make sure that the stories are reaching their intended audience. Anthony describes his daughters as both his initial "case study" and his "personal focus group," and he's happy to report that they've enthusiastically endorsed his storylines.

The comics include a pitch-perfect villain—Glitch—who wreaks havoc by placing bugs and viruses into codes in everyday technology. Ella the Engineer uses her super-coding skills to hack into systems, reprogram malfunctions, and save the day. Ella is helped along the way by her trusty computer Mack, her loyal tablet Tabby, and her smart aleck iPhone Smarty. Together, they make an irresistible team. While the comics contain puzzles and cryptograms for girls to practice their skills, Anthony's primary goal was to make the stories entertaining. "I wanted to not only show a hero who was a female lead and a computer science coder," Anthony explains, "but I also wanted to show kids that technology is actually intertwined into everything that we do."

Because Anthony wants to reach as many girls as possible, his comic books are available free online. Ella the Engineer also has her own Facebook and Twitter accounts where she posts news about girls and women in technology. Anthony wants girls to understand the social importance of software development and coding and spark creativity and confidence in building STEM skills. Most importantly, he wants girls to see STEM careers as inviting and fun.

The comic book series is part of a larger vision for expanding opportunities for girls in technology. Anthony envisions a tech world that's filled with skilled, imaginative, and successful women engineers who build, lead, and grow technology companies—"because they had a hero in Ella."

Since creating Ella, Anthony helped found SmartUp, a peer-to-peer learning platform that allows tech companies to share knowledge. He also became the General Manager of the Konrad Group, a digital innovation company. He's now thinking about "Ella 2.0." His dream is to get Ella the Engineer a movie gig so he can magnify her positive impact. He says he'll know that he's succeeded when he someday sees a giant, inflatable Ella floating past cheering crowds in a Thanksgiving Day parade.

In the meantime, Anthony has begun a new campaign for Ella the Engineer called STEM Figures, which connects the Ella comics with real-life female tech role models. Anthony is interviewing prominent women in the STEM field, including chief technology officers and tech entrepreneurs. He asks them what triggered their passion for math, science, or technology as young girls. Their stories are highlighted on his website, and they'll be woven into plotlines that will let Ella connect with the same events that got these successful female leaders excited about STEM careers.

Anthony is collaborating on this project with Jewelbots, which are programmable friendship bracelets that teach girls how to code. The bracelets are open source devices that let girls practice basic programming skills. Girls can program the bracelets to light up when a friend is nearby, send secret messages, or flash a rainbow when a group of friends get together. Anthony plans to have Ella the Engineer use her own Jewelbot to call upon the particular female STEM leader whose story inspired the comic episode. When Ella hits a roadblock, she can press her Jewelbot and the female STEM icon will appear in cartoon form to guide her through the challenge.

Ella the Engineer has already had an impact on Anthony's own daughters. His older daughter, Nicolette, decided to apply to her high school's STEM track. While Anthony's younger daughter, Ella, has proudly taken the books to school for show-and-tell, Anthony suspects that her spitfire nature will lead her to become a CEO. She's definitely learned from Ella the Engineer the importance of understanding technology for being an effective company leader one day.

How Dads Can Get Started

Luckily, if you're a dad who wants to fuel your daughters' interest in STEM, you don't have to create a new book series or comic superhero to have an impact. In addition to *STEAMTeam 5* and *Ella the Engineer*, several other children's books about girls in STEM are finding their way into bookstores. Check out Andrea Beaty's trilogy: *Rosie Revere, Engineer*; *Ada Twist, Scientist*; and *Iggy Peck, Architect*. Or try Tanya Lee Stone's *Who Says Women Can't Be Computer Programmers?* and Kimberly Derting's *Cece Loves Science*.

You can also follow the GeekDad technology blog and podcasts created by engineer dad Ken Denmead. Ken has a series of GeekDad project books for parents and kids, including *The Geek Dad Book for Aspiring Mad Scientists*. Another great resource is Mike Adamick's hands-on guide, *Dad's Book of Awesome Science Experiments*, which shows dads how to teach daughters chemistry with soap clouds, human biology with marshmallow pulse keepers, and physics with straw balloon rockets. If you need downtime while still being a stellar dad, have your daughters watch the PBS television show SciGirls, which highlights real tween girls using STEM skills to answer questions in their daily lives.

For dads who are looking for a perfect birthday present for daughters or their friends, there are terrific STEM-related games available online from The STEM Store. One of the best new toy lines was created by Debbie Sterling specifically for girls to practice STEM skills. Debbie studied mechanical engineering and product design at Stanford University, where she was shocked to see so few women in her program. Like Greg and Anthony, she decided there must be a way to get more girls excited about engineering.

Debbie spent time perusing toy stores, where she discovered that toys are highly sex-segregated. Even worse, she discovered that all the cool building and design toys are housed in the boys' section. She funneled her irritation into a new obsession: "disrupting the pink aisle." Debbie's goal was to design toys that would counter gender stereotypes and introduce girls to the joys of engineering. The result was an award-winning set of construction games with the girl-power title, "GoldieBlox."

Described by the *Boston Globe* as "an alternative to toys more concerned with looks than brains," the GoldieBlox construction kits allow kids to build contraptions to solve relatable challenges. In one set, girls help Goldie build a belt drive spinning machine for Goldie's dog, Nacho, to chase his tail and entertain the neighborhood pets. Another set lets girls design mansions with trapdoors, bridges, and balconies. There are even sets that teach girls how to safely launch female action figures careening down ziplines, skydiving, or speeding across aerial cable cars.

Debbie's husband Beau Lewis was so inspired by the concept that he left his job at the video production company Seedwell to join GoldieBlox as a co-founder in 2013. Beau has an engineering degree from Stanford, and he worked as a Program Manager at Microsoft and Zillow. Although he wasn't yet a dad, the mere thought of someday having a daughter was enough to motivate him to leave a lucrative tech career for the chance to make STEM-related toys for girls.

Debbie and Beau's passion and teamwork have taken the toy market by storm. GoldieBlox quickly expanded into books, apps, videos, and merchandise to inspire girls to become future engineers. Goldiblox has won multiple awards, including *Parents Magazine*'s *FamilyFun* Toy of the Year, and it became the first small business to have a Super Bowl TV ad after winning an Intuit contest that paid for a coveted thirty-second spot. But even with all of these accolades, Debbie and Beau's greatest reward is knowing they've built a platform to empower girls to pursue STEM careers.

In addition to filling girls' environments with STEM-inspired books, games, and toys, education experts say that dads can make a difference by engaging daughters in STEM-related outings and activities. By taking daughters to science and tech museums, going to the planetarium, and building things together in the backyard, dads can inspire an interest in STEM and grow daughters' confidence in math, science, and technology skills. Dozens of creative ideas for at-home science projects for girls can be found at the Go Science Girls website.

For dads who work in the STEM field, volunteering with an organization that teaches girls computer programming and other technology skills can also have a major impact. There are many organizations to choose from, including Girls Who Code, TechGirlz, Girl Develop It, CoolTechGirls, EngineerGirl, and Black Girls Code. Edward Stein is an EIT Director of Distribution Systems for Cardinal Health who carved out time to volunteer as a Program Planning Team Lead for CoolTechGirls, which provides mentors, internships, and career resources for girls who are interested in science and technology. "My thirteen-year-old daughter Megan is a big motivation for me," said Edward. "I enjoy providing her with opportunities to see herself in a future STEM career field which CoolTechGirls provides a forum for."

Girls Who Code is an excellent place for dads of daughters to get started. Founded in 2012, Girls Who Code seeks to close the gender gap in technology through education, mentorships, and school-to-work pipelines. Girls Who Code has reached almost 90,000 girls across all fifty states, and half of the girls in its programs are from minority or low-income families. The organization has nearly 5,000 college-aged alums who are choosing computer science or related fields as their majors at fifteen times the rate of the national average. At that pace, Girls Who Code could equalize women in entry-level tech jobs by 2027. Men can volunteer to facilitate a Girls Who Code after-school club for sixth- through eighth-grade girls or teach at a summer camp. Summer courses cover a range of topics, including website design, wearable technology, and iPhone app development.

TechGirlz also offers volunteer opportunities for dads of daughters. This organization focuses on engaging middle-school girls to build technology skills through free, interactive classes called "TechShopz." TechGirlz makes it easy for dads to run a workshop with online "TechShopz in a Box." These toolkits include workshop plans, curriculum, materials, and teaching guides that enable anyone to run a workshop for middle-school girls in their area. Dads of daughters can select from a wide range of TechShopz topics, including programming and coding skills, podcasting, website design, mobile apps, digital mapping, graphics and animation, game design, circuitry, network communication, artificial intelligence, robotics, and virtual reality. By open-sourcing their workshop plans, TechGirlz has tripled its enrollment, reaching over 10,000 middle-school girls around the country. Men can also sponsor a TechGirlz summer camp, assist with curriculum development, or help with outreach to tech professionals.

For dads of daughters who are in decision-making positions at technology firms, girls' coding organizations also offer opportunities for corporate partnerships. Girls Who Code has a pipeline-to-work initiative called #HireMe which allows partner companies to post job openings and internships and receive resumes from girls trained through Girls Who Code. Dads can also partner their companies with Girl Develop It, which offers software development classes to women. With programs in fifty-eight cities and over 55,000 members nationwide, Girl Develop It is always on the look-out for corporate sponsorships.

Increasing the pipeline of girls into STEM can also indirectly address the hostile work environment that plagues the tech industry. When women are equally represented in tech jobs and leadership roles, cultural shifts will likely follow. In the meantime, dads of daughters who work in the tech industry can help change their workplace culture by speaking up, empowering women to speak up, and taking women seriously when they do.

Dads of daughters are already showing themselves to be among the strongest male advocates for women in the STEM field. In 2013, researchers identified forty-seven men who were known for being gender diversity advocates in leadership positions at tech firms. Among the men in this group who were fathers, ninety-six percent had at least one daughter. When asked what had motivated them to become active in gender diversity efforts, many of them cited pivotal learning experiences with their daughters.

Mentoring women in STEM careers can happen informally on the job, or men can join an established mentoring program like the one created by Girls In Tech that focuses on professional women's career development. The Million Women Mentors initiative for advancing women in STEM careers also provides opportunities for dads to share their expertise, or dads can participate in the Men as Diversity Partners initiative created by the Society of Women Engineers.

In all of these ways, dads of daughters have opportunities to welcome girls into STEM, support women scientists, engineers, and mathematicians, and accelerate innovation. The first step is finding ways to replace the pervasive princess icon with far more powerful and exciting STEM role models for girls to emulate. That was one of Beau Lewis's primary motivations for leaving his tech job to co-found Goldiblox with his wife. Beau's inspiration came from the mere thought of being a *potential* father of a daughter. In explaining why he joined the movement to advance girls in STEM, Beau channeled the thoughts of many dads of daughters by writing a letter to his future daughter apologizing in advance for all of the ways that we inadvertently direct girls away from STEM careers and vowing to make a difference:

> **Dearest Zelda (daughter),**
>
> I'm afraid there is a 99.99 percent chance you won't grow up to be a princess.

I'm afraid I would rather you become an engineer.

I apologize that I wanted to have a boy....

I was afraid you wouldn't want to build a treehouse with me....

I was afraid that you wouldn't like ninja turtles and hot wheels....

I was under the impression that female role models existed to balance out the Barbie beauty queens, and that Bob the Builder and Lego Man weren't the only options.

I apologize that our country has fallen behind 200 other countries where girls are actually testing better than boys in math and science.

I apologize that I haven't done more to help improve the world for women.

I was under the impression that little girls grew up and had the same opportunities as men in the US workforce....

I was afraid that being a feminist was not for men.

I was afraid that helping little girls might seem creepy.

I am done apologizing.

I am no longer afraid nor easily impressed.

I am inspired....

I am doing something to make sure my daughter will know that she is more than just a princess.

Love,
Beau (Dad)

CHAPTER 4

Confronting Gender Bias

We've all heard the studies finding that assertive men are rewarded, while assertive women are viewed as "bossy," "bitchy," or "too aggressive." We all know that women are expected to be emotional, while men who display emotion are viewed as "weak." But those basic gender biases are just the tip of the iceberg.

Whether we're aware of it or not, gender stereotypes affect our thoughts and decisions, and they contribute significantly to women's workplace inequality. There's an entire array of leadership skills, competence, and expertise that we unconsciously associate with men. These biases often lead us to automatically devalue women's achievements and qualifications. In one revealing study, evaluators were given *identical* resumes, yet they were sixty percent more likely to say they'd hire the applicant when the resume had a man's name on top, rather than a woman's.

Even after women get hired and perform well, gender bias creates constant headwinds for advancement. Men receive the benefit of presumed competence, while women have to prove their ability again and again. Women are judged on their performance, while men are often judged merely on their potential. This is doubly unfair for women, whose actual performance tends to be underestimated, while evaluators overestimate the performance of men. Objective requirements are also applied rigorously to women but leniently to men. This means that women's mistakes get noticed more and remembered longer than men's. On the flip side, women's successes are often attributed to luck, while men's are attributed to skill. Women get less credit for accomplishments than men, and men tend to take credit for women's ideas far more than the reverse. Men also interrupt women more than they interrupt other men (and they interrupt far more than they get interrupted by women).

When women speak up and assert themselves, however, people like them less. In one study of actual performance reviews, sixty-six percent of women received negative feedback about their personalities—for example, "You can sometimes be abrasive"—while only one percent of men received similar comments. But it's a no-win situation. When women are nice and agreeable, they also get penalized—people still like them, but they're viewed as less competent. Agreeable women also don't get credit for the extra work they agree to do, while men get rewarded for doing the same things. One study of workplace evaluations discovered that men who stayed late to help prepare for a meeting got a fourteen percent increase in their performance reviews, while women who also stayed late got no increase at all. So if women agree to extra office tasks, they aren't rewarded, but if they refuse, they're penalized.

As harmful as gender stereotypes are for women in general, they're even harsher for women with children. When women become moms, their bosses and co-workers tend to view them as less competent, less intelligent, and less committed to their jobs. In one survey, forty-one percent of workers said they perceived working moms as less devoted to their careers than other workers, and more than a third judged mothers negatively for needing a flexible work schedule. It's no wonder that the percentage of women who report being worried to tell their bosses when they're pregnant has doubled in the last five years.

As a result of these gender stereotypes, employers set higher expectations on working mothers. That means that when moms perform just as well as other workers, they receive lower evaluations. When moms are late to work, for example, they're punished more severely than other employees who are also late. These harsher performance standards contribute to lower salaries and fewer promotions. While the gender pay gap for women overall is about eighty cents on the dollar, mothers get paid an average of only seventy-one cents for every dollar paid to men.

Gender biases also make it harder for moms to get hired in the first place. Stanford Sociology Professor Shelley Correll documented this bias by sending fake resumes to hundreds of employers. The resumes all had identical content, except that some mentioned the applicant's membership in a parent-teacher association. That tiny trigger indicating the applicant was a parent had dramatic effects on how employers responded. For women, the applicants whose resumes indicated they were moms were half as likely to be offered an interview.

The results were opposite for men. Men whose resumes indicated they were dads were slightly *more likely* to be offered an interview than other men. Other research has found a similar positive bias for fathers. When men have kids, they aren't viewed as less competent or less committed to their jobs. Instead, men tend to get more raises and promotions after becoming dads.

The differences in evaluations, pay, and promotions aren't because women actually become less productive and men actually work harder when they become parents. The disparity is because that's what employers *believe* they will do. That's the power of gender stereotypes. In implicit association tests, a large majority of both men and women more readily associate the word "career" with men and the word "family" with women, which spills into the workplace. Employers are acting on deeply ingrained biases that dads are breadwinners and moms are caregivers, and the effects are undermining women's equality. When asked to rate their most desirable employees, employers rank fathers at the top, followed by childless women and childless men, followed by mothers at the bottom.

Gender biases are particularly pernicious in male-dominated arenas. A survey of over 200 experienced women in the tech industry found extensive gender bias in everyday interactions. Many of these biases reflect a lack of respect for women's status and skills. For example, eighty-eight percent of the women said they'd watched a client or a co-worker ask a male colleague a question that should have been addressed to them. Forty-seven percent said they'd been asked to do "office housework" that male colleagues weren't asked to do, like taking notes in meetings or ordering food.

Women in tech also walk a tightrope navigating gender stereotypes about work and family. On one hand, women feel compelled to hide their status as mothers because of the career stigma that attaches to motherhood. Seventy-five percent of women reported being asked about their marital status and children during interviews, and forty percent felt the need to speak less about their family to be taken more seriously at work. On the other hand, being too explicit about career goals also had negative effects. Eighty-four percent of the women had been told they were "too ambitious"—a trait that's generally viewed positively for men.

Acting on gender bias often happens unintentionally by individuals who genuinely believe they're being fair and objective. So taking aim at gender stereotypes isn't cause for shaming or accusing men of wrongdoing—in fact, women hold implicit gender biases as well. But the unintentional and sometimes unconscious nature of gender bias doesn't mean that it doesn't have real consequences. It also doesn't mean that there's nothing we can do about it. Social scientists are discovering many ways that we can start disrupting gender biases and reducing their negative effects.

Dads of daughters are well-positioned to be leaders in this challenge, in part because daughters help dads question gender expectations. Dads of daughters are less likely than other men to believe that men should be breadwinners and women should be homemakers, for example. One study found that men's support for traditional gender norms decreased by eight to eleven percent while parenting school-aged girls. That's a great foundation for dads of daughters to start exploring unconscious bias and learning how to reduce its effects at work and at home.

Testing Your Bias

Clarissa Farr grew up in a family of teachers. After falling in love with Henry James's novels, she decided to become a teacher too. For fifteen years, she taught English and drama until setting her sights on running her own school. With a one-year-old baby in tow, she headed to Hertfordshire, England to become the Principal of a boarding school, where she served for ten years. Her dedication was rewarded in 2006 when she was named the High Mistress of St. Paul's Girls' School in London.

St. Paul's is one of England's most prestigious schools for academically gifted girls. Clarissa adored spending time with so many engaged and hardworking young women. "It's so energizing. It's so rejuvenating. They make me laugh. They challenge me. I learn something from my pupils every single day," she says. But most of all, Clarissa loved giving young women an extraordinary platform for success.

St. Paul's alumnae—known as "Paulinas"—include leaders in politics, science, law, education, and the arts. Parliamentarian Harriet Harman, politician Shirley Williams, author Petronella Wyatt, economist Joan Robinson, and scientist Rosalind Franklin all spent their childhood at St. Paul's. Former British Prime Minister Margaret Thatcher chose St. Paul's for her daughter, Carol, who became a journalist and author.

Yet over time, Clarissa started hearing troubling stories from her alumnae about workplace bias. Her former students were marching confidently into careers only to find pervasive double standards, sexist behavior, and higher barriers for women than for men. Clarissa knew that women were under-represented in leadership positions in the British workplace, and she knew that the eighteen percent gender wage gap was narrowing at a snail's pace. But the stories she heard from her Paulinas made the statistics personal. If the exceptionally well-trained women from her school were facing widespread gender bias, the problems must be even worse than the numbers suggested.

Clarissa joined forces with England's Girls' Schools Association to survey graduates aged twenty-five to thirty-five from girls' schools around the country to better understand their workplace experiences. The results were startling. seventy-one percent of the women reported having experienced or witnessed gender inequality in the workplace. Sixty-five percent said that women were unlikely to challenge sexist behavior out of fear that it would harm their chances for promotion. Gender wage discrimination was also rampant, with seventy-three percent of women ranking pay inequality as their biggest issue.

Clarissa was disturbed by these responses, but she also noted one data point that gave her an idea about how to address the problem. What caught Clarissa's eye was that seventy-five percent of the respondents said that men could do more to support women in the workplace. Up to that point, Clarissa had focused her efforts internally by creating the best educational experience for her students. The survey got her thinking instead about reaching out and engaging men.

Clarissa wondered how she could get men actively involved in supporting women's workplace equality. It dawned on her that she had access to some of the most influential men in London: the dads of the daughters at her school. Her students' fathers included attorneys, bankers, doctors, and other industry leaders who were in powerful positions to initiate change. So dads became the initial target of her work.

In 2016, Clarissa launched the Dads4Daughters initiative with the goal of engaging men in advancing gender equality. Her first step was to make a modest request to her students' fathers. She urged them to look around their workplaces and ask themselves a few questions. Would they want their daughters to be working there? Would their daughters feel comfortable in their work environment? Could they imagine their daughters becoming the CEO?

Clarissa's call to dads struck a chord in ways that impersonal statistics couldn't do. Her students' fathers responded with earnest requests to learn how they could better support women. Clarissa was overwhelmed by the response, and she realized what a powerful source of male engagement the father-daughter relationship can be. So she expanded her campaign to fathers everywhere. "We are urging men across the country, from all walks of life, to hold their organizations to account," explained Clarissa. "We hope that with the help of fathers, women will enjoy workplaces free from bias, pay inequality and glass ceilings."

To help dads translate their passion into action, the Dads4Daughters initiative invested in a valuable tool to educate men about unconscious gender bias. Clarissa teamed up with Split Second Research to develop the Dads4Daughters Test, which is available free online. The test is modeled after Harvard University's Implicit Association Test, which social scientists created to detect how strongly a person automatically associates various attributes with males or females. This type of implicit bias test measures gendered beliefs that individuals may not even know they have, even though the beliefs may affect their decision-making.

The Dads4Daughters Test uses what psychologists call an "affective priming approach," which has two phases. In the first phase, the test-taker quickly categorizes explicitly gender-related words—like girl, boy, she, he, hers, or his—as either female or male. The target word is flashed on the screen and the test-taker must press designated letters as quickly as possible to identify the word as female or male. For example, if the target word that's flashed is "hers," the test-taker must quickly press the letter "f" for female, but if the target word that's flashed is "he," the test-taker must quickly press the letter "m" for male. This first phase measures the test-taker's average response rate, which is used as a baseline for identifying gender biases during phase two.

In the second phase, the test-taker performs the same task of categorizing explicitly gender-related words like "she" or "he" as either female or male. However, in phase two, the screen flashes a "primer word" immediately before flashing each gender-related target word. The test-taker is told to ignore the primer words. But it turns out that's extremely hard to do. The primer words include twenty-four different personal qualities, roles, and jobs that have traditionally been associated with one gender or the other. Examples of primer words include powerful, weak, decisive, leader, manager, director, follower, supporter, engineer, pilot, surgeon, nanny, science, and math.

The test works by measuring how much the primer words affect the test-taker's response time when categorizing the actual target words. For example, the test will measure whether seeing a male-associated primer word (like "engineer") makes the test-taker slower to identify as female a target word like "she," or faster to identify as male a target word like "he." The stronger male or female association that the test-taker has with the primer word—i.e., the stronger the test-taker's implicit gender biases—the larger the impact will be on the test-taker's response times.

To illustrate, the test might flash the primer word "leader" before the target word "she." The test-taker is supposed to ignore the word "leader" and quickly press "f" to categorize "she" as a female word. If a test-taker doesn't implicitly associate the word "leader" with either men or women, then the primer word won't affect how quickly the test-taker categorizes "she" as a female word. However, if the test-taker strongly associates the word "leader" with men, the test-taker will be slower to identify the word "she" as female. That's because the initial primer word "leader" triggers thoughts about men, which must be overridden to get the test-taker's mind back on track to the task of categorizing "she" as female.

Conversely, if the primer word "leader" is flashed before a male target word like "he," a test-taker who strongly associates leaders with men will be even faster at categorizing "he" as a male word because the test-taker's thoughts have already been primed to think about men. This method can reveal unconscious gender biases that test-takers don't know they possess and may genuinely disavow, which is why it's so powerful.

After measuring the test-taker's response times with dozens of paired primer words and target words, the test calculates the strength of a test-taker's unconscious gender biases along four dimensions: professions, career fields, roles, and personal qualities. The results might show, for example, that a test-taker unconsciously stereotypes certain jobs or characteristics as male, even if the test-taker is truly committed to gender equality. Or the results might show that a test-taker who says that women are just as capable as men still unconsciously feels more comfortable with the idea of a male boss.

Implicit bias tests reveal that nearly all of us—men *and* women—are affected by gender stereotypes. So the results provide a dramatic jolt to almost all test-takers who perceive themselves to be unbiased workplace players. By helping people realize that they might inadvertently be part of the problem, the Dads4Daughters test is effective at getting men's attention and motivating them to act.

The test results alone don't tell dads what they can to do help, so the Dads4Daughters test also includes an action component. The test immediately provides each test-taker with a list of steps they can take to address the particular areas where they showed the most gender bias. Dads are asked to commit to several action items on the list. Some examples include: (1) I will mentor a colleague of the opposite gender. (2) I will be more aware of the language I use to describe male and female colleagues and the negative effects of certain adjectives. (3) I will listen to the experiences of female colleagues and sustain an open channel of communication with them. (4) I will not let men dominate a conversation in a meeting. (5) I will ensure that fifty percent of candidates interviewed for any job opportunity are female. Dads can print a pledge certificate with their selected actions, along with an affirmation stating: "I will celebrate my role as a father of a daughter to bring greater gender equality in the workplace."

By engaging dads to start addressing gender bias, Clarissa hopes that the Dads4Daughters initiative will not only create fairer workplaces for women, but also more welcoming workplaces for men. Men who want to be engaged fathers often find themselves marginalized in the workplace, and they understand the work/family conflicts facing women. "We feel that a lot of attention's been paid to the working mother," explains Clarissa. "We now want to celebrate the working father."

So the Dads4Daughters initiative focuses on giving dads the opportunity to make their workplaces better for their daughters, in part by supporting engaged fatherhood. Some of the pledge items on the Dads4Daughters Test are targeted at male stereotypes that contribute to inequality. One pledge item says: "I aim to make it more culturally acceptable for men to fulfill their roles as modern fathers, particularly by encouraging flexibility for both mothers and fathers." Another states: "I will not judge men or women to be less dedicated to their jobs if they have to devote time to their familial responsibilities." In this way, Dads4Daughters can start conversations about workplace flexibility that will benefit women and men alike.

Over 10,000 people have taken the Dads4Daughters test. Participants have spanned the globe from London to Ghana and have included men in an array of jobs from bus drivers to CEOs. Mark Wilson, the former CEO of the British insurance company Aviva, is one of the initiative's supporters. "It's up to all of us to take real action to bring about a world that works for women as well as men," says Mark. "As a dad with daughters, I'm right behind the Dads4Daughters campaign. We know that a workforce that truly reflects the community we live in has got to be a good thing."

How Dads Can Get Started

Fathers who want to learn more about gender bias should begin by taking the Dads4Daughters Implicit Bias Test. For all of us, it's both humbling and enlightening to see how we can support gender equality, but still be affected by gender stereotypes. At the end of the test, take the Dads4Daughters Pledge and select a few recommended actions to focus on at your job.

Another excellent tool for combatting gender stereotypes is the "50 Ways to Fight Bias" card deck available from LeanIn.org. You can purchase the cards for $35 or get the same information free in video format. The cards and videos allow you to set up interactive sessions with workplace colleagues to learn about how gender bias affects hiring, pay, and promotions. The activities work best in groups of six to eight people to promote discussion, sharing personal experiences, and brainstorming solutions. The LeanIn.org website also offers advice for individuals to serve as discussion moderators, which would be a terrific role for dads of daughters.

Each card in the "Fight Bias" deck contains four components for discussion. The card highlights a specific example of gender bias in the workplace. The card identifies why that type of bias occurs. The card explains how that form of bias contributes to inequality.

And most importantly, the card offers advice about how bosses or co-workers could respond to the situation.

Here's an example from one of the cards, which starts by describing a common scenario involving gender bias: "A woman suggests an idea in a meeting and it falls flat. A few minutes later, a man suggests the same idea and gets an enthusiastic reaction." The card explains why this situation occurs and why it matters for women's equality: "Because we tend to underestimate women's performance and overestimate men's, we often don't give women as much credit for their ideas. Getting credit for ideas is important—it's often how employees get noticed. When people don't feed heard, they may also stop speaking up and sharing their views. Over time, if their contributions go unseen, it can slow their advancement." After reading this information, participants discuss the scenario, share personal stories of similar experiences, and brainstorm what to do if they encounter this situation. Participants can then review the flip side of the card, which offers advice. This card suggests an easy response: "You can remind everyone that the idea originated with your woman colleague: 'I think [name] made that point a few moments ago. I like this direction.'"

Another resource for men who are interested in challenging gender bias comes from the #LeanInTogether initiative, also launched by LeanIn.org. This initiative offers men tips for becoming "Workplace MVPs" who speak out for gender equality at their jobs. The tips include reminders of common gender stereotypes for men to watch for, like the expectation that men should be confident and assertive while women should be compassionate and nurturing, the assumption that men are more committed to their careers, and the fact that men's performance is often overestimated compared to women, who tend not to take or get credit for their contributions. The #LeanInTogether website encourages men to take small but powerful steps to combat these biases, like making sure that women get time to talk at meetings, speaking up when women are interrupted or have their ideas stolen, and evenly distributing mundane office housework like notetaking, event planning, and training new employees.

Another resource for male allies is the "Bias Interrupters" program from WorkLife Law. Bias interrupters are specific changes that individuals or companies can make to hiring, evaluation, promotion, and compensation practices to reduce gender bias. One of the crucial first steps is using metrics to audit workplace systems and reveal where gender biases are strongest. Metrics should measure whether men are consistently receiving higher performance evaluations, more promotions, and higher pay than women. Metrics should also assess whether women's ratings fall after they have children, and whether women or men lose ground after taking parental leave or seeking flexible hours.

The Bias Interrupters website offers toolkits for redesigning performance evaluations to reduce gender bias. The toolkits help employment decision-makers set performance criteria linked to job requirements, rather than using subjective assessments like "culture fit" or "executive presence," which open the door for bias. The toolkits also teach employers how to gather evidence to support ratings on each criterion, which reduces the tendency to apply standards more leniently to men. This also minimizes gendered reactions to similar behavior—like assessing men as leaders when they ask for a raise, but viewing women as aggressive when they do the same. In addition, this reduces the "halo and horns effect," which is the tendency to assume that if a male worker has one particular strength, he's stellar across-the-board, while assuming that if a female worker has one particular weakness, she's generally deficient. The toolkits also establish separate ratings for performance versus potential to avoid the bias of promoting men based on expectations, while requiring women to have documented achievements.

Another easy Bias Interrupter is for managers to stop relying on employees' self-promotion to share achievements. Relying on self-promotion disadvantages women who tend not to talk about their own successes as much as men, in part because they are liked less when they do. Managers can set up formal systems for submitting employee accomplishments, which get distributed in a monthly company email. Another effective practice is not making assumptions that working moms wouldn't want challenging assignments or can't travel, and to instead simply ask them about their preferences. To learn more about concrete steps for combatting gender bias, encourage your company to sign up for a Bias Interrupters Training session at your workplace.

A final step that dads of daughters can take to help disrupt gender bias is to use Karen Pressner's "flip it to test it" technique—and ask your male colleagues to do the same. Karen is the Global Head of Human Resources for Roche Diagnostics, but despite her leadership success, she noticed that even she held unconscious stereotypes about women.

To disrupt her own biases, Karen started making mental reverse-gender comparisons to assess her interactions. When a woman asked her to evaluate whether she was being paid fairly, for example, she forced herself to think about whether her response would be the same if a man made the request. Discovering that her answer was "no," she realized the effects of deeply ingrained stereotypes of men as breadwinners who provide for their families. This inspired Karen to launch #FlipItToTestIt, which offers companies training to combat gender bias.

Dads of daughters can practice this technique both at work and at home. If you find yourself asking a female colleague to order food for a meeting, for example, consider whether you'd make the same request of a male colleague. If someone on your hiring team criticizes a female candidate for bragging about her accomplishments, ask the team member if they'd have the same reaction if it was a male candidate hyping his achievements.

The same thing applies when doling out chores and rewards at home. If you ask your daughter to help with household tasks, consider whether you'd expect the same from a son. When you pay your son for doing household chores, ask yourself if you'd pay your daughter the same amount. In case you're wondering, this is where the pay gap inadvertently starts. The American Time Use Survey revealed that girls aged fifteen to nineteen spend an average of 15 percent more time doing chores like cooking, cleaning, yard care, and pet care than boys the same age. But boys earn an average of twice as much as girls for doing chores each week. It's no wonder that these patterns repeat themselves in the workplace, but dads of daughters can break the cycle.

One dad who's trying to make a difference is Will McDonald, the Director of Public Policy and Corporate Responsibility at Aviva. Will took the Dads4Daughters test and became convinced that fathers have a unique opportunity to become workplace leaders for gender equality. "I want my kids to grow up in a world where the limits to what they achieve are not set down by what gender they are," says Will. "But to see real change, we need to harness the power of dads at work. After all, dads don't stop being dads when they walk through the office door."

CHAPTER 5

Rethinking Masculinity

On October 15, 2017, actress Alyssa Milano asked her Twitter followers to reply “me too” if they’d ever been sexually harassed or assaulted. She thought it might help reveal the magnitude of abuse that women face. The response was overwhelming. Within the first day, the hashtag was shared over 500,000 times on Twitter. Within forty-five days, #MeToo posts on Facebook had topped eighty-five million across eighty-five countries. In a few short weeks, #MeToo became a status, a movement, and a wake-up call.

Alyssa’s tweet came in the wake of serial sexual assault allegations against movie mogul Harvey Weinstein, as well as other entertainment industry leaders. What #MeToo revealed was that those were not isolated incidents. Women from all walks of life face the risk of sexual harassment, assault, and rape. Although Alyssa’s tweet brought global attention to #MeToo, it actually originated in 2006 when activist Tarana Burke used the phrase to express solidarity with sexual assault victims, particularly girls and women of color, who face even higher rates of sexual violence.

The statistics are deeply disturbing. In one survey of American women, eighty-one percent said they had experienced some form of sexual harassment or assault. One in five women have been the victim of rape or attempted rape, and one in five female college students have suffered sexual assault on campus. Each year, around 125,000 rapes are reported in the US alone. Other surveys report that one in three women have been sexually harassed at their jobs, often by men in positions of power—that's thirty-three million women who've faced sexual harassment while trying to make a living. Today, women aren't even safe online, with forty-one percent reporting incidents of cyber sexual harassment.

What's particularly frightening is that the statistics capture only part of the story, as most sexual misconduct goes unreported. Less than two percent of women who are sexually harassed confront their perpetrators, instead altering their own behavior by avoiding locations where they feel vulnerable, changing work assignments, or quitting their jobs. Three out of every four women who are sexually harassed at work never report it to anyone, and only one out of ten women file a formal complaint. Women's low rates of reporting sexual misconduct stem from rational fears about not being believed, facing retribution, or losing their jobs. In criminal cases, there's often a particular lack of will to investigate and prosecute. For every 1,000 sexual assaults and rapes, only 230 are reported to the police, and only five lead to felony convictions.

While most incidents of sexual harassment are committed by strangers, the majority of sexual assaults and rapes are perpetrated by people the victim knows—acquaintances, friends, family members, or partners. That compounds the low reporting rate because sexual violence by non-strangers tends not to be taken seriously. Victims often find themselves being blamed, so they keep quiet, which has helped shield a domestic violence epidemic in the US. One in four women will suffer severe physical violence at the hands of an intimate partner during her lifetime, making domestic violence the leading cause of injury to women.

So what role can be played by the majority of men who aren't directly part of the epidemic? By the men who treat women with respect? By the men who are appalled by the sexual abuse of women? By the men who want to protect the women in their lives and create a safer future for their daughters? One critical role for men is to start challenging our cultural norms of masculinity that fuel the epidemic. Sexual assault starts with a culture that teaches boys and men to be strong, non-emotional, aggressive, dominant, predatory, and controlling. It starts with a culture that teaches boys and men to objectify, demean, and devalue girls and women. It starts with a culture that fiercely polices boys and men who break these rules and show any sign of compassion, caring, or vulnerability. It also starts with silence—good men who ignore the misconduct of other men.

Men can make a difference by openly discussing and re-writing our society's deeply ingrained rules about what it means to be a "real man." Caring dads of daughters are well-positioned to lead this movement toward a healthier masculinity. In the end, this path will not only make the world safer for girls and women, it will also improve the wellbeing of boys and men.

Breaking Out of the Man Box

Tony Porter was born in Harlem and grew up in the Bronx. Like most boys, he learned the rules of manhood at an early age. When he was about twelve, he remembers a tough sixteen-year-old boy in his neighborhood who was sexually abusing a girl who was mentally disabled. The older boy was pressuring him and other young boys to do the same. While Tony didn't succumb to the pressure, he also didn't speak up and instead pretended to follow along. That's because challenging the older boy's behavior would have destroyed his own reputation and made him a target for abuse himself. This was just one small example of what Tony now calls "The Man Box"—the limiting and harmful way that we socialize boys to understand what it means to be a man. As Tony explains:

> *Growing up as a boy, we were taught that men had to be tough, had to be strong, had to be courageous, dominating—no pain, no emotions, with the exception of anger, and definitely no fear—that men are in charge, which means women are not; that men lead, and [women] should just follow and just do what we say; that men are superior, women are inferior; that men are strong, women are weak; that women are of less value, property of men, and objects, particularly sexual objects.*

Over time, Tony started realizing how these harshly enforced rules set the foundation for gender-based violence. He also began seeing how these rules trap men as much as they demean women. Tony didn't see his own father cry until Tony was twenty-one years old, and it took the death of his teenage brother to move his father to tears. While his father's grief was totally understandable, his dad made a point of not crying in front of his mom and sisters, and he apologized to Tony for showing emotion. He also praised Tony for not shedding his own tears. This didn't seem like a healthy or authentic way for anyone to be living.

Once Tony had daughters and he started worrying about their safety, he felt an obligation to do more. It wasn't easy for him to admit—as a good man who treated girls and women with respect—that he was still part of the problem. If he sat back and tolerated the Man Box rules and the culture of male violence against women that they produced, then he was complicit. "Ending violence against women and girls is primarily the responsibility of men," Tony realized, including kind and well-meaning men like himself.

To help others escape the Man Box, Tony co-founded A CALL TO MEN, an organization that supports boys and men in learning a more respectful approach to masculinity. A CALL TO MEN partners with schools, companies, sports teams, and government agencies to train boys and men in how to build healthier relationships and prevent gender-based violence. In 2017, A CALL TO MEN quickly responded after the #MeToo revelations. The organization teamed up with the Joyful Heart Foundation, which supports sexual assault survivors. Together, they launched the #IWillSpeakUp and #SupportSurvivors campaigns to teach men how to take responsibility for creating a safe environment for women and girls.

Being the dad of daughters played a major role in spurring Tony to action. "A lot of what motivates me is the world I want to see for my daughters," he says. After explaining his journey to break out of the Man Box in his moving TED Talk, Tony splashed a photo of his youngest daughter, Jade, on the large screen behind him. "This is the love of my life," Tony said, and she's the reason for his call to action to other men:

> *In the world that I envision for my daughters and yours, and how I want men to act and behave, I need you on board. I need you with me. I need you working with me and me working with you on how we raise our boys, teaching them to be men. We can show our boys that it's okay not to be dominating. That it's okay to have feelings and emotions. That it's okay to promote equality. That it's okay to have a woman who you are just friends with and that's it. That it's okay to be a whole person. That our liberation as men is tied to their liberation as women.*

In his training sessions, Tony doesn't hesitate to tap into men's emotions as fathers of daughters to help men understand the importance of healthy masculinity. "I advise men all the time to envision the world they would want for their daughters and other girls that they love and care about," Tony explains. "I usually follow that statement with a question: in that world, how do you want to see men acting and behaving?"

This question can even impact young men in high school and college who have no plans to become fathers anytime soon. In school workshops, Tony often starts by asking young men to talk about common phrases they use to describe women, like "fresh meat." The young men tend to laugh, joke, and take very lightly any suggestion that the words do real harm. Then Tony asks them to imagine themselves in twenty-five years having the same conversation with their daughters sitting in the room. "You can hear a pin drop," says Tony. "These young men, in this moment, transition mentally from young college men to fathers, and they immediately begin to process and view this issue differently."

While Tony's message often resonates deeply with dads of daughters, the father-daughter relationship can also pose unique challenges to embracing healthier masculinity. Scott Davis is a trainer for A CALL TO MEN, and he's also the dad of two daughters, Sara and Rosalie. Having daughters motivated Scott to become an ally for women's safety. But the relationship also made it difficult for him to challenge one of the most conventional notions of masculinity: the fiercely protectionist father-daughter instinct. "Having daughters didn't exempt me from my complicity in a culture of masculinity that views women as objects, as less than, and as the property of men," explains Scott:

> *In fact, having daughters motivated me to elevate my "real man" status. The most common advice I got as a father was, "better get a shotgun." Because a real man protects his women. I needed to double down on projecting my willingness to perpetrate violence and simultaneously reinforce that my daughters were my property. They belonged to me, and anyone crossing the line would feel my wrath... My daughters gave me perfect cover for reinforcing my existence in the Man Box. I was able to dive in headfirst, justifying it with fatherly love.*

Eventually, Scott realized that by enacting aggressive protectionism of his daughters, he was actually reinforcing the culture of violence against women. "Far from protecting my daughters with my crazy dad love," says Scott, "I was actively participating in creating a dangerous environment."

The hardest lesson for Scott was that he couldn't keep his daughters safe by being a stronger protective force. That's why he got involved with A CALL TO MEN. "Showing up for my daughters," says Scott, "means I need to show up for everyone impacted by the violence of manhood."

Tony Porter recently took this message to the professional football players in the National Football League, where athletes personify hyper-masculinity. Living up to those expectations gives NFL players their hero status, but it has a dark side. When compared to similarly-paid men in other professions, NFL players have a much higher rate of domestic violence. Between 2012 and 2013 alone, fifteen NFL players were arrested for committing violence against women. As of 2015, forty-four active players had been accused of sexual assault or domestic violence. In a recent survey, over two-thirds of both football fans and non-fans agreed that the NFL has a serious problem with domestic violence.

Despite this public awareness, the league hasn't seemed committed to addressing the problem. League administrators tend to be lenient on players who commit domestic violence, often ignoring their own policy of imposing a mandatory, six-game suspension. Some teams even draft players with a known history of domestic abuse. So instead of waiting for the NFL to take action, Tony went directly to the players to address the problem.

Tony became an NFL advisor to educate players about healthy relationships and respectful manhood. He worked with more than twenty teams as part of a life skills curriculum. Tony was moved by the players' responses. "To experience the candor and emotion elicited by a topic often considered to be a 'woman's issue' from the most adored and seemingly aggressive athletes in the world was very powerful," says Tony. But he was most impressed by the men who had daughters. The dads didn't just hear Tony's message, many committed to becoming role models for other men.

One of the results of Tony's partnership with the NFL is a book called, *NFL Dads Dedicated to Daughters*. The book shares the stories of over seventy NFL fathers who've been motivated by their daughters to change what it means to be a "real man" and become advocates against domestic violence.

The NFL dads who participated were committed to becoming role models for healthy masculinity. "I am living in a way that shows how much I value women in my personal life," says Kevin Mawae, a former center for the Tennessee Titans. "My hope is that more men will stand up and speak out on violence against women for the sake of their daughters as well."

Lorenzo Alexander, a Buffalo Bills linebacker, agrees. "I take it upon myself to behave in a way I would want another man to treat my daughter: with love and respect." Sometimes this requires NFL players to challenge their own notions of masculinity and reveal a more caring side.

"Each time I try to fall back into the routine of what society defines as 'manly' behavior," says Hall-of-Famer Jerome Bettis, "the look on my daughter's face, her smile, and sometimes her laugh reminds me that it's okay to be sensitive and vulnerable."

The NFL dads also pledged to speak up when they see men mistreating women. "Sometimes I hear guys use degrading words when they talk about women," says former linebacker Andra Davis. "It's unnecessary, and I make a point to challenge them on their language. Taking a stand on how men treat women is important to me, because I have three daughters who mean more to me than words can express."

Brian Waters, a six-time Pro Bowl member, also credits his three daughters as motivation for speaking up. "As men, we live by the code that tells us to stay out of other people's business," says Brian. "But, we can't continue to do that if violence against women is going to stop."

Holding other men accountable for their conduct toward women was a theme echoed by many of the NFL dads who joined the project. "As a devoted father who wants a better world for his daughters, I think it's important for my voice to be heard on the issue of domestic violence," says Bertrand Berry, a former defensive end for the Arizona Cardinals. "We need to speak up and out.... Tasteless jokes, embellished stories about encounters with women, and being silent when we know that a man is mistreating a woman are contributing factors and must stop for positive change."

Deshea Townsend, a former player and current NFL coach, agrees that men have an obligation to set standards for other men. "I love my daughters so much and want them to have a life that is free of violence and intimidation," says Deshea. "For the well-being of all of our daughters, I hope that more men will speak up on this issue and hold their sons, brothers, fathers, cousins, and teammates accountable for their actions."

As popular icons of masculinity, NFL dads are in a unique position to shift gender norms and prevent violence. "Some men choose not to confront domestic violence because they think they're good guys, so it's not their problem," explains Deon Grant, a former safety for the New York Giants. "But in the long run, we aren't going to be around forever to protect our little girls. We should all consider it our problem because we have the power to affect the world they live in now and possibly impact the future."

Matt Ware, a former defensive back for the Arizona Cardinals, agrees that all men have a responsibility to prevent domestic violence, and he credits his daughter for helping him "mature as a man" and recognize this role. "Women have led the fight against domestic violence alone for way too long," says Matt. "We want our mothers, wives, sisters, and daughters to be safe and receive the same respect that we expect for ourselves." These heartfelt sentiments from some of the nation's most popular athletes—men who've built their reputations on aggressive play—is a credit to Tony Porter's work through A CALL TO MEN and to the power of the father-daughter relationship.

Dads are also leading the way in preventing sexual assault on college campuses. In 2015, Illinois Republican House Representative Rodney Davis spoke about his daughter in front of a packed audience at the University of Illinois. "As a father of a daughter heading off to college in the fall," he said, "nothing is more terrifying than hearing the statistic: 1 in 5 women have experienced sexual assault since entering college."

Davis gave this speech to launch a rally by the It's On Us organization, which was created by Former Vice President Joe Biden in response to President Obama's White House Task Force to Prevent Sexual Assault. It's On Us engages male students in preventing sexual assault. The organization has worked with students on over five hundred college campuses by teaching about consent, bystander intervention, and supporting sexual assault survivors. Along with training, the organization asks men to take the It's On Us Pledge, which requests four commitments: "To recognize that non-consensual sex is sexual assault. To identify situations in which sexual assault may occur. To intervene in situations where consent has not or cannot be given. To create an environment in which sexual assault is unacceptable and survivors are supported."

It's On Us is one of several organizations that have shifted focus away from teaching women self-defense to instead focus on male involvement in prevention. Two other groups that train men about violence prevention, respectful relationships, and healthy masculinity are Men Stopping Violence and Men Can Stop Rape.

Futures Without Violence is another organization that's engaging men in their roles as dads, coaches, and educators to prevent violence against women. One of its most successful programs is Coaching Boys Into Men (CBIM), which works with high school athletic coaches to teach male athletes about respecting women. CBIM has created a "Coaches Kit" to give male coaches the skills and resources to promote respectful behavior among their male players and reduce sexual assault. The kit also offers CBIM Cards with topics and instructions for coaches to lead discussions about healthy relationship skills.

Because male athletes are revered by their peers, they hold incredible power to establish rules for behavior at their schools. They're the ones who can make it cool to act respectfully toward girls. Many of the high school athletes who've participated in CBIM report that they often check each other's behavior just by saying the words, "boys into men," when they see disrespectful behavior. When a popular male athlete invokes that simple phrase, it's usually enough to shut down misconduct by his peers.

The CBIM program has been used in the US, India, and South Africa. To test its success, sixteen high schools with over 2,000 male athletes participated in a study in which half of the schools taught the CBIM program and half did not. In later surveys, male athletes who had CBIM training reported that were less likely than untrained athletes to have engaged in abusive or disrespectful behavior toward girls and were more likely to have intervened when witnessing misconduct by their male peers.

Male coaches take their mentoring role seriously and are often among the most influential voices in boys' lives. This makes high school athletics a perfect forum for shaping lifelong attitudes and behaviors in young men—both on and off the playing field. Many professional athletes support CBIM's training of healthy relationship skills and its message that "violence never equals strength." Former NFL Quarterback Doug Flutie is one father of a daughter who has leant his voice to the effort. "There's nothing better than excelling at a game you love," says Doug. "There's nothing worse than thinking your accomplishments as a player outweigh your responsibilities as a person."

In the US, we typically think of gender-based violence in terms of sexual harassment, assault, and rape, but male dominance over women's bodies comes in different forms in different cultures. No matter what form male dominance takes, it requires courageous men to break the cycle. Kebebe Muntasha learned this as both the father of a daughter and the headmaster of a primary school in Ethiopia. As in many African and Middle Eastern countries, young girls in Ethiopia are routinely forced to undergo female genital mutilation—also known as FGM or cutting—as part of deeply ingrained cultural beliefs that incorrectly link FGM to chastity, cleanliness, family honor, and marriageability.

FGM involves the total or partial removal of a girl's female genitalia. It has no medical benefits and can have devastating effects, including hemorrhaging, infections, difficulty urinating, developing cysts, post-traumatic stress disorder, and other mental health issues. FGM is also a major cause of sexual dysfunction, infertility, and childbirth complications, including maternal and fetal deaths. Today, over 200 million girls and women are living with the traumatic aftermath of FGM.

Kebebe began educating himself about FGM after he noticed a rise in absenteeism among adolescent girls at his school. He discovered that they were recovering from FGM, which often kept them out of school for long periods of time. Some girls never returned. Kebebe's first instinct was to protect his own daughter, whom he defiantly declares will never be subjected to FGM.

But Kebebe wanted to do more, so he contacted Plan International for advice. He learned ways to start changing the cultural norms around FGM so that his community could keep girls safe, healthy, and in school. He began openly discussing the issue with his students, many of whom have become outspoken opponents of the practice. Kebebe also launched the "Uncut Girls Club" at his school, which gives girls a place to discuss FGM and other practices that harm girls and women. With over fifty members, the club has also become a source of advocacy outside the school, where students are educating their families and friends. "I am no longer embarrassed," shared Alem, a teenage girl who's a member of Kebebe's group. "I dare to speak out about the perils of FGM."

Kebebe is particularly gratified that boys are becoming advocates, often after losing a sister or mother to childbirth complications from FGM. "Many boys in our school have joined the effort and publicly announced that they will marry a girl who has not been cut," he explains. Kebebe's hope is that the eradication of FGM will be a first step toward full equality for girls in his country by allowing them to stay in school, where he's seen their ability to excel. He is most proud that one of his daughter's goals is to become the Chair of the Uncut Girls' Club.

How Dads Can Get Started

The easiest way for dads of daughters to foster healthier masculinity is to become "Dadfluencers" by proudly displaying your daddy love. Journalist Emily Dreyfuss coined the phrase "Dadfluencers" to describe fathers who are boldly sharing the joy, struggles, caring, vulnerability, and deep connection they experience by being engaged parents. On Instagram, there are 3.7 million photos and videos tagged #dadlife that share images of men doing everyday parenting. By encouraging men to connect with other men in positive ways, Dadfluencers are starting to rewrite the rules of masculinity. By normalizing men's caregiving role, engaged dads are turning compassion into a manly quality.

"The more people see fathers actively fathering," says Emily, "the more it becomes a normal part of society." By challenging the notions of men as aggressive, dominant, controlling, powerful, and non-emotional, Dadfluencers can disrupt the cultural norms that fuel abuse and violence against women. Each small step in sharing the emotional journey of being a dad can help foster healthier relationships and create a safer world for women and girls.

In addition to modelling healthy masculinity, dads of daughters can also speak out when other men mistreat girls and women. It's also important to speak out when men police other men for not being sufficiently "masculine." Question behavior that demeans women and applaud men who show compassion and treat women with respect. If you're hesitant to step into other men's business because you're not sure it's your place, take ten minutes to watch Tony Porter's 2010 TED Talk, which *GQ Magazine* lists as one of the "Top 10 TED Talks Every Man Should See." You can also read Tony's book, *Breaking Out of the "Man Box": The Next Generation of Manhood*. Tony makes a persuasive case for why fostering healthier masculinity and combatting gender violence is every man's responsibility.

Dads can also find support from other male activists who have thought about how our culture of toxic masculinity fuels our epidemic of sexual assault and domestic violence. These men have thoughtful advice for other men who want to get involved. Several of these game-changing books include Paul Kivel's *Men's Work: How to Stop the Violence that Tears Our Lives Apart*; Jared Yates Sexton's *The Man They Wanted Me To Be: Toxic Masculinity and a Crisis of Our Own Making*; and Mark Greene's *Remaking Manhood: Stories from the Front Lines of Change.*

Mark is a Senior Editor for the Good Men Project, which shares stories, research, and resources for men who want to connect with other men to foster healthier manhood and build stronger relationships. One of the most important things that Mark has learned is that breaking down the Man Box doesn't just make girls and women safer, it also improves the lives of boys and men. When men are freed to live authentic, compassionate, and connected lives, they are happier and healthier as well. He shares these insights in his book, *The Little #MeToo Book for Men*.

Dads can also break the cycle of gender violence by educating their sons about gender equality. Even men who proudly self-identify as feminists sometimes need a reminder that empowering girls is only one piece of the puzzle. Canadian Prime Minister Justin Trudeau is a good example. He's been an outspoken advocate for women's advancement and equal pay. He was recently telling his wife Sophie how proud he was of raising their daughter Ella to be a confident and ambitious young girl. "I talk to Ella all the time about how she can do anything she wants, and she's just as good as any man," he was saying, when Sophie stopped him cold. "That's great," she said. "But how are you saying that to our sons as well? How are you training your sons to be focused on women's rights and women's opportunities the way you're focused on telling your daughter that she can be anything?"

This was one of the few times that Prime Minister Trudeau has ever been at a loss for words. Looking back, he sees that moment as a turning point. He's now just as focused on raising his sons to be gender equality advocates as he's focused on empowering his daughter to reach for her dreams.

Educating our sons can take many forms. If you have a teenaged son, talk to him about consent and have him sign the It's On Us Pledge before heading to college. For younger boys, talk about respect, empathy, and tolerance. Teach boys to do caregiving work—of their pets, younger siblings, grandparents, and other family members. Teach boys to care for themselves as well. Encourage boys to be friends with girls, which fosters stronger communication skills and healthier adult relationships. Let boys know that anger isn't their only permissible emotion. Until age five, boys cry the same amount as girls, but then they learn that showing vulnerability isn't allowed. Most importantly, let boys follow their interests—even if it's dress-up, art, or ballet. Why is this important? In journalist Claire Cain Miller's article, *How to Raise a Feminist Son*, she offers the best answer: "[B]ecause women's roles can't expand if men's don't, too."

CHAPTER 6

Being More Than Just a Sports Fan

Sixty-one minutes into the 2019 World Cup finals, Megan Rapinoe's brilliant penalty shot pushed the US Women's National Soccer Team into the lead. Eight minutes later, midfielder Rose Lavelle threaded her way through a string of defenders to score the only other goal of the match. That clinched the US team's record-breaking fourth World Cup Championship. Within minutes, the 58,000-person crowd erupted in chants of "Equal Pay! Equal Pay! Equal Pay!"

The fight for equality in sports has been an uphill battle that didn't start with Megan, Rose, or their other teammates who've become household names after a billion viewers watched their World Cup matches. The US women's team solidified its place its history when Carli Lloyd lead her teammates to their third World Cup championship in 2015. Over twenty-five million Americans were riveted to their TV sets for the final match. At the time, it was the most-watched soccer match—women's or men's—in US history. The team has been a powerhouse since the 1990s. Millions of fans will never forget watching the women's dramatic victory in a penalty shoot-out during the final game against China in the 1999 World Cup.

The 1999 championship team included soccer icons Julie Foudy, Kristine Lilly, Briana Scurry, Michelle Akers,

Brandi Chastain, Joy Fawcett, Carla Overbeck, and Mia Hamm—a group of women who are often called "the Title IX babies." These women were among the first generation of girls to grow up with a federal law that opened doors to competitive high school teams and college scholarships.

Title IX of the Education Amendments Act of 1972 was the brainchild of Oregon Representative Edith Green. Outraged by the hundreds of educational programs that were only open to boys, Edith snuck in a small amendment to a sprawling education funding bill. The amendment prohibited any public school receiving federal financial assistance from discriminating against students because of their sex. While that sounds like an obvious requirement for public schools, the amendment sparked highly emotional opposition.

Many Congressmen thought the idea of equal educational funding was ludicrous, but Edith campaigned relentlessly for Title IX. With the support of Representative Patsy Mink and Senator Birch Bayh, Edith cajoled the bill through Congress with the amendment intact. President Nixon signed the bill on June 23, 1972, and it took effect a year later.

For nearly three years, Title IX languished without the backing of agency regulations to direct its use. The US Department of Health, Education, and Welfare (HEW), which was tasked with writing Title IX's regulations, was stymied by internal disagreements and rancorous public opposition. The most contentious issue was whether the agency should apply Title IX to sports.

School administrators were understandably worried about the financial impact of Title IX being applied to athletics because schools nationwide spent dramatically less on sports programs for girls than for boys. In the early 1970s, there were 170,000 male college athletes, but only 30,000 females athletes. The University of Michigan spent $2.6 million on men's sports and *nothing* on women's sports. The University of Washington had an annual budget of around $2 million for men's sports, but only $18,000 for women's varsity teams. The school district in Waco, Texas spent $250,000 for seven competitive boys' sports, but just $970 on one competitive sport for girls. None of these schools were anomalies.

Luckily, many of the HEW officials were dads of daughters who knew first-hand about the second-class treatment of girls in school athletic programs. So when HEW finally issued its regulations for Title IX, the agency included a rule requiring schools to provide girls an equal opportunity to compete in sports. Although HEW made a huge concession that schools don't need to spend the same amount of money on girls as boys, the regulations demanded that girls get the same quality of coaches, equipment, locker rooms, and travel as boys.

Despite high hopes for Title IX to equalize school sports programs for girls, the law hasn't had the full impact its creators had hoped. While Title IX pushed many schools forward, progress has been hampered by lackluster enforcement, limited investigative resources, and school officials who are often indifferent to Title IX's requirements. Almost fifty years after Title IX's enactment, nearly 4,500 public high schools still have major gender disparities in their sports programs. That means that twenty-eight percent of all public high schools are likely still failing to comply with Title IX. This translates into 1.3 million fewer chances for our daughters to play high school sports than our sons.

Things aren't much better at the college level. Top college programs spend only twenty-eight percent of their sports budgets on female athletes, and men get $190 million more than women in annual college athletic scholarships. There are 63,000 fewer college team slots for women than for men. Women are also largely invisible in the collegiate coaching ranks. Only two percent of head coaches for men's college teams are women, and almost none are in high-profile sports like football and basketball. Title IX has also had the unintended effect of reducing the percentage of women head coaches for women's college teams. As the funding for women's programs increased, men started coaching women, so the percentage of women serving as head coaches for women's teams has dropped from ninety to forty-three percent.

The inequality is even starker in professional sports, which aren't covered by Title IX. The average salary for male professional basketball players is seventy times larger than for female players. There are fifty-two male NBA players whose individual salaries exceed the combined salaries of *all* the women in the WNBA. The problem is compounded by the media, which devotes just two to four percent of its sports coverage to female athletes. That makes it hard for girls to grow up with women's teams to support and women's sports figures to idolize.

Inequality even plagues the US Women's Soccer Team, which has not only dominated the world stage, but has also far out-performed the US Men's Soccer Team. While the women's team has four World Cup championships and four Olympic gold medals, the men's team has none. The women's team is ranked 1st in the world, while the men's team is ranked thirtieth. The women's team also has a larger fan base and produces higher annual revenues than the men's team. But the men still earn more money when they lose than the women earn when they win.

In the World Cup, women are paid $4,950 per game, while men are paid $13,166. That's bad enough, but it pales in comparison to the prize money. The 2019 women's World Cup prize money was $30 million, while the 2018 men's World Cup prize money was $400 million (and the US Women's Team became world champions, while the US Men's Team didn't even qualify to participate). In 2015, the women's team generated almost $20 million more revenue than the men's team, but the women were paid only a quarter of what the men earned. That year, the women's team received $2 million for winning its third World Cup Championship, while the 2014 men's team received $9 million for getting knocked out in the round of sixteen.

Because of the women's winning record, the US Women's Team played nineteen more matches then the US Men's Team from 2015 to 2018, yet still got paid less. Male players also get better medical benefits, safer playing conditions, and more money for travel expenses. As a result, twenty-eight members of the US Women's Team have filed a sex discrimination lawsuit that's pending in court—a move that the men's soccer team supports.

In the midst of this glaring inequality, sixty-six percent of American men describe themselves as sports fans (seventy-six percent for upper-income men). Yet their daughters are getting fewer sports opportunities and lower quality athletic programs than their sons. It's time for dads of daughters to become more than just sports fans—not just because girls are being deprived of the same opportunities to compete and earn a living, but also because girls are missing out on tremendous benefits from athletic participation. We all know that sports develops life skills like goal setting, perseverance, discipline, resilience, competitiveness, teamwork, and the ability to perform under pressure. But the pay-off for female athletes is even bigger.

Sports participation significantly improves girls' health and wellbeing. Girls who are athletes have higher self-esteem, a better body image, and more confidence than other girls. They also have lower rates of depression and less risk of teen suicide. Girls who participate in sports are less likely to smoke or use drugs. Athletics also strengthens girls' bones and reduces their risk of obesity, which lowers the future risk of osteoporosis and chronic illness. In high school, female athletes are less likely than other girls to have an unwanted pregnancy, and they're more likely to either abstain from sex or use contraceptives. What dad can argue with those outcomes as a positive pay-off from sports?

The time that girls spend on the playing field also pays off in the classroom. Girls who play sports typically earn higher grades than other girls in math and science. Sports participation increases girls' commitment to academics and their desire to go to college. Female athletes have a lower high school dropout rate and are seventy-three percent more likely than other girls to earn a bachelor's degree. This success comes in part from female athletes' ability to set priorities, organize their work, and manage their time. Girls who play sports are also more achievement-oriented, independent, and self-motivated than other girls. This prepares female athletes particularly well for male-dominated careers.

The skills that girls gain from sports outlast their time in the field, on the track, or at the gym. Female athletes are more prepared for demanding careers because they create larger, achievement-based networks, which are valuable in today's workforce. Although women are still under-represented in the executive ranks of the corporate world, sports are helping close the gap. A study of over 400 women executives at large companies found that eighty-two percent had played organized sports in junior high, high school, or college. Of the women executives who were former athletes, eighty-one percent said that playing sports had improved their teamwork ability, sixty-nine percent said it had developed their leadership skills, and fifty-nine percent said it had given them a competitive edge in their careers.

These findings were confirmed in a survey by Ernst & Young's Women Athletes Business Network. The survey included over 800 senior managers and executives at large companies around the world. Ninety percent of the women reported having previously participated in sports, including ninety-six percent of all women in C-suite positions. The higher the level of sports competition, the higher up the corporate ladder the women rose.

Many of today's prominent women business leaders are former athletes, and they credit their sports experience as one reason for their success. Weili Dai, the billionaire cofounder of Marvell Technology Group, learned valuable lessons while playing basketball in China. "The basketball court is the foundation for everything," she says. It made her a quick thinker and a creative problem-solver, and it gave her the self-confidence and positive attitude to excel. Other women CEOs shared a similar path from athletic fields and gyms into business leadership positions. Former Rice University basketball player Lynn Laverty Elsenhans became the first woman to run a major oil company as Sunoco's CEO. Former Indian cricket player Indra Nooyi became the CEO of PepsiCo. Meg Whitman, former CEO of eBay and Hewlett-Packard—who was named among the world's 100 most powerful women—played squash and lacrosse at Princeton University.

All of this data represents a pretty phenomenal return on a dad's investment in girls' athletics. But with stark inequalities remaining in sports programs at every level, there is still enormous work to be done. Looking back on the early years of Title IX offers some compelling stories of dads of daughters who first opened up playing fields for female athletes. Dubbed the "Dadfly Army," these devoted dads of daughters joined the early fight to expand sports opportunities for girls, and they're looking to recruit new dads to their team.

The Dadfly Army

In the mid-1990's, Herb Dempsey was enjoying a quiet retirement from careers as both a teacher and a police officer. He had earned the time to slow down, relax, and hang out with his five children. He loved sitting in the stands cheering for his kids at a soccer game or volleyball match. But that all changed in a bitter cold moment on a hard bleacher seat. It was there that a spark of indignation pushed Herb back into action.

Herb was braving a freezing rain and windstorm to watch his younger daughter's junior high soccer game.

The girls were turning blue wearing lightweight summer uniforms in 29°F sleet. Herb noticed that the boys on the football team were faring much better. They were practicing with warm-ups, rain slickers, and blankets to keep them cozy on the sidelines. Herb turned to the father sitting next to him and said, "This is crap."

Herb had the same reaction years earlier while watching a video of his older daughter's high school homecoming gala. His daughter Jen's volleyball team had just finished a stellar year, placing seventh in the state tournament. That same year, the football team had a disappointing 3-6 season. That didn't matter come gala time when the football team was treated like royalty. Cheerleaders in fancy gowns escorted the football players to a place of honor in the front row, while the girls' volleyball players couldn't even get seats.

At the time, Herb was still a full-time public school teacher and a part-time police officer, so he only had time for passing irritation. But once he was retired and saw his younger daughter get the same second-class treatment, he was fed up. He wasn't about to sit by quietly and let another daughter "get the fuzzy end of the lollipop."

Herb had a few strengths working in his favor. He had experience with the inner workings of public school systems from thirty-three years as a teacher, and he had strong investigative skills from twenty years on the police force. He also knew how to organize folks into action. He'd been the president of a 600-member teachers' association, so he'd mastered the art of herding cats. But Herb's most important assets were a belief in equality and a passion for battle. "I'm Irish," says Herb, "and I just love to fight."

Herb confronted the principal of his daughter's school about the shoddy clothing for the girls' soccer team. Herb's a persuasive guy, and it didn't take long for the principal and the school district to come up with better uniforms for his daughter's team.

Herb could have rested on this victory and returned to his peaceful retirement. Instead, he became a pit bull. He suspected that his daughter's experience wasn't unique, so he started investigating girls' sports throughout his school district. He was disgusted by what he found. He expected some level of differential treatment between girls' and boys' teams, but he found rampant discrimination. To measure the disparities, Herb devised a fairness scorecard, which rated girls' and boys' teams on a list of criteria. He looked at the number of sports available, coaching quality, equipment, practice and competition schedules, travel funding, training facilities, and medical treatment. The scoring gap between girls' and boys' sports was often shockingly large. "I found that the program is operated by old men, who employ younger men, who deliver a superior and well-funded program to very young men," Herb explained.

Herb knew that his charisma and persuasion skills would only go so far, so he decided to learn some law. Through his research, he stumbled onto Title IX. The law looked great on paper, but it hadn't translated into meaningful changes at many schools even twenty years after its enactment. Herb was one of the first dads to understand that Title IX doesn't enforce itself—it was a tool with a lot of potential, but someone had to put it to use.

Herb taught himself some basic legal skills and started filing Title IX discrimination cases for every sports inequality he found. In one case, he revealed how a boys' baseball team had two top-quality baseball fields, one with a new $9,000 outfield fence, while the girls' softball team played on a "barely improved cow pasture." In another case, he challenged a school's decision to shorten girls' soccer games from eighty to thirty minutes because their playing field didn't have lights and it got too dark to play full games in the evenings. In another case, he fought a school's practice of always scheduling boys' games on Friday nights, while girls' teams never got the premier timeslot. This made it harder for girls' parents to attend games, and only boys' events got the backing of pep band rallies and after-game dances.

While the most common Title IX complaints address unequal playing fields and locker rooms, Herb also challenged other unfair practices. He went after schools that allocated a lower percentage of student body funds for girls' athletics than for boys. He took on schools that didn't give female athletes equal access to athletic trainers. He even called out inferior end-of-season banquets for girls' teams. While boys' teams often celebrated at restaurants, girls' teams were usually relegated to the school cafeteria.

Herb didn't win every complaint he filed, but he kept on fighting. Before he knew it, he'd racked up thousands of Title IX discrimination complaints. In addition to working the legal angle, Herb also played on public opinion. When a problem involved a visible inequality, like a lower-quality sports field for a girls' team, he would send photos to local newspapers, which printed side-by-side comparison shots. Herb enjoyed surfing images on

Google Earth to find the shoddy sports facilities for girls without even leaving home.

Herb soon became more than just a local celebrity. He became an expert resource for other parents who wanted to challenge discrimination in their own daughters' sports programs around the country. Herb enthusiastically recruited other dads to join his fight.

Herb's relentless pursuit of athletic equality prompted *Sports Illustrated* to dub him a "Dadfly." The title comes from the word gadfly, which the dictionary defines as "a person who stimulates or annoys other people especially by persistent criticism." The word takes it meaning from the literal gadfly, a tiny insect whose life's work is to incessantly bite cows, horses, and other livestock. Despite the term's root, Herb wears his Dadfly title with pride. He even has a business card that describes his post-retirement profession as: "Instigator and agitator. Certified problem creator using Title IX and state equity law." When asked about his own daughters' reactions to his Dadfly status, Herb recalled an interview of his youngest daughter for a local newspaper. "He's crazy," his daughter had said. "But it's a good kind of crazy."

While Herb has been labelled the "mother of all Title IX fathers," there was an entire Dadfly army supporting female athletes in Title IX's early years. These fathers channeled their outrage over poor treatment of their daughters into action that has benefited a generation of girls who followed.

Paul Bucha Sr. was one of these early heroes. As an Army colonel, he probably didn't realize that he was honing his skills for future gender equality battles when he helped future President Eisenhower plan the Normandy invasion. But after he retired, Paul spearheaded a class action lawsuit to allow his daughter, Sandra, to swim on her high school team. The lawsuit lost because it was filed before Title IX became law, but Paul's efforts brought much-needed attention to the inequalities in girls' high school sports. His daughter became a champion marathon swimmer and a criminal law attorney.

Pat Egan, a construction contractor in Kentucky, was an even more unlikely candidate to become a gender equality advocate. He despises political correctness and steers clear of activism. But his outlook changed when his daughter Chrissi landed a spot as a pitcher on the softball team at Pat's high school alma mater. After an outstanding 36-8 season, Pat had lost patience for the girls' inferior treatment. While the boys had a high-quality practice field at the high school, the girls used a dilapidated field several miles away. "It's horrible," said Chrissi. "There are dips in the field. The fence is falling apart. There are weeds everywhere." While Pat never imagined himself getting into a fight over girls' softball, he couldn't stand by any longer. So he did some research and filed a Title IX suit on behalf of his daughter's team.

Another Dadfly, who probably surprised himself more than anyone when he became an advocate for girls' athletics, was hardworking firefighter Ron Randolph. As a registered Republican who had never heard of Title IX, Ron did not consider himself a feminist. He still doesn't believe that girls and boys should play on the same teams, but after watching the shoddy treatment of his daughter, Mimi, and her high school softball team in Oklahoma, he became a proponent of equal opportunities for girls. He saw it as a matter of basic fairness. If he gave $10 of his tax money to public schools, then he thought $5 should go to his daughter and $5 should go to his son. But every year, the boys' teams kept getting better fields, better uniforms, and better facilities.

During his off-duty time, Ron attended a college seminar to learn about Title IX. He was probably the only firefighter in the room. He shared what he learned with other parents at his daughter's school and together they asked the district to spend $35,000 to remodel the girls' softball field. The school district refused, which ended up being a short-sighted decision. Armed with knowledge of Title IX, Ron filed a lawsuit. When the suit finally settled, the district was forced to spend $275,000 to build a state-of-the-art girls' softball facility, which triggered thirteen similar lawsuits across Oklahoma.

One of Ron's comrades-in-arms was Russell Johnson, a pipe fitter by trade, who describes himself as a frustrated dad more than an angry one. When he moved his family to Gadsden, Alabama for a better job, he had no idea what his three athletic daughters would find at their new public schools. Russell was shocked by the lack of support for girls' sports. "I was heartbroken," he says. The boys' baseball team had a nice field at the high school with a locker room attached to the dugout. The girls' softball team had to practice at a city park, where they'd often get kicked off when the city had other plans. The girls had lousy uniforms and nowhere to change into them, and they were given hardly any equipment. Their season was often cut short because the school couldn't be bothered to reschedule girls' games when they were rained out.

Russell was beyond annoyed, but he wasn't sure what to do. "Title IX didn't mean nothing to me," he said. "I had no clue." He talked with local school officials, who were pleasant, but unresponsive. So, like many parents who don't know where to turn, Russel started searching the Internet. It was during these frustrated surfing sessions that Russel learned about Title IX. He wanted to help his daughters and the other girls in his district, so he figured out how to file a complaint. In response, the school district obtained the exclusive right to a city field for the girls' softball team, provided access to a nearby coliseum for the girls to use the locker room, bought the girls new uniforms, shoes, and equipment, and hired additional coaches for the girls' teams. The district also agreed that the new high school slated for construction would include equal sports facilities for girls and boys.

Although this original Dadfly army made major progress in advancing gender equality in sports, there are still many battles to be fought. Bruce Cloer is a dedicated dad who enjoyed watching his daughter play on her school sports teams in Rockland County, New York. He noticed that her teams rarely got to play on the nicest fields or at the best times, even though at that point Title IX had been the law for over thirty years. When Bruce complained, school officials told him that it was because "girls don't take sports as seriously as boys." For a Dadfly, those are fighting words. Bruce went over their heads and talked to league officials, but he got the same response.

So Bruce contacted the Women's Sports Foundation for advice and started reporting Title IX violations at school board meetings. He also hosted a Title IX workshop on the 2007 Girls and Women in Sports Day. He invited fifty school administrators to attend, and he introduced them to two early Title IX beneficiaries: Olympic soccer player Carla Overbeck and WNBA basketball legend

Teresa Weatherspoon. The administrators also got advice about how to comply with Title IX, and Bruce handed out “Save Title IX” t-shirts and posters to get parents to join the fight. His efforts had a big impact, and school administrators started working with him to equalize girls’ sports in their district.

Many of these outspoken fathers were primed to become Dadflies in the athletic arena even though they had no track record of social activism. They often had experienced the benefits of sports themselves while growing up and they simply expected their daughters to have the same opportunities they did. Former major league pitcher and baseball manager Dallas Green is a perfect example. After playing for the Philadelphia Phillies and managing the New York Mets, there was no way Dallas was going to tolerate a Little League baseball program that excluded his little girl. So he leant his name to a lawsuit that opened up Little League baseball diamonds to girls around the country.

In addition to playing sports themselves, many dads also recalled a pivotal moment in sports history that challenged their stereotypes about women athletes. There’s an entire generation of dads who remember being gripped by the epic tennis match between Bobby Riggs and Billie Jean King on September 20, 1973. At the time, Billie Jean was one of the world’s top women tennis players. Having proven herself on the court, she began demanding equal pay for female tennis pros. When her demands went nowhere, she and eight other top women players created their own tennis tour.

Billie Jean’s audacity irritated tennis pro Bobby Riggs, a previous Wimbledon and US Open champion. Bobby proudly described himself as a male chauvinist pig and was openly disdainful of female athletes, who he thought lacked the strength, skill, and competitive intensity of men. “If a woman wants to get the headlines,” he would say, “she should have quintuplets.” Bobby’s arrogance and adoration of publicity lead him to challenge Billie Jean to a match to prove that even at age fifty-five he could beat any player on the woman’s tour. Billie Jean initially refused, not wanting to amplify Bobby’s voice. But after Bobby beat Margaret Court, a top Australian player, Billie Jean felt she had no choice but to accept the challenge.

Billed as the “Battle of the Sexes,” the match used the best-of-five format from the men’s tour rather than the best-of-three format that was used in women’s matches at the time. Billie Jean trained with an intensity that was fueled by having much more at stake than just the $100,000 prize money. She did not disappoint. Billie Jean didn’t just beat Bobby Riggs. She crushed him, winning handily in straight sets: 6-4, 6-3, 6-3. Bobby’s trouncing sent a message that not only empowered young girls around the globe, but that also laid the foundation for future dads to become allies in the fight for sports equality. Decades later, Billie Jean often found herself approached by men in their forties and fifties who told her that watching her match had changed their expectations for their daughters. “They’re the first generation to insist that their daughters and sons have equal opportunities,” said Billie Jean.

As Title IX approaches its fifty-year anniversary in 2022, most of the original Dadfly army will be grandfathers. This recognition has prompted *Sports Illustrated* writer Alexander Wolff to caution schools from easing up on their commitment to sports equality. “Gender equity obstructionists and backsliders, beware,” he warns, having taken to heart Herb Dempsey's newest battle cry. "You know who's worse to deal with than fathers?," says Herb, "Grandfathers!"

Coach Pop

Gregg Popovich is both the dad of a daughter and one of the all-time greatest coaches in the NBA. Known to many as "Coach Pop" or just "Pop," Gregg is the head coach of the San Antonio Spurs. He has over 1,000 game wins under his belt and five NBA championships to his credit. He's been named the NBA Coach of the Year three times and is the longest serving active coach of all US major sports leagues. In addition to being disciplined, he's rather cantankerous and has been described as a "professional grouch." So when Gregg speaks out on behalf of women—like supporting the Women's March and calling out President Trump's misogyny—people take notice.

People also noticed when Gregg took action to advance women in the NBA, which has been an almost exclusively male haven since its inception. In 2014, Gregg hired Becky Hammon as the first full-time female coach in NBA history—actually, the first full-time female coach in any of the four major men's professional sports in North America. Becky was imminently qualified for the assistant coaching job and has a basketball IQ that's "off the charts." She played professional basketball with the WNBA for sixteen seasons and was a six-time All-Star team member. In 2011, she was named one of the WNBA's top fifteen players of all time.

With these stellar credentials, Becky's appointment as an assistant NBA coach should have been unsurprising, except that she's female. Becky credits Gregg for being the first head coach to simply judge her on her qualifications. "He sees me as a person that knows basketball," says Becky. "He didn't care that I was a woman. What he cared about was can I help the team and will I do a good job." While many people have called Becky a "barrier breaker," she reserves that term for Gregg. "Pop leaned in for me, big time," she says. "I might have been the tool, but he thrust me through that ceiling."

Although Gregg's decision to hire Becky was pathbreaking, he did it without fanfare or self-congratulatory speeches. For Gregg, it was just another solid management decision for his team. Becky did such a good job as an assistant coach during the 2014–2015 season that Gregg selected her as the head coach for the Spurs' summer league team in Las Vegas in 2015—another first for a woman in the NBA. Becky lead the Spurs to the Las Vegas Summer League championship title, and in 2016 she was the first woman to be part of an NBA All-Star coaching staff.

Many of Gregg's insights about women's leadership capabilities have come from being the dad of a daughter. During the summer of 2013, Gregg spent weeks trying to recover from his team's stunning defeat in the NBA finals, which would have given the team its fifth NBA championship. In game six of the series, the Spurs had a seemingly insurmountable five-point lead with only twenty-six seconds left, yet the Miami Heat miraculously pushed the game into overtime and stole a victory, which lead to the championship title going to Miami in game seven. The series marked the Spurs' first-ever loss in the NBA finals. Needless to say, Gregg took the loss very badly. "I've been quite lugubrious," he told a reporter weeks later. When asked what that meant, he said: "As sad as you can possibly be."

Gregg's daughter, Jill, is the one who finally helped him move forward. After seeing her dad moping around for weeks, she'd had enough. In words that could have been scripted by Pop himself, Jill piped up: "OK, Dad, let me get this straight: You won four championships, and you go to a fifth Finals. Other coaches lose all the time. But poor Greggy can't lose because he's special. Can you please get over yourself? End of story." Gregg stared at his daughter and then burst into laughter, knowing that he'd been on the giving side of the "get-over-yourself line" many times. "That started me on the path to recovery," says Gregg. His next big coaching moves were to take the Spurs back to the NBA finals in 2014, where he took home his fifth championship title, and to hire Becky Hammon to coach his team.

How Dads Can Get Started

Although Herb Dempsey and Coach Pop set the bar high for Dadflies, there's still lots of work to be done and many smaller ways that dads of daughters can contribute to the Dadfly army. The easiest thing that dads can do is watch women's sports events with their daughters. Watching women's sports gives daughters role models and helps them imagine themselves as athletes. On a larger scale, more viewers leads to more media coverage, which leads to more sponsors, more revenue, and more opportunities for female athletes. Watching fierce women compete is also an enjoyable way to spend time with your daughter while supporting women's equality at the same time.

For dads who see inequality in their daughters' school sports teams, a little Title IX knowledge goes a long way. Schools that violate Title IX risk losing federal funding, which gives dads leverage to get school officials' attention. Title IX requires every public school to designate one employee as a Title IX coordinator and to have a procedure for filing and resolving complaints. Talking with a school's Title IX coordinator and using a school's internal process is usually a good first step that may prompt improvements to girls' sports programs without needing legal action.

If a conversation with a school's Title IX coordinator fails to persuade, dads can file a legal complaint. Unlike many laws, Title IX allows anyone to file a complaint, not just the direct victim of discrimination. While dads are welcome to get a lawyer involved, they can also file a complaint on their own. The US Department of Education's website has a free guide, *How to File a Discrimination Complaint with the Office for Civil Rights*, with easy-to-use instructions. The complaint can be submitted with an online form or by mail or email, and it just requires basic information about how a school is treating a girls' team less favorably than a boys' team. The Office for Civil Rights will investigate and seek an agreement from the school to comply with Title IX.

Sometimes it can be hard to tell if a girls' team is receiving unequal treatment, particularly at the college level. There are several helpful tools to gather information. The National Women's Law Center offers a checklist to assess the equality of sports programs. Available free online, the checklist is called: *Check It Out: Is the Playing Field Level for Women and Girls at Your School*? The guide helps users compare girls' and boys' programs on various criteria, including the number of athletes, budgets, equipment, scheduling, travel, coaches, locker rooms, facilities, medical services, recruitment, scholarships, and publicity.

A Title IX coordinator should be willing to share data on these checklist items, but if you encounter reluctant school officials, the data is also available online. Public schools are required by the Equity in Athletics Disclosure Act to file annual reports about their sports programs with the federal government. The reports include information about student participation, staffing, revenues, and expenses for all women's and men's teams. This data is housed on the Equity in Athletics Data Analysis (EADA) website. The EADA allows anyone to request a report about the sports programs at any public college or university, get comparative data on multiple schools, or get data on trends at a particular school over time. This can give you concrete data to support a complaint if you suspect, like Herb Dempsey, that your daughter is getting "the fuzzy end of the lollipop."

If you have questions along the way, the Women's Sports Foundation also has a useful guidebook: *Step by Step: A Practical Guide to Assessing and Achieving Gender Equity in School Sports*. In addition to an investigation checklist, the guide provides conversation scripts for meeting with a school administrator or Title IX coordinator, sample letters to school officials, and sample Title IX complaints. The guide also explains how to enlist media and contact state officials.

There are also smaller ways that dads of daughters can support female athletes that don't require becoming a part-time detective or an amateur attorney. One way for men to help women athletes get recognized is to use the Women's Sports Foundation's online forms to nominate a female athlete for an annual award, including Sportswoman of the Year, the Wilma Rudolph Courage Award, or the Billie Jean King Leadership Award.

Dads of daughters can also improve sports culture just by speaking out against gender bias when you have the opportunity. British professional tennis player, Andy Murray, did this flawlessly during a recent press conference at Wimbledon. Andy had just suffered a surprising loss in a quarter-finals match to American Sam Querrey. During the press conference after the match, which was probably the last place Andy wanted to be, he found a way to make his two daughters proud by calling out a journalist for subtle sports sexism.

The journalist began what sounded like an innocuous question. "Sam is the first US player to reach a major semi-final since 2009," said the journalist, "how would you describe the—" But before he could finish, Andy interjected.

"Male player," Andy said.

"I beg your pardon?" replied the journalist.

"Male player, right?" Andy repeated.

"Yes, first male player, that's for sure," said the journalist, finally realizing his mistake. Andy was of course referring to the many successes at major tennis tournaments by US players Serena and Venus Williams, among others. Serena is a twenty-three-time grand slam champion who's racked up twelve tournament victories since 2009 alone. When Andy's mom, Judy, heard the interview, she proudly tweeted: "That's my boy."

Of course, not all dads of daughters are three-time Grand Slam tournament winners and two-time Olympic tennis champions who speak at televised press conferences. But that didn't stop thousands of dads from advancing women's equality in the cycling world just by lending their support. As of 2013, women cyclists weren't allowed to participate in the world's most prestigious cycling event: the Tour de France. Four of the world's top female cyclists decided to make a change. Dutch Olympic champion Marianne Vos, British world champion Emma Pooley, Caribbean national champion Kathryn Bertine, and British World Triathalon Champion Chrissie Wellington joined forces to convince the Amateur Sports Organization (ASO) to include women in the Tour de France.

The campaign included an online petition, which explained how women had been excluded from the premier endurance event for its entire hundred-year history. Women cyclists also get fewer races, less TV coverage of their events, and much smaller prize money. The petition urged people to sign their support for having a women's Tour de France.

The petition garnered over 97,000 signatures. Between forty and fifty percent of the supporters were men, many of whom signed specifically because they were dads of daughters. The website asked supporters to explain their reasons for signing, and the comments were filled with fathers' dreams for their daughters' future.

One dad wrote: "I'm an avid cyclist and have three daughters who have always asked me, 'Daddy, where are the girls,' when watching the Tour all of their lives. They now are starting families and it would be so nice for their kids to be saying, 'come on girl,' instead of, 'where are the girls.'" Many dads who signed the petition had daughters who were athletes, so they'd seen girls' abilities and the benefits from sports.

"As a father of two athletic girls," wrote one dad, "women are extraordinary in their work ethic and should not be second class citizens in cycling."

Another dad agreed: "I want my daughter to grow up in a world where she is treated equally to everyone else and does not see that she might be held back because she is a women." Hundreds of other dads shared similar hopes.

One dad from the Netherlands—apparently a man of few words—summed of the sentiments of all the dads who signed the petition, writing simply: "I have a daughter."

ASO leaders heard these passionate responses, and the petition did its job. Beginning in 2014, women cyclists have participated in their own Tour de France known as La Course, an annual one-day road race for elite women cyclists. La Course became an official part of the Union Cycliste Internationale Women's World Tour in 2016. The winner of the inaugural La Course was Marianne Vos, one of the four women who launched the petition. Future winners will likely include the daughters and granddaughters of the many Dadflies who have cared enough to agitate for their dreams.

CHAPTER 7

Engaging Other Men

Hank Aimes earned his reputation as a tough, conservative, no-nonsense laborer through years of hard work in the local iron mine. He was a quiet leader in his tight-knit Northern Minnesota town, which revolved around the male-dominated mining industry. Hank's world views about men and women were deeply tested when his daughter, Josie, dared to get a job at the mine. Josie was a single parent, and the mine was her best opportunity to provide for her kids. Hank didn't think it was an appropriate place for his daughter. Unfortunately, he understood the work environment all too well. Josie became a constant target of sexual harassment, assault, and degrading abuse from her male co-workers. After getting no help from the owners, Josie filed a sex discrimination lawsuit against the mine.

Hank had his father-daughter turning point during a union hall meeting while Josie was defending her decision. Belligerent men in the crowd shouted over her and refused to let her talk. Hank strode to the podium and took the microphone from his daughter's hand.

"My name is Hank Aimes and I've been a ranger all of my life," he said to the rowdy men, who initially thought he was siding with them. "I've never been ashamed of it until now," Hank continued, quickly disabusing them of that notion. "You know, when we take our wives and our daughters to the company barbecue, I don't ever hear nobody calling them those names like bitches and whores and worse. I don't ever see nobody grabbing them by their privates or drawing pictures of them on the bathroom walls... So what's changed? She's still my daughter. Isn't she?... You're all supposed to be my friends, my brothers. Well, right now I don't have a friend in this room. In fact, the only one I'm not ashamed of is my daughter." As Hank lead his daughter out the room, a few grateful claps turned into a wave of applause from men who finally found empathy by sharing a father's perspective.

If this sounds familiar, that's because it's a scene from the 2005 Warner Brothers movie, *North Country*. Hank Aimes was played by actor Richard Jenkins, who's himself the father of a daughter, and Josie was played by Charlize Theron. The movie was successful—and the scene was effective—because it tapped into something very relatable. It tapped into our intuitive belief that invoking the father-daughter relationship can be a compelling way for men to convince other men to think more deeply about gender equality.

Social science research suggests that our intuitions are correct. Making the father-daughter relationship salient enables some men to become more empathetic to girls and women. It can also move men from empathy to action. Researchers have found that taking someone else's perspective is most likely to motivate supportive conduct when a person feels a sense of unfairness and a vested interest or an emotional stake in another's well-being. Asking men to view the world through the lens of a daughter's father is one way to trigger the emotional connection and outrage that's needed to turn understanding into advocacy.

Business professors Rebecca Ratner and Dale Miller have identified two other benefits when men invoke their father-daughter relationship while advocating for women's advancement. First, it helps some men overcome concerns about how their support for women might be perceived by others. Second, it can make other men more responsive to their message. In their study, Ratner and Miller set out to understand why more men don't voice support for women's leadership initiatives. They found that some men are sympathetic to gender equality efforts, but they feel like it's not their place to speak up. In studying the reactions that outspoken male allies received in response to their advocacy, Ratner and Miller found that men's hesitancy is well-founded. When male advocates lacked an obvious self-interest in women's workplace equality, their colleagues—both men *and* women—often responded with surprise, anger, and resentment.

According to Professors Ratner and Miller, these are typical reactions to someone who seems to be violating "the norm of self-interest." If it's not clear why you're advocating for someone else, people tend to question your motives. In addition, they tend not to listen to your message. This means that if men identify a vested interest in women's advancement, it can validate their participation. Ratner and Miller refer to this process as "granting standing." Invoking one's father-daughter relationship is one way to achieve this effect and allow others to respond with a more open mind. Similarly, asking other men to consider how their daughters might feel, or asking them to support gender diversity on their daughters' behalf, can make some men more willing to advocate for equality.

Catalyst researchers have made similar findings when attempting to discover the most effective ways to engage male allies for women. Catalyst interviewed thirty-five male business leaders who actively supported gender equality initiatives. The researchers compared those interviews with survey responses from 178 businessmen who hadn't shown a commitment to women's advancement.

Unsurprisingly, the outspoken male advocates tended to have high levels of awareness about gender bias. But that wasn't enough by itself to predict which men ultimately spoke up. Some of the men who weren't active supporters were also knowledgeable about sex discrimination. So why did they remain on the sidelines? There were two main reasons. Some men stayed quiet because they feared disapproval from their male peers who might view them as less masculine if they supported gender equality. Others were inactive because they didn't feel a personal stake in the outcome, even though they understood that gender bias existed.

Invoking the father-daughter relationship is one way to overcome these barriers to becoming male allies. When men link their support for gender equality to their responsibility to care for their daughters, their support is sometimes more easily perceived as "masculine," which can empower some men to speak up. Encouraging other men to think about their father-daughter role can also be an effective way to help them make a personal connection to gender equality and fuel a strong enough sense of unfairness to get involved. When one of the outspoken male allies in the study was asked about the characteristics he'd seen in other strong male allies, he said that many of them, like himself, had "a very personal investment in improving the lives of our daughters."

This research suggests that dads of daughters can be particularly effective at engaging other men in gender diversity efforts. The stories in this chapter highlight dads of daughters who have made their mark by actively recruiting other male allies to the cause.

yWomen

All eyes in the crowded auditorium in Atlanta turned to watch as Jeffery Tobias Halter walked onstage wearing a pressed blue suit, a crisp white shirt, a sharp necktie, and a pair of size fourteen bright red pumps. Jeffery smiled as a few uncomfortable giggles and a wave of curious whispers let him know that he'd grabbed the crowd's attention. The words, "Wanted: Male Engagement," were illuminated on the screen behind him. Jeffery's goal at this 2015 TEDx Talk was to convince businessmen to start prioritizing women's advancement at their companies. The shoes were just his hook. His plan was to use the father-daughter relationship to reel men in and pull them on board.

Jeffery's journey to his red-heeled equality pitch in Georgia began years earlier while working in sales training at the Coca-Cola Company. In 2000, Coca-Cola faced a $200 million discrimination lawsuit, and company officials launched a diversity program in hopes of avoiding future litigation. At the time, Jeffery knew nothing about diversity initiatives. He'd been working at Coca-Cola for fourteen years. When he saw the job posting seeking someone to run a diversity education program, he thought it was joke. But Coca-Cola leaders thought otherwise and they picked Jeffery to be the new Director of Diversity Business Development. Jeffery was as surprised as anyone by this sudden shift in career path. "I'm a straight white guy," thought Jeffery. "What the hell do I know about this diversity thing?"

Selecting Jeffery for the job turned out to be a brilliant decision. When he stepped into the position, Jeffery found what he described as "literally the bad diversity training that you've all seen on episodes of *The Office*." So he threw himself into the challenge with an open mind and a salesperson's tenacity.

Despite his hard work, Jeffery admits that it took him years to discover the most effective motivator for engaging men in workplace gender diversity efforts. At the time, Jeffery's daughter was a sophomore in college, where she began reading about the gender wage gap. Seeing his own daughter burdened with learning the reality of gender pay discrimination, Jeffery felt an obligation to speak out for women's workplace equality. Since then, Jeffery has worried about his daughter every day. "I know what she's going to face in getting her career off the ground and in advancing in a male-oriented organization," he says. "My daughter is less likely to make the same amount coming out of school as my son will, even if she negotiates for it."

Jeffery admits that this was a blind spot for him for almost twenty years at Coca-Cola before he'd internalized both the power and the responsibility that fathers of daughters have to advocate for women's equality. Over time, his motivation was also fueled by talking with other dads. As the diversity programs director, Jeffery frequently attended conferences about women in business. He made it a habit to seek out the other men in the audiences and ask them why they were there. "I'm doing this for my daughter," they would often say.

This inspired Jeffery to focus full-time on engaging men in gender equality initiatives. After twenty-six years at Coca-Cola, including twelve years heading diversity programs, Jeffery left to become the Founder and President of a gender consulting company called YWomen. The "Y" represents the Y chromosome to highlight the importance of engaging men to become advocates for women's rights. The company's goal is to educate male business leaders about why gender diversity is critical to their companies' success, and to get men committed to advancing women into leadership roles.

Having since worked with companies around the globe, Jeffery has learned that inspiring male allies requires two components—the "head part" and the "heart part." The head part is the business case that demonstrates how gender diverse leadership increases a company's financial success. Jeffery makes this case persuasively in his book, *Why Women: The Leadership Imperative to Advancing Women and Engaging Men*.

But the heart part of the equation requires more than just compelling data. The heart part requires tapping into men's empathy and personal sense of fairness. To achieve the head and heart connection, Jeffery unabashedly invokes the father-daughter relationship in personal and often urgent terms. Jeffery's view is that fathers of daughters have a responsibility to become visible and outspoken advocates for women's equality.

When talking with other dads of daughters, Jeffery doesn't pull any punches. "It's your job to do every little bit you can to enhance women's equality in the workplace now so you can somewhat level the playing field for your daughters' future," he says. "[M]en who embrace male advocacy and become male champions, will at least be able to look their daughters in the eye and say, 'Yes, I tried to do my part to make this a better world for you.'"

Jeffery has even provided his own twist on Madeleine Albright's well-known saying that there's "a special place in hell for women who don't support other women." Jeffery warns instead that there's "an extra special place in hell for those fathers of daughters, who, once they make the connection of the real issues facing women in the workplace, still choose to do nothing about it."

In the end, Jeffery's pitch to powerful businessmen to become advocates for women's equality is straightforward: "We owe it to our daughters." In appreciation for other dads' commitment, Jeffery dedicated his book "to the fathers of daughters who realize the incredible responsibility they have for supporting the advancement of women in the workplace and the world."

Jeffery's work at YWomen caught the attention of Betsy Myers, who served as the Director of the White House Office for Women's Initiatives and Outreach during the Clinton Administration. "Engaging men in the advancement of women," says Betsy, "is truly the new frontier for every company in America." Jeffery's focus on the father-daughter relationship resonated with Betsy, who agrees that that no amount of data alone can move men "from passive participants to active champions." Betsy invited Jeffery to be the keynote speaker at a symposium on Engaging Men to Advance Women in Business in 2013. One talk lead to another, which is how Jeffery found himself perched upon a pair of red heels at the Centennial Park Women's TEDx event in Atlanta. The purpose of the event was to bring together men and women to explore new ways to support women's advancement.

Before swapping his red heels on stage for a more comfortable and less colorful pair of loafers, Jeffery explained to the TEDx audience his initial apparel selection:

> *Believe it or not, these are a great visual aid for the state of engaging men in women's leadership advancement... First, they represent discomfort, certainly for me at this moment. More importantly, they represent the discomfort that men have in even wanting to have this conversation with women in the workplace. Most men are afraid we'll say or do the wrong thing, and so we choose not to engage. They're also a great visual aid around men and women having very different experiences in the workplace.*

After returning to more traditional footwear—and making the business case for gender-diverse leadership teams—Jeffery launched into his father-daughter campaign:

> *Most men, when we leave for work, we put on our suit of armor and we don't even think about our family. We just go out and do battle... As a boomer dad, though, I tried to be a good father. Whether it*

> *was dance or soccer, I made the game. I supported my daughter. I made sure she went to a great college. But the day she graduates and makes seventy-eight cents to my son, I choose to do nothing. I choose to stop advocating for one of the most important people in my life. Fathers of daughters in this country need to be outraged that organizations and society only value our daughters at seventy-eight cents on the dollar. Only men can choose to fix that. We've got to get angry, and we've got to do so with a sense of urgency... It's about fathers of daughters realizing the responsibility they have to drive change in this country for their daughters and for their sons.*

This message has found receptive business leaders around the country. YWomen's clients have included General Mills, Kimberly-Clark, Deloitte, Walmart, McDonald's, Clorox, and other Fortune 500 companies, as well as Target, Sodexo, Cisco, American Express, Johnson & Johnson, Proctor & Gamble, and Cummins, all of which have leadership ranks made up in part of fathers for whom Jeffery's pitch was hard to ignore.

Jeffery's message also gives men a ready response to male colleagues who may look negatively on their outspoken support for women. Jeffery learned this lesson himself at Coca-Cola when he moved from sales into diversity training. Other salesmen initially chided him for his new position, which they saw as a hit to his masculinity, but Jeffery discovered a powerful response. "I'm not doing this for you or to prove anything," he would say, "I'm doing this for your daughter."

"All of the sudden," says Jeffery, "they got it."

YWomen also offers a strong antidote to the messages that tend to let men off the hook by holding women responsible for their own low pay, second-class employment status, and limited advancement. This narrative began in the federal courts in the 1970s and 1980s when judges refused to use discrimination laws to hold employers responsible for the lack of women in prestigious, high-paying jobs. Judges gave men a pass by attributing women's absence at the top of the workplace hierarchy to women's own "lack of interest" or "personal choice."

In *EEOC v. Sears, Roebuck & Co.*, for example, a federal court rejected a sex discrimination claim alleging that Sears had a nationwide practice of failing to hire and promote women into well-paid commission sales jobs. At the time, Sears was one of the largest merchandise retailers in the country, and it had a stunning absence of women in commissioned sales. Despite the glaring statistics, the court accepted the company's argument that women were simply less interested in the far more lucrative commissioned positions selling cars and building supplies than they were in the lower-paying, non-commissioned jobs selling clothing and cosmetics.

The idea that women are responsible for their own lack of workplace advancement has reached beyond the courtroom and became embedded in popular culture. Bookstores are flooded with self-help books for women seeking to break through the glass ceiling. The most famous book in this genre is Facebook COO Sheryl Sandberg's best-selling book, *Lean In: Women, Work, and the Will to Lead*. Other titles include the following:

- Nice Girls Don't Get the Corner Office: 101 Unconscious Mistakes Women Make that Sabotage Their Careers
- Pushback: How Smart Women Ask—and Stand Up—for What They Want
- See Jane Lead: 99 Ways for Women to Take Charge at Work
- The Go-Getter Girl's Guide: Get What You Want in Work and Life (and Look Great While You're at It)
- The Confidence Code: The Science and Art of Self-Assurance—What Women Should Know
- Hardball for Women; and
- How Women Rise: Break the 12 Habits Holding You Back from Your Next Raise, Promotion, or Job.

The problem isn't that these books lack useful advice. The problem is the lack of a similar set of books targeting male leaders who hold far more power to accelerate women's progress. Jeffery hopes to balance things out by focusing more on the role that men can play in advancing women. He understands that tapping into the inspiration from the father-daughter relationship is just the first step. Even highly motivated dads may need training to translate their empathy into action, so to support dads of daughters who want to get involved, Jeffery launched the "Father of a Daughter Initiative," which is available on the YWomen website.

This initiative asks dads to sign a pledge committing to at least one specific activity to support women's advancement at their companies. The pledge states:

"As the father of a daughter, I will LISTEN, LEARN, LEAD and have the WILL to advocate for the recruitment, advancement, retention and equitable treatment of women in the workplace." The pledge lists a variety of actions that men can take to support women's advancement, and dads are asked to select a few specific steps on which to focus their efforts. Some of the action items include mentoring or sponsoring a female colleague, advocating for workplace flexibility, learning more about women's experiences at their company, and encouraging women to apply for promotions and seek stretch assignments.

For Jeffery, the most important action item on the pledge list is a promise to engage other fathers of daughters in conversations about women's advancement. He describes father-to-father advocacy as "the next holy grail." The challenge, says Jeffery, "is figuring out how we get men to invite other men into this conversation." To answer that question, Jeffery's been creating male engagement circles to support inspired fathers in recruiting other men to the cause. One easy suggestion to get things started is for dads to simply ask other dads: Would you want your daughter to work for our company? "That's the next milestone," says Jeffery, "men reaching out to other men." And if donning painful red heels is what it takes to jumpstart those conversations, the discomfort is well worth the gain.

Male Champions for Change

Glen Boreham was the Managing Director of IBM Australia/New Zealand, where he lead 15,000 employees and was responsible for over $4 billion in annual revenues. In his free time, he enjoyed skiing, watching sports, and drinking a good glass of wine. Twice named among the top five leaders in the information industries, Glen spent a lot of time both on and off the job thinking about global business strategy. Gender equality, however, hadn't quite made it to the top of his priority list. That changed in 2010 when he got a phone call from his friend, Liz.

Elizabeth Broderick is an Australian lawyer who tenaciously worked her way into the partnership ranks of a global commercial law firm. Although Liz was a model of women's empowerment, she didn't describe herself as a feminist during much of her legal career. Two events nudged Liz into what she calls "late onset feminism." While she was a junior attorney, she was sexually harassed by one of her firm's most important male clients. "I could say no and risk the firm losing one of their largest clients, or I could go along," recalls Liz. "It wasn't really a choice." She received a second jolt when she became a mom. "It wasn't until I had my first child," she says, "and my husband's career continued to develop while mine, I saw, could go to a very different place without some kind of intervention—that I started to realize maybe it isn't equal after all."

Liz decided to make a career shift in 2007 when she took a fifty percent pay cut to become Australia's Sex Discrimination Commissioner. The Commissioner is the federal government official who enforces sex discrimination laws and leads public education and outreach about women's workplace equality. During her first few years as Commissioner, Liz focused on women advocates. She entered the job believing that women working together was the key to achieving workplace equality. But she got frustrated seeing women constantly being asked to change how they acted, networked, or negotiated, instead of focusing on institutional barriers to women's success. "You know what?," she told herself, "this isn't going to change until you get men taking the message of gender equality out to other men." So she came up with a new plan: "We need decent, powerful men to step up beside women to create a more gender equal world."

Liz established the Male Champions of Change (MCC) in 2010. Her goal was to get male CEOs to spearhead male engagement for advancing women into leadership positions. But how does a female government worker get powerful men to commit time, energy, and resources to advancing women's equality? Liz wisely started with the dad of a daughter.

Liz's first phone call was to Glen Boreham at IBM. Liz asked Glen to start using his influence to engage other men to create better work environments for women. She began with data, reminding Glen that women held only three percent of CEO positions in Australia's top two-hundred companies and filled only seventeen percent of board seats. Then she appealed to Glen as a father. Glen had twins—a boy and a girl. So for Glen, the data meant that his daughter would face a very different world than his son. "That just does not seem fair or smart," said Glen.

After his conversation with Liz, Glen became a founding member of the Male Champions of Change, and he started recruiting others. The group quickly grew to around thirty men from industries across the private and public sectors. The men met four times each year, and no stand-ins were allowed. That may sound trivial, but it meant that around thirty of the most influential male leaders in Australia were getting together, face-to-face, once every quarter, solely to discuss women's advancement. Once they got in a room together, Liz found that they were determined to hold each other accountable for results. "This issue is not beyond our intellectual capacity to solve," said one founding member. "Excuses are just that!"

At the meetings, the men discussed their experiences with gender diversity—including successes, failures, and frustrations. They shared ideas, data, and strategies, and they established specific goals. Most importantly, all members had to regularly conduct gender diversity audits at their own organizations and publicly report their progress. The MCC website has become a repository for the group's reports.

One of MCC's initial strategies was to recruit other men to the team. The members began by sending letters to over 150,000 business leaders in Australia urging action on women's workplace equality. They speak at events around the globe to make the case to other male leaders about women's advancement. While they're at it, they use their influence to get more visibility for women at high-profile events. They've all taken a "Panel Pledge" stating that they won't appear at conferences where women aren't adequately represented as speakers.

With the men of the MCC pushing each other and holding each other accountable, the group is starting to achieve results. Glen Boreham reached his initial goals for IBM Australia/New Zealand by having fifty percent women on the executive board and increasing female interns from twenty to forty-six percent. Ben Rimmer, the CEO of the City of Melbourne, also made progress as an MCC member and dedicated dad. "My daughter," says Ben, "simply expects the world to be equal. At some point during the next ten years, I fear that she will discover that it is not really all that equal—at least, not yet." So Ben focused on ensuring that the City's business grants support women entrepreneurs and that City contractors are committed to gender diversity. More than 150 men have joined forces across Australia and New Zealand to set up industry-specific groups supporting women in architecture, property, STEM, fire and emergency, and sports.

Elizabeth Broderick stepped down as Commissioner in 2015, but she didn't relax for long. In 2016, Liz became a United Nations Special Advisor tasked with taking the Male Champions of Change global. "Men taking the message of gender equality to other men," says Liz, "that is what will change the picture of gender equality."

#LeanInTogether

Stephen Curry isn't just a six-time NBA All-Star. He isn't just a three-time NBA champion with the Golden State Warriors and a two-time league MVP. He isn't just one of the greatest shooters in NBA history. Steph is also the devoted dad of two daughters, Ryan and Riley.

Steph recently penned an essay called, "This is Personal," in which he asked men to join him in the daily fight for women's equality. Steph has learned from many strong women in his life, including his mom and his wife, Ayesha. But he acknowledges that having daughters added more urgency to his belief that all men have a responsibility to support equal opportunities for girls and women. "[S]uddenly seeing things through the eyes of these daughters of ours," said Steph, "I'd be lying if I didn't admit that the idea of women's equality has become a little more personal for me, lately, and a little more real." Steph candidly shared his hopes for his daughters' future:

> *I want our girls to grow up knowing that there are no boundaries that can be placed on their futures, period. I want them to grow up in a world where their gender does not feel like a rulebook for what they should think, or be, or do. And I want them to grow up believing that they can dream big, and strive for careers where they'll be treated fairly. And of course: paid equally.*

The most important thing that Steph learned from his daughters, however, is that everyone has a stake in gender equality, which motivated him to take his message to other men. "I think it's important that we all come together to figure out how we can make that possible," said Steph. "Not just as 'fathers of daughters,'" but as advocates for a better world. In his view, "You're not world class if you're not actively about inclusion."

In 2018, Steph hosted a basketball camp for girls. He was blown away by the girls' work ethic and intensity—both on and off the court. He used the opportunity not just to coach basketball, but to set up discussions with successful women in sports and business. Connecting young girls with women role models is something that all men can do to inspire girls to dream big. "Let's work to close the opportunity gap," says Steph. "And let's work *together* on this."

Steph has also lent his voice along with other NBA stars to support the #LeanInTogether initiative, created by LeanIn.org. This initiative engages men to play an active role in challenging gender bias and advancing women's equality in three areas. It inspires men to become more involved fathers. It encourages men to share responsibilities at home. And it asks men to become women's advocates at their workplaces. Steph's message to other men is pretty simple. "I'm in," he says. "Are you?"

How Dads Can Get Started

As a dad, one of the most impactful things you can do to support your daughters' future is to engage other men in discussions about gender equality. YWomen's Father-Daughter Pledge is a terrific springboard for conversation. Print out the Pledge from the YWomen website and select a few action items from the pledge list to support women in your workplace. Sign the pledge and display it prominently in your office so that women—and other men—can see your commitment and approach you with questions. Encourage your male colleagues to do the same. Touch base with each other often to discuss progress, challenges, and successes on your pledge commitments.

Dads of daughters can also check out Julie Kratz's Pivot Point website for advice on engaging men in conversations about supporting women at work. To set up formal discussions, join the Forté Foundation's Male Ally Initiative, which provides a free toolkit for companies to establish male ally groups using lesson plans, facilitator guides, and consulting services. You can also sign up to receive free weekly emails from LeanIn.org, which offers tips for men to support other men in becoming women's advocates.

Another way to engage men in conversations about women's equality is to ask them to spend a few minutes on one of two powerful online activities. They're both short and easy to complete, and their results are hard to ignore. One is the Dads4Daughters Implicit Bias Test described in Chapter 4. Because nearly everyone who takes the test is surprised by their own level of implicit gender bias—and because the test offers non-judgmental support for making progress—the test can be a great kick-starter for engaging other men. The other is the Male Advocacy Profile, which is available on the YWomen website. The Profile is a set of twenty questions that help men assess their current level of commitment to women's equality, along with suggestions for becoming a stronger ally. Sharing links to these two online tools with your male colleagues, friends, and family members is one way to get productive conversations started.

Lastly, be sure to have a ready reading list available to share with other men who seem interested in gender equality. Begin with Steph Curry's "This Is Personal" essay, and ask your male friends for their reactions. Books to have on your go-to list should also include: Jeffery Halter's *Why Women: The Leadership Imperative to Advancing Women and Engaging Men*; Brad Johnson and David Smith's *Athena Rising: How and Why Men Should Mentor Women*; Joanne Lipman's *That's What She Said: What Men and Women Need to Know (and Women Need to Tell Them) about Working Together*; Julie Kratz's *One: How Male Allies Support Women for Gender Equality*; and Rania H. Anderson's *WE: Men, Women, and the Decisive Formula for Winning at Work*.

At the top of your list should be Michael Kaufman's *The Time Has Come: Why Men Must Join the Gender Equality Revolution*. Michael has spent four decades engaging men to promote gender equality. In 1991, he co-founded the White Ribbon Campaign, one of the largest networks for men to end violence against women. With compassion, humor, and insight, Michael's book shares what he's learned about the most effective ways for men to engage other men in advancing women's rights. Here's some of his wisdom in a nutshell:

> *Approach men as allies. Reach out to men with positive messages of change. Challenge our fellow men but carry the banner of empathy and compassion... Encourage men to honestly examine our own privileges and mistakes, but don't assume collective guilt or blame... Understand the capacity of men for change; understand the capacity of men for decency and love.*

Michael's most important insight—and one that's critical as men take up the challenge to engage other men—is that it's not just girls and women who benefit from a more equitable world. "It turns out," says Michael, "that the gender equality revolution will mean that our lives as men will be changed for the better too."

CHAPTER 8

Flexing Empathy Muscles

At a time when we need empathy more than ever, empathy is on the decline. Some tenacious researchers have actually measured the drop. They devised a standardized test of empathy skills and administered it to US college students for thirty years starting in 1979. Students got less empathetic each year. Over time, scores fell thirty-four percent on "perspective taking," which measures the ability to understand other people's points of view. Scores plummeted forty-eight percent on "empathic concern," which measures the tendency to feel and respond to people's emotions. Unfortunately, the trend seems to be getting worse. Starting in 2000, the decline in empathy began accelerating.

Social scientists haven't just been studying empathy levels, but also figuring out how empathy can inspire fair treatment of others. It probably won't surprise most dads to hear that the father-daughter relationship is a powerful source of empathy skill-building, and that the skills dads develop can motivate action to advance gender equality.

So what is empathy and how does it work? Social scientists define empathy as "the cognitive ability to understand a situation from the perspective of other people, combined with the emotional capacity to comprehend and feel those people's emotions." In simpler terms, empathy is engaging both your brain and your heart on behalf of others. Although we may think that empathy is a trait that some have and some don't, it's actually a skill that can be learned and improved. But just because people have empathy doesn't mean they'll always react by supporting others. So there are two questions that researchers are studying: how to build empathy, and how empathy sparks action.

Researchers have found that we are more likely to empathize with people we like or know well, people who feel close or familiar, and people with whom we identify. The more knowledge we have about someone, the more likely we are to respond empathetically because we can more easily see the world from that person's perspective. This means that when men consciously connect their father-daughter relationship to their other roles, it increases their empathy for girls and women.

Of course, having a daughter isn't the only way for men to gain empathy on gender issues, but any path to growth is a positive thing. The knowledge, familiarity, and caring that dads have for their daughters can increase men's ability to identify with the experiences of other girls and women. This can be particularly important for men at work. Many dads have gained empathy for women colleagues after hearing about their own daughters' experiences of sex discrimination or by seeing their adult daughters juggling work/family conflicts.

Empathy is also critical in the workplace because it affects how we explain the causes of people's behaviors—what social scientists call "causal attributions." Most of the time, we fall into a predictable attribution pattern, which bolsters our self-esteem.

We tend to attribute our own successes to enduring personal characteristics, like our own intelligence or creativity. And we tend to chalk up our own failures to fleeting situational factors, like unfair treatment or bad luck. This helps us feel in control and responsible when we succeed, while letting us off the hook when we fail.

The problem is that we tend to make the opposite attributions for other people's behavior. We're less likely to explain other people's successes by assuming they're brilliant, clever, or talented. What's worse, we tend to attribute other people's failures to permanent personal deficits, like lack of intelligence, low skill, or poor judgment. This is problematic because attributing other people's struggles to their personal attributes makes it less likely that we'll act on their behalf. If we believe that their outcomes are due to personal flaws, their results tend not to strike us as unfair.

Perhaps the most important effect of empathy is that it changes our typical explanations for other people's shortfalls. Specifically, empathy helps us reach the same kinds of explanations for others' failures that we tend to make for our own. When we empathize with others, we're more likely to attribute their struggles to situational factors rather than personal flaws. This shift allows us to look for barriers that block people from success, instead of blaming people for their own inability to succeed.

This effect of empathy allows male leaders to understand the obstacles contributing to women's workplace inequality. It allows men to pay attention to the effects of informal mentoring practices, inadequate childcare and nursing facilities, inflexible work hours, and other barriers to women's advancement, rather than attributing the lack of female leaders to a lack of interest, skills, or commitment. It's that deeper understanding that allows men to be effective women's allies.

The link between empathy and women's equality can be seen in many different arenas. To illustrate the importance of empathy—and see how dads of daughters can lead the way—we'll take a look at a few gavel-wielding fathers who are making a difference.

Donning an Empathetic Robe

William Rehnquist is one of the most conservative Supreme Court Justices in US history. His path to the high court seemed almost preordained. He grew up with Republican parents who admired President Herbert Hoover, which naturally lead him to law school. After graduation, he practiced law in Arizona while becoming active in Republican politics. He made his first splash as a speechwriter for Senator Barry Goldwater's presidential bid in 1964, and he built his reputation lobbying against civil rights and against federal government regulation.

When Richard Nixon became president in 1968, he hired Rehnquist as an Assistant Attorney General in the Office of Legal Counsel, which advises the president. Hoping to ratchet back the Supreme Court's liberal shift under Chief Justice Earl Warren, President Nixon nominated Rehnquist as the Court's 100th Justice in 1971. Fifteen years later, President Ronald Reagan elevated Rehnquist to become the Court's Chief Justice. In that role, Rehnquist is widely credited with (or maligned for) launching a conservative legal revolution. So Rehnquist was definitely *not* the Justice that women's advocates wanted at the Court's helm to decide a critical case involving gender equality.

The case began when an all-too-familiar work/family conflict left a dedicated worker unemployed. William Hibbs was toiling in relative obscurity as a social worker at the Nevada Department of Human Resources. In 1997, William's wife was injured in a car accident and needed neck surgery, so William asked his boss for time off to care for her. A dispute arose about his return date, and William got fired. He lost his income and medical insurance just when he needed them most.

William sued his employer—the State of Nevada—for violating the Family and Medical Leave Act (FMLA), which President Bill Clinton signed in 1993. The FMLA is one of the few federal laws in the US that helps employees keep their jobs when family issues arise. The law allows employees who meet certain criteria to get time off from work to care for close family members who are seriously ill or to care for a newborn baby or newly-adopted child. The FMLA is limited because it only applies to large companies and only requires *unpaid* leave, so millions of workers are either excluded or financially unable to take time off. But it's still a lifeboat for many workers who would otherwise lose their jobs and health insurance during a family crisis.

In response to William Hibbs's lawsuit, Nevada's lawyers argued that Congress overstepped its authority in applying a federal law to state governments. In legal circles, this is called a federalism question—an ongoing debate about how our Constitution divides up power between our national and state governments. In short, Nevada argued that the US Constitution doesn't allow the federal government to tell a state government what to do with its workers.

Despite the technical nature of the case—and the fact that the employee was a man—the case had huge implications for women's equality. Although women have entered the workforce in record numbers, women still provide far more family care than men. That's true even in families where a woman is the primary earner, and even when a woman's husband is unemployed. Without the FMLA, many employers simply fired women who needed time off to care for a sick child, an ailing parent, or a new baby. Men who'd like to help have often been understandably reluctant to take time off because the stigma for men taking family leave can be even greater than for women. Men who take caregiving leave are often ridiculed at work and end up with lower pay and fewer promotions.

The FMLA took two important steps to address these problems. First, the law gives women protected leave time so they can care for their families without losing their jobs or medical insurance. This is crucial now that women are the sole or primary earners in over forty percent of American families. Second, lawmakers understood that the way to break down gender stereotypes in the long run is to encourage men to become more equal caregivers. So Congress designed the FMLA to protect both women *and* men.

Because the FMLA is such an important foundation for workplace equality, advocates kept a close eye on William Hibbs's case. When the Supreme Court accepted the case, advocates were devastated. If the Court ruled against William, more than sixteen million state and local government workers would lose their right to family leave. Women's equality would take a major step backwards.

With Rehnquist sitting as the Chief Justice, women's advocates predicted a virtually certain loss. Rehnquist posed two major roadblocks for keeping the FMLA's family leave protections for state employees. The first was that Rehnquist was an ardent states' rights supporter. For years, he led a conservative block of Justices known as the "Federalism Five"—including Antonin Scalia, Clarence Thomas, Anthony Kennedy, and Sandra Day O'Connor—to many 5-4 rulings striking down a record number of federal laws.

But that wasn't the biggest hurdle in William Hibbs's case. An even larger problem was Rehnquist's record on women's rights. When Rehnquist was in the Nixon Administration, he wrote a memo urging the President to reject the Equal Rights Amendment, which would have guaranteed equal rights for women. Rehnquist warned that the "fanatical" desire for gender equality would jeopardize traditional gender roles and "hasten the dissolution of the family." While on the Supreme Court, he was one of only two Justices who dissented in the landmark case of *Roe v. Wade*, which recognized women's Constitutional right to abortion. In the 1990s, Rehnquist was an outspoken opponent of the Violence Against Women Act, which funds federal prosecutions for domestic violence and sexual assaults. Needless to say, the FMLA's future looked bleak indeed.

Because of Justice Rehnquist's record, women's advocates assumed that he'd vote to strike down the FMLA in William Hibbs's case, along with the other three men in his voting block. Court watchers assumed that the liberal block—Justices David Souter, Ruth Bader

Ginsburg, Stephen Breyer, and John Paul Stevens—would vote to uphold the FMLA. So the outcome was expected to rest on the shoulders of Justice Sandra Day O'Connor. Given the line-up, even Hibbs's own attorney, Nina Pillard, expected to lose. One of her colleagues placed her odds of winning at a dismal five percent.

Women's advocates were stunned when the Supreme Court issued its decision in *Nevada Department of Human Resources v. Hibbs* in 2003. It was a 6-3 ruling upholding state governments' obligation to follow the FMLA's family leave rules. Advocates were even more stunned when they learned that the author of the majority opinion was Justice Rehnquist, who joined the four liberal justices along with Justice O'Connor. Stunned doesn't begin to describe the reaction from feminists reading Rehnquist's opinion. What they found wasn't his typical discourse on federalism. Instead, they found a compassionate recognition of the work/family conflicts that disadvantage women.

Justice Rehnquist began by explaining that the FMLA's goal is to prevent gender discrimination in the workplace. If states had a history of discrimination, that could justify the FMLA as federal regulation of unfair state conduct. So the issue was whether states had discriminated against women before the FMLA was enacted. Although Rehnquist had shown little understanding of women's experiences in *Roe v. Wade* in 1973, he was surprisingly insightful about the workplace biases facing women in 2003.

Rehnquist chronicled how states had designed their employee leave policies to treat women differently from men. In Rehnquist's view, these policies were built on "the pervasive sex-role stereotype that caring for family members is women's work." But his understanding went even deeper as he explained that discouraging men from taking family leave was also part of the problem. He blamed these "mutually reinforcing stereotypes" for causing women to shoulder the bulk of caregiving responsibilities and for employers viewing women as less committed employees. In a final phrase that's become a mantra for working moms, the seventy-nine-year-old lifelong conservative concluded that a federal family leave law was a necessary bridge across "the faultline between work and family."

Legal pundits were initially at a loss to explain how Justice Rehnquist went from rejecting a woman's fundamental right to choice in *Roe v. Wade* to an empathetic understanding of gender stereotypes in *Hibbs*. Some even wondered if his colleague, women's rights advocate Justice Ruth Bader Ginsburg, had ghost-written the opinion. Even Ginsburg's husband asked her if she was the real author. Although Ginsburg didn't write the decision, she admitted that it was "a delightful surprise" to read Rehnquist's opinion, and she was happy to cast her vote alongside him. So what could explain Justice Rehnquist's enlightenment? A look at his personal life during the thirty years between *Roe* and *Hibbs* leads to one persuasive conclusion: Rehnquist had become a dad of daughters.

Rehnquist and his wife, Natalie Cornell, had two daughters, Janet and Nancy, and one son, James. Rehnquist's wife died from cancer in 1991, leaving him the sole parent, and he was an engaged and loving father. During the years leading up to *Hibbs*, Rehnquist's daughters grew up, started working, had children, and most importantly, struggled while balancing careers and motherhood. Rehnquist was particularly involved with his older daughter, Janet, who was an attorney. After Janet got divorced, she often dealt with childcare challenges while building her career as a single mom. The same year that Rehnquist decided *Hibbs*, he often left Court early to pick up his granddaughters from school when Janet needed help with childcare.

Justice Ginsburg saw firsthand the impact that Rehnquist's daughters had on his views. "When his daughter Janet was divorced," she explained, "he became more sensitive to things that he might not have noticed." Former Justice Department Official Randolph Moss agreed: "Having a child who is a woman with a career has to have some effect on his thinking about the role of women in the workplace."

Justice Rehnquist died in 2005, two years after the *Hibbs* case, leaving three proud children and nine grandchildren. At Rehnquist's funeral, his daughter, Janet, spoke about how their dad always put family first. His granddaughter, Natalie, talked about how he'd taught her to play bridge, fan-tan, and poker—including how to look in window reflections to peek at an opponent's cards. Justice Ginsburg was moved by Natalie's eulogy, and she marveled at how few people had known the empathetic dad side of Justice Rehnquist. As the dad of daughters—and the granddad of granddaughters—Justice Rehnquist left his mark far beyond being the Supreme Court's conservative revolutionary.

After *Hibbs*, two researchers wondered whether the father-daughter effect on Justice Rehnquist was unique. They wanted to know if judges who are dads of daughters are generally more empathetic to women. In 2015, Emory Professor Adam Glynn and

Harvard Professor Maya Sen gathered data on 224 federal appellate court judges. They recorded how each judge ruled in a total of 990 women's rights cases between 1996 and 2002. The cases involved claims of sex discrimination in employment and education, pregnancy discrimination, and reproductive rights.

The study found strong support for a father-daughter effect. The researchers compared judges with the same total number of children. Within each group, male judges with at least one daughter had a more pro-women voting record on gender-related cases than male judges who had only sons. Having at least one daughter translated to an average seven percent increase in cases in which a male judge voted pro-women. The effect was even bigger for male judges who had only one child. In that group, having a daughter instead of a son translated to an average sixteen percent increase in feminist votes. Although that may sound insignificant, a sixteen-point shift is more than the baseline difference in voting records between male judges who are Democrat versus Republican.

Although the father-daughter effect crossed political lines, it varied for judges with different political ideologies. The shift toward a more pro-women voting record was larger for male judges who were appointed by Republican presidents. That's because judges appointed by Democratic presidents started with more left-leaning voting records, so Republican-appointed judges had more room to shift their voting patterns when they had daughters. For conservative judges, having a daughter was a trigger for becoming more empathetic. "By having at least one daughter," Professor Sen explains, "judges learn about what it's like to be a woman, perhaps a young woman, who might have to deal with issues like equity in terms of pay, university admissions or taking care of children."

The empathy that grows from the father-daughter relationship appeared to drive not only Justice Rehnquist's opinion in *Hibbs*, but also Justice John Paul Stevens's opinion in another case six years later. The case began when thirteen-year-old Savana Redding was marched out of her middle-school math class into the Assistant Principal's office. The male Assistant Principal asked Savana whether she had any prescription or over-the-counter medication, which would violate school policy. Savana's interrogation was prompted by an uncorroborated accusation from another student, who'd been found with several prescription-strength ibuprofen and one over-the-counter naproxen.

Savana told the Assistant Principal that she didn't have any pills and hadn't given any pills to the other student. Savana was an honor student without any prior school violations, but the Assistant Principal still proceeded to search her backpack. Finding nothing, he ordered his administrative assistant to take Savanna to the school nurse's office for a strip search.

In the nurse's office, the two women made Savana remove her jacket, shoes, socks, stretch pants, and shirt. Savana sat in her bra and underwear while the two adults examined her clothes and found nothing. They ordered Savana to pull her bra away from her body, revealing her breasts, to see if any pills would fall out. Again, they found nothing. Then they ordered Savana to pull out the elastic on her underwear away from her body, revealing her pelvic area. Once again, no pills were found. Hiding her head so the adults couldn't see that she was about to cry, Savana was finally allowed to get dressed. But instead of returning to class, she was forced to sit outside the Assistant Principal's office for over two hours. School officials never contacted Savana's parents during the entire incident.

Savana felt embarrassed, frightened, and violated. She described the search as "the most humiliating experience I ever had," and she suffered lasting trauma that eventually caused her to drop out of school. Her parents knew that the school had crossed a line. Student strip searches are so degrading that some schools have banned them entirely. So Savana's parents sued the school, the Assistant Principal, the administrative assistant, and the school nurse, claiming that they had violated Savana's Fourth Amendment Constitutional right to be free from unreasonable searches.

Savana's case made it to the Supreme Court, which at the time had eight men and only one woman, Justice Ginsburg. During the oral arguments when the Justices questioned the attorneys for each side, Justice Ginsburg was mortified by the callous behavior of her male colleagues on the bench—described by one commentator as "a pack of giggling schoolboys."

Justice Steven Breyer began by asking Savana's attorney why a strip search was a big deal when children change clothes for gym class all the time. Justice Ginsburg could barely contain herself as she jumped in to state the obvious: kids changing for gym class is nothing like girls being stripped to their underwear by authority figures accusing them of wrongdoing. But Justice Breyer was unfazed. "In my experience when I was eight or ten or twelve years old, we did take our clothes off once a day, we changed for gym," he said. "And in my experience, too, people did sometimes stick things in my underwear." After a stunned silence in the courtroom, uncomfortable laughter erupted. But instead of recognizing the absurdity of Breyer's defense for strip-searching a girl for ibuprofen, Justice Antonin Scalia agreed with his rationale.

"You've searched everywhere else," said Scalia, so "the drugs must be in her underpants."

Justice Ginsburg wasn't just appalled by her male colleagues' questions, she was also worried what the case could mean for girls in schools nationwide. While she could easily put herself in the position of a thirteen-year-old girl and understand the impact of the school officials' conduct, her colleagues could only see the case through their own eyes. "They have never been a thirteen-year-old girl," she said. "It's a very sensitive age for a girl," which her male colleagues didn't understand. "Maybe a thirteen-year-old girl is different from a thirteen-year-old boy in terms of how humiliating it is to be seen undressed," she explained. But the male Justices only imagined their own reactions.

When the Court issued its opinion in *Safford Unified School District v. Redding* in 2009, women's advocates shared a sigh of relief. The Court majority held that the school's strip search of Savanna was unconstitutional. But the relief was overshadowed by the Court's refusal to hold the three school officials responsible. That decision was based on a legal rule called "qualified immunity," which allows officials to avoid paying damages for constitutional violations if the right that they violated wasn't clearly established in the law. Qualified immunity allows a government official to essentially say, "I didn't know that what I was doing was unconstitutional when I was doing it, so I shouldn't have to pay." Seven male Justices—including those who had shown an embarrassing lack of empathy for Savana during oral argument—accepted the qualified immunity defense. That let the school officials off the hook, even though the Court recognized that their conduct violated Savana's Constitutional rights.

Justice John Paul Stevens stood alone with his female colleague, Justice Ginsburg, to say that the school officials *should* be held responsible for their actions—a conclusion that required an empathic connection with Savana's plight. When Justice Stevens joined the Supreme Court, nobody could have predicted his ability thirty-four years later to understand how the abuse of school authority would affect a thirteen-year-old girl. Justice Stevens was a white, wealthy, Protestant, conservative, antitrust lawyer, who was appointed by President Nixon to a federal appellate court in 1970, before being elevated to the Supreme Court in 1975 by President Gerald Ford.

Despite his upbringing, Justice Stevens broke ranks with the seven other male Justices by putting himself in Savana's position and understanding how she felt humiliated and degraded. For Justice Stevens, the case wasn't even close. He saw it as "clearly outrageous conduct." "It does not require a constitutional scholar," he chided his male colleagues, "to conclude that a nude search of a thirteen-year-old child is an invasion of constitutional rights of some magnitude." Professor Sonja West and journalist Dahlia Lithwick agreed. "[I]t takes not a constitutional scholar," they explained, "but an adult with the empathy to understand that stripping a young girl to her underwear isn't the same as sending her to the locker room to change for gym class."

As the only male on the Court who understood this distinction, Justice Stevens demonstrated remarkable empathy for an eighty-nine-year-old man. How was Stevens able to see this case through Savanah's eyes when his seven male colleagues were unable to do so? The answer: Justice Stevens had three daughters of his own—Kathryn, Elizabeth, and Susan.

The empathy that Justice Stevens gained from being the father of daughters was used as a rallying cry after the case to get men to speak out against the majority's opinion. In one blog post criticizing the case, the headline implicitly called fathers to action. "Supremes Don't Care if School Officials Strip Search Your Daughter to Look for Advil," the headline read.

Justice Stevens retired from the Court a year after the *Redding* case, but women's advocates still praise him for his compassion. "Stevens used empathy not to skew or manipulate," explained West and Lithwick, "but to consider the effects of his decision on real people and to accept that the law can look quite different depending on where you're standing. That's part of what made him such a great justice, and it's a quality the president should bear in mind in selecting his replacement."

This call for empathy fell on responsive ears. Barack Obama was President at the time, and he has long believed that empathy is essential for judges to reach fair decisions. "We need somebody who's got the heart, the empathy, to recognize what it's like to be a young teenage mom," he said, "the empathy to understand what it's like to be poor or African American or gay or disabled or old."

While the research on judges who are dads of daughters supports President Obama's insights, his comments were surprisingly controversial. They sparked a heated political debate that editor Richard Just dubbed "The Empathy War." Some commentators equated judicial empathy with an inability to follow the law. Empathy became such a toxic concept that it became known simply as "the E-word."

But empathy is absolutely necessary for fairness and impartiality. As Law Professor Thomas Colby explains, a non-empathic judge who believes that he's acting as a neutral umpire—someone who "thinks that he is simply calling objective balls and strikes"—will end up unwittingly giving undue weight to his personal perspective. What a non-empathic judge fails to realize, explains Colby, "is that he *is* seeing the case from a particular perspective—his own—and is mistaking that perspective for an unbiased, neutral one."

The empathy that's needed to combat bias can come from many sources, including being the dad of a daughter. During his Senate confirmation hearing, conservative Justice Samuel Alito, Jr. acknowledged this in his own life. "When I get a case about discrimination, I have to think about people in my own family who suffered discrimination...because of gender," he said, "and I do take that into account."

The importance of empathy was most evident in the biggest women's rights victory of the century, *Roe. v. Wade*, which legalized abortion by recognizing that women's right to privacy includes the fundamental right to choice. The *Roe* opinion is another example of the father-daughter effect, at least for the Justice who became the surprise author of the majority opinion: Harry Blackmun. "On Harry's improbable journey," says journalist Linda Greenhouse, "becoming a feminist icon was perhaps the most improbable destination of all."

Justice Blackmun was a lifelong Republican who attended Harvard Law School. He began his career practicing tax law, trusts and estates, and civil litigation. President Eisenhower appointed Blackmun to a federal appellate court in 1959, and President Nixon nominated him to the Supreme Court in 1970, in large part for his staunch conservative record. Blackmun was recommended for the job by conservative Supreme Court Justice Warren Burger, who was the best man at Blackmum's wedding. When he was appointed, Blackmun was rated as more conservative than two of the most conservative Justices currently on the Court, Justices Clarence Thomas and John Roberts.

Although Justice Blackmun's conservative record earned him a seat on the Court, it didn't reveal what ended up being his most valuable preparation for his most important case. That came from the work that he shared with his wife, Dorothy Clark, as the father of three daughters—Nancy, Sally, and Susan. A few years before *Roe v. Wade*, his middle daughter, Sally, had an unplanned pregnancy at age nineteen during her sophomore year in college. She dropped out of school to get married and have the baby, but she had a miscarriage less than three weeks after the wedding. Her marriage ended, and she went back to college, attended law school, re-married, and had two daughters of her own. Sally's struggles gave her dad insight into the choices and challenges that women face when pregnant.

When *Roe v. Wade* reached the Supreme Court in 1973, Justice Blackmun reached out to deepen his understanding even more. After hearing the oral arguments, Blackmun asked his daughters for advice. His youngest daughter, Susan, later recounted the conversation they had with their dad while he was working on the case:

> *"What are your views on abortion?" he asked his three daughters over dinner. Sally's reply was carefully thought out and middle of the road, the route she had taken all her life.... Nancy, a Radcliffe and Harvard graduate, sounded off with an intellectually leftish opinion. I had not yet emerged from my hippie phase and spouted out a far-to-the-left, shake-the-old-man-up response. Dad put down his fork mid-bite and pushed back his chair. "I think I'll go lie down," he said. "I'm getting a headache."*

But a headache was a small price to pay for the sixty-four-year-old Justice to expand his thinking by seeking out women's perspectives, which helped him write one of the most empathic opinions in the Court's history. Writing for the majority, Blackmun explained the numerous ways that women are harmed by state laws that criminalize abortion. He talked about the medical risks that women face from pregnancy. He acknowledged how having children can burden women financially, physically, and mentally. He recognized the pain for all involved when a woman is forced to bear a child while being unable to provide the care that a child demands. By viewing the issues through the eyes of women who face difficult decisions about pregnancy, Justice Blackmun had no trouble concluding that a woman's ability to make her own reproductive choices is a Constitutional right.

The need for empathy is growing as *Roe v. Wade* comes under increasing attack. In 1992, the Supreme Court lowered the standard for assessing the legality of state restrictions on abortion in *Planned Parenthood v. Casey*. Over Justice Blackmun's strenuous objection, the Court allowed restrictions on abortions as long as they don't impose an "undue burden" on a woman's right to choose. This new standard makes judicial empathy critical. "A judge cannot strike that balance in any given abortion case," explains Professor Colby, "without empathizing with the woman, trying to understand, from her perspective, the extent to which the regulation burdens her right to choose."

Justice Blackmun wrote a powerful dissent in *Casey* as one of his final cases before he retired in 1994. He chastised the Court's majority for failing to consider women's perspectives, and he objected to the "undue burden" standard because he doubted his colleagues' ability to empathize with pregnant women. Blackmun's concerns have been prophetic. Since *Roe*, state legislatures have enacted over 1,000 restrictions on abortion access. In the wake of these developments—as well as increasing attacks on access to contraceptives—Justice Ruth Bader Ginsburg clings to one source of hope for men's capacity to grow their empathy skills. "I think daughters can change the perception of their fathers," she explains, which allows her to remain cautiously optimistic.

While judges who are dads of daughters have been making progress on women's rights, that doesn't replace the need to get more women appointed to the bench.

Women judges are ten percent more likely than male judges to rule in favor of women in federal appellate cases involving sex discrimination claims. Women judges also influence their male colleagues' votes. On federal appellate courts where cases are decided by three-judge panels, male judges are twelve to fourteen percent more likely to vote for a female plaintiff in a sex discrimination case if at least one of the other judges is a woman.

Having judges who are dads of daughters may also advance this long-term goal of appointing more women judges. Having a daughter not only affects how judges decide cases, but also who they hire as law clerks. Law clerks work closely with judges for one- or two-year periods to conduct research, prepare judges for oral arguments, and sometimes draft opinions. Law clerk positions with federal judges or Supreme Court Justices are among the most prestigious jobs for new attorneys, and they're a pipeline into top law firms, law faculties, and judgeships.

Because Supreme Court law clerk jobs open doors to the most influential legal positions, ensuring equal access to judicial clerkships is critical to advancing women's equality in the legal profession. Unfortunately, women have been highly under-represented in the Supreme Court law clerk ranks. Not a single woman was hired as a Supreme Court clerk in its first 150 years of existence. It wasn't until 1944 that a Justice hired the first woman clerk, and it took twenty-two years for another Justice to hire the second. Since 1998, less than a third of all Supreme Court law clerks have been women, even though the majority of law school graduates have been women during that time.

One Supreme Court Justice who opposed hiring women clerks was William Brennan, Jr., who joined the Court in 1956. Justice Brennan enforced his "no women" policy for his first eighteen years on the bench. But in 1974, he had a change of heart and hired his first female clerk, Marsha Berzon. Marsha was imminently qualified, but many other women who had sought the position for the prior eighteen years had also been qualified. So what had changed?

Right before hiring Marsha, Justice Brennan's daughter had gotten divorced, and she and her baby had moved in with him. Brennan's daughter was re-establishing her career, which meant that someone had to pick-up her baby from daycare every evening. Because Brennan's daughter often didn't get off work before the daycare center closed, Justice Brennan often left Court early to pick-up his granddaughter and care for her until his daughter got home. This experience paved the way for Brennan's willingness to hire Marsha, who also left Court at five o'clock each evening to get her son from daycare. Sadly, Justice Brennan died three years before Marsha Berzon was herself appointed as a federal appellate judge in 2000. Grandpa Brennan surely would have been proud.

Justice Blackmun's support of women went beyond his opinion in *Roe v. Wade* to his law clerk hiring as well. Blackmun hired more women law clerks than all other sitting Justices combined. Blackmun's former clerks include Karen Nelson Moore and Diane Wood, both of whom later became federal appellate judges.

Despite these advances, women are still under-represented in the judiciary. Only four of the 113 Supreme Court Justices have been women. Women make up just thirty-six percent of federal appellate court judges and thirty-three percent of federal trial court judges. There are still six federal district courts that have never had a female judge. So while we press for more women judges, having judges who are dads of daughters at least broadens the perspectives of the men on the bench. "If we can't in fact have a court that looks like America," says Professor Sonja West and journalist Dahlia Lithwick, "we should seek a court that feels for America."

In addition to judges, there's another group who can also play a powerful role in advancing women's equality in our justice system: jurors. In trial courts around the country, jurors decide discrimination cases every day. Seasoned trial attorney Robin Workman has been studying juries for over twenty-five years. In her experience, there's one type of ideal juror in sexual harassment and sex discrimination cases: dads of daughters.

Robin says that dads of daughters make good jurors because they don't need a legal explanation of wrongdoing. "They know where the line is, and they know when it's been crossed." Why? Because they naturally ask themselves whether the conduct is something they'd want their daughters to face. "You get a dad who's got a daughter who's gone through the travails of high school, or difficult bosses at jobs, and then it hits home," says Robin. "Dads of daughters just have a better empathic scale."

How Dads Can Get Started

The easiest way for dads to build empathy for girls and women—which is a crucial step to becoming effective male allies—is to pay attention to their own daughters' experiences. Do what Justice Blackmun did when he wanted to understand women's perspectives before deciding *Roe v. Wade*: ask your daughters about their views. Pay particular attention to the external barriers that your daughters face in achieving their goals. Next, find other women with diverse backgrounds and experiences—perhaps friends of your adult daughters—and do the same thing. Your goal is not to solve their problems. Your goal is to listen, learn, and see the world from a new vantage point.

Gender strategist Jeffery Halter offers the same advice to men who want to become more empathic women's allies in their workplaces. Jeffery has discovered that male leaders who want to advocate for women tend to understandably attack the challenge by—you guessed it—*leading*. But leading without empathy is unlikely to be a successful formula for supporting women. According to Jeffery, the first step isn't to lead. The first step is *to listen*.

Jeffery has found that becoming a male ally is a four-step process: listen, learn, lead, and have the will. Listening is the most important step because it builds the empathy that's necessary to lead effectively. Listening helps men understand the organizational, social, and cultural barriers that often prevent women from reaching their full potential. Women and men are having very different workplace experiences, so without empathy, even the most well-intentioned men may not appreciate the changes that are needed.

The hardest part about listening to women is getting conversations started in ways that empower women to talk candidly about their experiences. For male leaders who often hold positions of power in their workplaces, that's not always an easy task. In the wake of #MeToo, many men are afraid they might do or say something wrong, and they may not know how to launch these discussions. After talking with many male leaders about these concerns, Jeffery has devised some practical tools to support men's empathy-building goals in a format that builds trust and supports men to become effective gender equality leaders.

The practical tools are what Jeffery calls "Gender Conversation QuickStarters." These ready-made "meetings in a box" facilitate workplace conversations between men and women about gender equality. Each QuickStarter contains three items. First, the QuickStarter identifies a topic for discussion, which gets men and women on the same page. Some of the topics include unconscious bias, gender stereotypes, sexual harassment, how workplace culture disadvantages women, and why women's advancement is good for business. Second, the QuickStarter includes a link to an article or video to share background information for the discussion. Third, and most importantly, the QuickStarter includes specific questions to literally get the conversation started.

Male leaders can use Jeffery's Gender Conversation QuckStarters in staff meetings, one-on-one discussions, or small-group settings. The QuickStarters set one important ground rule: assume good intent by all participants. The materials remind participants that someone might say something that seems wrong or inappropriate, but that can lead to deeper understanding. By structuring a safe setting to discuss difficult gender issues, these tools can support men—and women—in building the empathy that's needed to work together to advance women's equality. To get started, dads of daughters can visit the YWomen website and sign up for an e-newsletter to receive the Gender Equality QuickStarters for free.

For men who aren't in positions to establish formal conversations in their workplaces but who still want to build empathy to become effective women's allies, Jeffery also offers advice for having informal conversations with women. He suggests taking a trusted woman colleague to lunch or coffee and asking this straightforward question: Do you believe men and women are having different experiences at the company? "Then be quiet and genuinely listen," says Jeffery. "Don't interrupt, don't be defensive or justify company policies, just shut up and listen." After ten minutes of listening, Jeffery's advice is to humbly ask a second time: What else don't I know? After ten more minutes of listening, he suggests asking one more time: And what else?

In Jeffery's experience, asking several times for more information—while listening non-defensively—is what empowers women to open up about the causes of inequality that are often invisible to men. "Listen so others will speak," is Jeffery's mantra. Why? Because hearing about women's different experiences is what builds the empathy that empowers men to become effective leaders for advancing women. "When you talk, you know what you know," says Jeffery. "But when you listen, you know what they know and what you know."

Men who'd like to build empathy to support gender equality in their workplaces have several other resources from dads who were inspired by their daughters to study the connection between empathy and leadership. Dr. Relly Nadler is an executive coach with clinical psychology training. Relly's research had long supported the notion that empathy is a critical leadership skill and a foundation for effective mentoring. But in trying to figure out how to build empathy, his early insights came from his interactions with his daughter McKensey.

When Relly talked with his daughter, he found himself becoming more attuned to others' emotions and increasing his ability to take others' perspectives. He discovered that there's actually a physiological explanation for his growth. "What we know about neuroscience is that emotions are contagious," Relly explains. Men become more attuned to emotions from spending time with their daughters, and they bring their increased emotional IQ into the workplace. That makes them stronger leaders, particularly in understanding the barriers facing women.

Relly shares his insights about building empathy to become a better leader in his management guidebook, *Leading with Emotional Intelligence*. The book offers practical advice for business leaders on developing empathy to communicate and collaborate more effectively. The book also explains how empathy boosts a company's bottom line by increasing employee morale, loyalty, and productivity.

Another great resource is John Gerzema and Michael D'Antonio's book, *The Athena Doctrine: How Women (and the Men Who Think Like Them) Will Rule the Future*. John is the CEO of Harris Insights & Analytics, a research firm that analyzes social changes to support organizational growth. Michael is a Pulitzer-Prize winning writer and journalist. More importantly, John and Michael are fathers of daughters, which helped them build their own empathy skills.

The Athena Doctrine explains the importance of empathy to leadership success. Empathetic leaders can build more inclusive workplaces and diverse leadership teams, which increases innovation. John's research shows that so-called "female characteristics"—empathy, authenticity, and collaboration—are precisely the skills that leaders need to solve today's challenges. John's goal is to re-brand these characteristics not as "female," but as leadership skills. His book invites men into the gender equality conversation by encouraging them to re-think what it means to be a strong leader. "Leave it to two fathers of daughters to show us how men and women alike are using empathy and collaboration to solve problems big and small," says Arianna Huffington, the former editor-in-chief of *The Huffington Post*.

In the book's acknowledgements, John and Michael thank "the goddesses of wisdom in our lives," who include John's daughter, Nina, and Michael's two daughters, Amy and Elizabeth. John and Michael particularly appreciated how the patient and supportive women in their lives "nodded approvingly" at their ideas, "without ever asking why it took us so long to reach such obvious insights."

CHAPTER 9

Drinking the Daughter Water

The gender pay gap in the US is stunningly large and painfully persistent. For full-time employees, women earn an average of eighty cents for every dollar earned by similarly-educated men doing similar work. The gap is even larger for women of color, with African American women earning sixty-two cents and Latinas earning fifty-three cents for every dollar earned by men. The overall gender wage gap has hardly changed in the last fifteen years. At the current rate of progress, most working women will never experience wage equality during their lifetime.

The wage gap exists even in the gig economy, which supposedly removes gender bias through online platforms. A study of over a million Uber drivers found that the hourly earnings of male drivers exceed female drivers by seven percent. In other non-traditional work relationships, the numbers are even worse. Among independent contractors, men earn nearly twenty-two percent more than women. Among the self-employed, men out-earn women by twenty percent. Even among temp workers, the gender wage gap is fifteen percent.

If we throw parenthood into the equation, the gender gap becomes a chasm. Among full-time, year-round workers, moms make an average of seventy-one cents for every dollar earned by dads. This is the result of both a "motherhood penalty" *and* a "fatherhood bonus." When women become moms, their incomes decrease, but when men become dads, their salaries actually go up. This differential treatment can't be explained by real performance differences. Pay gaps between moms and dads exist even after controlling for qualifications, experience, education, types of jobs, and number of hours worked. Over time, the gap really adds up. The average working mom misses out on $16,000 each year, with an average lifetime loss of over $400,000.

While the parenthood wage gap crosses education levels, ages, races, locations, and occupations, that doesn't mean it affects all women equally. The gap is wider for moms of color, and it's most extreme for women who can least afford the loss. Men with the highest incomes get the biggest pay increases when they become dads, while women with the lowest incomes face the biggest pay losses when they become moms. White men receive the highest fatherhood bonuses, while women of color face the largest motherhood penalties. Perhaps most disturbing is that while the overall gender wage gap is decreasing—although at a glacial pace—the gap between moms and dads is growing.

All of this depressing news exists despite the fact that gender pay discrimination has been illegal for most workers since Congress enacted the Equal Pay Act of 1963 and Title VII of the Civil Rights Act of 1964. But lawsuits are an expensive and inefficient way to solve the problem. Many women don't even know that their male colleagues are getting paid more for doing the same job because many employers keep their pay data a tightly-held secret.

The gender pay gap has also persisted in part due to the insidious myth that women are responsible for their own low pay because they don't negotiate as well as men. In 2003, Linda Babcock and Sara Laschever fueled this storyline with their book, *Women Don't Ask: Negotiation and the Gender Divide*. Using interviews and social science research, this book revealed that women are indeed less likely than men to initiate pay negotiations in some situations.

What the "women don't ask" narrative fails to recognize, however, is that women's tendency not to initiate pay negotiations as frequently or aggressively as men is highly rational behavior. Research shows that employers react more negatively to women than to men who attempt to negotiate their wages. Employers are more resistant to and take tougher positions against women for engaging in the same self-advocacy for which men are rewarded. Workplace evaluators—male *and female*—tend to penalize women for seeking higher pay by concluding that they are less likeable, overly aggressive, intimidating, and bossy, and by being less willing to work with them in the future. In short, when men and women both ask for more money, men typically get a raise, while women get hostility. So women have very good reasons for neither asking too often nor negotiating too hard for higher pay.

Facebook COO Sheryl Sandberg acknowledges this problem in her book, *Lean In*. "[W]e need to recognize that women often have good cause to be reluctant to advocate for their own interests, because doing so can easily backfire," she cautions. Because employers expect men to advocate on their own behalf, there's no downside when men ask for a raise. "But since women are expected to be concerned with others,"

Sheryl explains, "when they advocate for themselves or point to their own value, both men and women react unfavorably." This puts women in a perilous position when negotiating for equal pay—what Sheryl describes as "trying to cross a minefield backward in high heels."

Even though the "women don't ask" storyline could have triggered much-needed scrutiny of employers' biased responses to pay negotiations, the reaction was instead to blame women themselves. In no time, the market was flooded with books telling women how to fix their perceived negotiation deficiencies, which were purportedly at the root of the gender pay gap.

Several years after publishing *Women Don't Ask*, the same authors wrote a follow-up book titled, *Ask for It: How Women Can Use the Power of Negotiation to Get What They Really Want*. This book is described as the action plan that women need "to ask effectively, in ways that feel comfortable to you as a woman." In another book, *Why Women Earn Less: How to Make What You're Really Worth*, author Mikelann Valterra similarly targets women with a self-help guide for tackling the gender wage gap:

> *This book is a practical, step-by-step guide for under-earning women who are ready to turn their lives around. It demystifies the process of under-earning, explores its underlying psychological and emotional issues, and offers practical advice and strategies to help overcome it. Why Women Earn Less explains how you can be better paid for the work you do. It maps out, on a practical level, how to overcome the bad*

> *habits that contribute to earning less than you deserve.*

Holding women responsible for their own "under-earning" even found its way into a bill introduced in Congress to address unequal pay. The Paycheck Fairness Act (PFA) was intended to expand sex discrimination laws by providing stronger legal remedies for unfair pay. Buried at the end of the bill was a section titled, "Negotiation Skills Training for Girls and Women." Had this bill ever passed, this section would have authorized the Secretaries of Labor and Education to establish a grant program for selected public agencies, nonprofits, and community-based organizations to "carry out an effective negotiation skills training program that empowers girls and women."

While the authors of these books and initiatives surely have women's best interest at heart, they fail to place responsibility for unequal pay on the individuals in power who are setting the unfair wages: employers. Despite recognizing the risks that women face by seeking fair pay, even Sheryl Sandberg has focused her advice on how women can improve their negotiation skills. She advises women to adopt a "communal approach" to pay negotiations. According to Sheryl, this approach requires "smiling frequently, expressing appreciation and concern, invoking common interests, emphasizing larger goals, and approaching the negotiation as solving a problem as opposed to taking a critical stance."

The problem isn't that this is bad advice. It's actually well-founded in negotiation research. The problem is in placing the burden to fix the gender pay gap on women's own shoulders. Jeffery Halter, founder of the gender consulting firm YWomen, thinks that more responsibility should be placed on male leaders—particularly dads of daughters. “We don’t need another workshop for women,” says Jeffery. “We need fathers of daughters to be outraged that our daughters earn less than our sons!” “Every CEO has the information on pay equity,” explains Jeffery, but “as long as women are the only ones talking about these issues there is no reason to change.”

Research supports Jeffery’s belief in the potential for dads of daughters to help tackle the gender pay gap. Male CEOs who have a daughter tend to have smaller gender pay gaps in their companies than at other male-lead firms. A study of over 10,000 Danish companies found that when a male CEO’s firstborn child is a daughter, the gender pay gap in his company decreases an average of 2.8 percent. That may sound trivial, but the economic impact is significant. While the study was being conducted, the gender wage gap in Denmark was 21.5 percent. That means that women were earning an average of 78.5 cents for every dollar earned by men. Closing the gap by 2.8 percentage points eliminates thirteen percent of the total gender wage gap—*just by having a male CEO become the father of a firstborn daughter*.

Business Professor David Gaddis Ross was one of the study’s primary researchers. He says that when a male CEO has his first daughter, it’s like “a switch flips,” and he suddenly pays more attention to gender issues. The impact of a firstborn girl was largest in smaller companies where CEOs have more direct control over pay rates, and the pay gap closed the most for highly educated women in a new dad’s firm. The impact was smaller when a male CEO’s first daughter arrived after he already had a son, and additional daughters didn't add to the effect. There's something uniquely powerful when a man's first child is a girl.

If that much progress can result simply from a male CEO having a daughter, imagine what dads of daughters could accomplish if they actively set their sights on eliminating the gender pay gap. Getting men sufficiently outraged to prioritize pay equity was the goal of a clever initiative launched in Australia, which discovered that tapping into dads' expectations for their daughters' futures is a great way to take aim at pay discrimination.

The Daughter Water Campaign

In 2014, the CEOs of more than 3,000 Australian companies received surprise packages in the mail. Each package contained a small bottle with a mysterious liquid labeled, "Daughter Water." The new product launch included a YouTube video titled, "Introducing Daughter Water," which lured curious viewers with an intriguing question: "Can a drink close the gender pay gap?"

The video opens to the back of a male CEO standing in a luxurious office talking intently on his cell phone. A narrator explains that researchers have discovered that a company's gender pay gap shrinks when a male CEO has a daughter. The CEO then turns around to reveal an adorable baby—with pink socks, a pink onesie, and a pink cap—cooing happily in an infant carrier strapped to his chest. The scene shifts to a boardroom meeting in a high-rise office where the CEO—baby still in tow—draws a picture on a whiteboard of a male symbol with a large dollar sign and a female symbol with a smaller dollar sign. The baby smiles as her CEO dad erases the small dollar sign next to the female and replaces it with a larger one. The narrator continues:

> *Introducing Daughter Water, the latest breakthrough in pay inequality. Daughter Water is formulated using a potent combination of old wives' tales to help CEOs have a baby girl. Gender selection technology implement tools are placed in an X formation beneath the tank. This releases X chromosomes upwards into the water where they form pairs, feminizing the molecules. Every bottle is rigorously gender checked using the ring swing test. Can a drink really help you have a daughter? Probably not. Can a drink close the pay gap? That's up to you.*

The video directs viewers to a website to see if their own employers are taking action on equal pay.

The website was run by Australia's Workplace Gender Equality Agency (WGEA), which was created by Australia's Workplace Gender Equality Act of 2012 to help advance women's workplace equality. The goal of the WGEA's "In Your Hands" campaign was to get CEOs to conduct a formal gender pay analysis at their firms. The CEOs who received Daughter Water samples were the leaders of the nearly seventy-four percent of Australian companies that had never completed pay studies.

WGEA officials were having a hard time getting CEOs to act, and they needed to grab their attention. So they turned to the marketing agency DDB Sydney to design a pay equity campaign to raise awareness about the gender pay gap and motivate CEOs to do something about it. The idea was based on the encouraging data showing that male CEOs with daughters had smaller gender pay gaps in their companies than at other male-lead firms. Recognizing the power of the daughter-father relationship, the designers came up with the Daughter Water campaign. They hoped that the fake Daughter Water product would help male CEOs have their own light-bulb moments and prioritize gender pay equity in their firms.

When the Daughter Water campaign began, the gender pay gap in Australia had risen to a twenty-two year high of 18.2 percent. That gap translates into an average lifetime earnings deficit for moms of around $1.2 million relative to dads. For parents who have at least a bachelor's degree, the deficit for moms rises to $1.5 million. Closing that gap would not only help women, but would boost Australia's GDP by an estimated eleven percent.

WGEA Director Helen Conway acknowledged that the Daughter Water campaign was an unconventional tactic for a government agency, but she felt that Australia's rising gender pay gap demanded a creative approach. "It is a slightly ridiculous way of attracting attention to this issue and getting people to focus on it," admitted Helen. "But every year we talk about the pay gap, and we have equal payday and nothing changes."

The Daughter Water campaign not only tapped into the power of the father-daughter relationship, it was also backed by public persuasion. The WGEA's website, which YouTube viewers were encouraged to check out, started publishing gender pay data for all Australian companies.

Employees, customers, and investors quickly discovered that they could find out exactly how companies stacked up on pay equity. The website also allowed individuals to ask the WGEA to email individual CEOs—either to praise their efforts or urge them to improve.

But it wasn't enough to just catch the attention of CEOs with bottles of Daughter Water. Nothing would change if the CEOs didn't know what to do about the problem. So the WGEA provided toolkits to help employers analyze pay data and reduce disparities. "[O]nce we raise that awareness," explains Helen, "we provide them with the wherewithal to fix any problems they have."

One of the WGEA's most valuable tools is a Gender Pay Gap Calculator, which was created in partnership with Mercer, a global employment consulting firm. The calculator provides step-by-step instructions for analyzing a firm's pay data. The WGEA also offers a technical guide, an eLearning module, and a sample data set for illustration. The WGEA's website has pay equity briefings for company directors, CEOs, and managers, which include practical tips for establishing fairer pay practices.

The WGEA was careful to strike a positive tone, rather than shaming CEOs. "We know employers don't set out to pay women less," the website explained, "however gender bias can creep into performance, talent development and pay decisions to create instances where women are paid less than men for doing the same job." So the focus was on carrots rather than sticks.

One of the WGEA's incentives was an online report card that graded companies on pay equity. When business leaders made significant progress, the WGEA honored them with the title, "Pay Equity Ambassador," and highlighted their companies on the agency's website. To become Pay Equity Ambassadors, executives had to conduct a formal gender pay analysis, reduce pay disparities, and communicate their findings to their employees. Pay Equity Ambassadors also had to endorse a Pay Equity Pledge acknowledging the link between fair pay and business success. Companies could also receive an Employer of Choice for Gender Equality Citation, and industry groups could become Pay Equity Official Supporters by publicizing the WGEA's pay equity resources and hosting webinars about equal pay.

During the Daughter Water campaign, the WGEA's pay equity resources were downloaded nearly 4,500 times. Since the launch, over one-hundred Australian CEOs, directors, and senior executives have achieved Pay Equity Ambassador status. Over one-hundred Australian companies have earned the Gender Equality Citation, and twenty-seven industry groups have become Pay Equity Official Supporters. That's a pretty good return on a few thousand bottles of apparently quite potent Daughter Water.

The UK's government agency tasked with advancing gender equality has also tried creative campaigns to spur action on gender pay equity. In the early 2000s, the UK's Equal Opportunities Commission (EOC) launched the "Close the Gap" initiative. Like Australia's Daughter Water campaign, this initiative also tapped into the power of the daughter-father relationship. One poster in the Close the Gap campaign depicted a smiling young boy sitting next to a cross-armed, pouting young girl. The tagline read: "Prepare your daughter for working life. Give her less pocket money than your son." The poster explained that even after forty years of equal pay law, women were still paid less than men, and it directed readers to the agency's website to learn how to take action.

The EOC's Close the Gap campaign was later picked up by *Grazia*, an international women's magazine. In 2014, *Grazia* launched the "Mind the Gap" campaign, which played off the ubiquitous warning in the London underground that reminds passengers to be careful as they step over the space between the train door and the station platform. At the time, British women were earning an average of sixteen percent less than men, and the gap had doubled for women in their twenties in the prior four years. *Grazia*'s Editor-in-Chief Jane Burton specifically reached out to dads of daughters to support the campaign, reminding them that their daughters' future was at stake.

The Mind the Gap initiative had a specific objective. The goal was to collect 100,000 signatures on a petition demanding a change to the UK's sex discrimination law. The existing law already prohibited gender pay discrimination, but it was difficult to enforce because most women had no idea if they were getting paid less than men. The petition asked lawmakers to change the law to require large companies to publish annual data on their male and female hourly wages. Gloria De Piero, who was the Shadow Minister for Women and Equalities in the British Parliament, supported the amendment, and she knew that dads of daughters held power to make a difference. "This is not a man versus woman fight," said Gloria. "Men should be with us on this. It's their daughter...who is suffering. Let us all pull together and finally close this pay gap for good."

How Dads Can Get Started

Not all dads of daughters are in positions to directly change employers' pay-scales, but all dads can make a difference. One concrete step is supporting pay transparency at your workplace. Allowing employees to know how much their co-workers are paid is critical for closing the gender pay gap. If nobody knows whether men and women in the same positions are getting paid the same, it's easy for unequal pay to exist and hard to do anything about it. Without pay transparency, sex discrimination laws may accomplish very little. Making pay data public also increases pressure on companies in other ways. Nearly a third of workers say they won't apply to a company that they know has a gender pay disparity, and two-thirds of American customers say they are less likely to buy products from companies that they know pay women unfairly.

Dads of daughters can also start changing work culture by talking about their compensation with co-workers, asking bosses to disclose employees' salaries, and encouraging their daughters to seek employers with accessible pay data. If employers are resistant, you can mention that pay transparency not only helps close the gender pay gap, but also increases employee performance, job satisfaction, and loyalty. When employees believe they are underpaid, they're more likely to switch jobs. So ensuring equal pay can save companies money by decreasing turnover. Men can also rest assured that the law will protect their efforts. The National Labor Relations Act prohibits most employers from retaliating against employees for talking about compensation or criticizing pay practices.

Some dads of daughters *are* in positions to directly affect compensation at their companies. For those dads, instituting pay transparency—and educating colleagues about why it's important for achieving gender pay equity—can send a powerful message. As more companies begin disclosing pay data to their employees, the pressure increases on other companies to do the same.

Some companies may be unwilling to disclose pay data out of fear of getting sued. To address this concern, companies can first conduct an internal pay audit to address any gender pay gaps. The WGEA's Gender Pay Gap Calculator and toolkit are an excellent resource for company leaders to conduct this important self-assessment. Dr. Andrew Chamberlain, the Chief Economist at Glassdoor, has also created a step-by-step guide for employers to analyze pay gaps by comparing similarly-situated male and female employees. The guide is available free online, with the accompanying computer code and sample data sets for illustration.

Dads of daughters in corporate leadership positions can also make managers aware of the gender biases that affect pay negotiations in ways that de-value women—particularly mothers. Formalizing the pay negotiation process, setting salaries based on objective criteria, and regularly conducting pay audits can ensure that women are paid fairly. LeanIn.org has many resources to help, including checklists for establishing fair hiring, performance evaluation, and promotion practices, which can reduce gender bias that results in unequal pay.

It's also important to be forward-looking in pay-setting rather than basing salaries on what a new employee made at a former employer. Basing current pay on an employee's prior pay perpetuates past inequality rather than solving the problem. Some state legislatures have recognized this issue and enacted laws that prohibit employers from even asking job applicants about their prior pay.

Tackling the gender pay gap is a daunting task that will require small steps from as many men as possible. While Australia's Daughter Water campaign moved quite a few dads to action, there's one sure indication of its success in getting men engaged in the challenge. In 2015, the Urban Dictionary added an entry for the phrase, "daughter water." Founded in 1999 by Aaron Peckham, the Urban Dictionary is a crowdsourced online collection of words used in popular culture. The Urban Dictionary defines "daughter water" as: "The mystical 'tonic' where fathers of daughters become far more aware of the impact of diversity and sexism issues because they see the world through their daughters' experiences." The Urban Dictionary even provides a sample use of the phrase in a sentence: "He became far more aware of the plight of women in the workforce after he drank the Daughter Water." For all the dads who want to make things better for their daughters, let's raise a glass of Daughter Water and toast to the coming demise of the gender pay gap.

CHAPTER 10

Investing in Women Entrepreneurs

Successful entrepreneurs all share a few essential traits: aggressiveness, independence, competitiveness, extroversion, and a willingness to take risks. At least, that's what we've grown up believing. That's how we've seen entrepreneurs portrayed in the media. That's the impression that students get in business school. There's just one problem with this "lone warrior" persona of successful entrepreneurs. It's wrong.

Researchers have discovered that none of the male-associated traits that we connect with successful entrepreneurs actually correlate with entrepreneurial success. In fact, there is no single successful entrepreneurial personality. The only trait that correlates with entrepreneurial success is conscientiousness—which isn't a trait that's viewed as particularly masculine. This might be amusing if it didn't have real-world consequences. But our masculine stereotypes about entrepreneurs put women at a major disadvantage.

From small business owners to high-tech innovators, women entrepreneurs have immense talent to offer. Yet their contributions are being blocked and under-valued at every turn. There are more than eleven million women-owned businesses in the US, but they're far more likely than male-owned businesses to be very small or solo ventures. Only two percent of women-owned businesses ever hit the $1 million revenue mark, which is reached 3.5 times more often by businesses owned by men.

This isn't due to a lack of skills or a shortage of good ideas. It's largely because women are excluded from the networking circles that support start-up success. Most importantly, women have a much harder time than men getting credit and financial backing. Financing networks often operate through referrals, which leaves most women out of the loop. As a result, women are more likely than men to invest their own money in their businesses instead of getting outside capital. Women also have less access to incubators, which are physical spaces where entrepreneurs, investors, lawyers, and accountants work side-by-side to launch new ventures. In a study of 18,000 firms that were started through incubators, only six percent were run by women.

It's hard for women to make headway in a community where men have amassed most of the start-up experience, control most of the money, and network mostly with other men. This is unlikely to change anytime soon because male entrepreneurs and male investors tend to mentor, support, and invest in entrepreneurs who are just like themselves. Social scientists have a fancy name for this obvious but problematic phenomenon: "homophily." In lay terms, it means that people like to hang out with similar people.

In the start-up world, this has serious negative effects. The most obvious is that entrepreneurs end up looking just like the venture capitalists (VCs) who fund them. Ninety-one percent of VCs are men, eighty-six percent are white, eleven percent are Asian, and the majority went to Harvard, Stanford, or the University of

Pennsylvania. Venture-backed entrepreneurs look nearly identical: ninety-one percent are men, eighty percent are white, sixteen percent are Asian, and most have degrees from a similar set of universities. This doesn't just result in gender inequality. It also results in an enormous loss of talent and innovation.

The lack of funding for women entrepreneurs is particularly glaring in Silicon Valley, where the premier VCs are mostly men, who invest mostly in start-ups run by other men. Venture capital firms play a critical gatekeeping role for entrepreneurs by deciding which emerging companies to finance. Partners at VC firms select early-stage companies with growth potential, and they provide funding in exchange for an ownership stake. So VC partners effectively decide which start-ups live and which start-ups die.

In Silicon Valley, that god-like role is played almost exclusively by men. Men make up eighty-nine percent of the investment decision-makers at the top seventy-two VC firms in the country. Ninety-two percent of the top-tier VC firms don't have a woman on their senior investment teams, and seventy-two percent have never hired a female investor. So it's not surprising where the money is flowing. In 2016, VCs poured $64.9 billion into male-founded start-ups, but only $1.5 billion into start-ups founded by women. Start-ups with at least one female founder got only nineteen percent of all seed funding, only fourteen percent of early-stage funding, and only eight percent of funding in late-stage venture rounds. That means that most female entrepreneurs' ideas never see the light of day.

As dismal as these investment numbers are, the reality facing women entrepreneurs is far worse. In 2017, a flood of investigative reporting revealed the pervasive culture of sexual harassment that female founders endure from male investors—a problem that's gone unchecked in the start-up community for years. The ouster of Justin Caldbeck from Binary Capital and Dave McClure from 500 Startups gave the public just an inkling of the epidemic. Dozens of female entrepreneurs came forward to share deplorable accounts of sexist comments, unwanted advances, and sexual misconduct by male investors.

While the percentage of VCs who are women has hardly changed over the past twenty-five years, dads of daughters are beginning to chip away at this impenetrable male stronghold. Harvard Business Professor Paul Gompers and economist Sophie Calder-Wang studied 1,400 partners at nearly 1,000 VC firms from 1990 through mid-2016. They discovered that VC firms with male senior partners who have daughters are more likely to hire women partners into their firms. Having a male senior partner with a daughter increases the chance the firm will hire a female investor by twenty-four percent.

Hiring women partners, in turn, significantly increases a VC firm's financial success—whether measured by individual deal outcomes or overall fund performance. One explanation for this success may be that the pool of female investor candidates is particularly talented because women have been excluded from VC firms for so long. Gender diversity may also produce better investment decisions by bringing a broader perspective when assessing start-ups. Women VC partners may also attract more diverse investment opportunities from more diverse entrepreneurs.

The father-daughter impact at VC firms also has a positive ripple effect for women entrepreneurs. When a VC firm has a senior male partner with a daughter, the firm not only hires more women investors, but those women are more likely than men to invest in women-run start-ups. So dads of daughters aren't just diversifying the investment community (and making more money for their firms in the process). The women partners are also paying it forward by investing in women entrepreneurs.

This is a good first step, but there's a long way to go. The male-dominated start-up community has not only pushed many talented women out, it's also deterred many women from entering in the first place. A 17-country survey found that women are less likely to consider entrepreneurship as a career than men. Women are also less confident than men in their entrepreneurial skills—even though most of us are mistaken about the skills that matter. Several dads of daughters are finding ways to encourage more girls and women to start running their own businesses. Their stories can help rewrite what it means to be an entrepreneur.

The 5by20 Initiative

When you think of Coca-Cola, you probably think of slick ad campaigns with famous sports stars, catchy jingles, and cans and bottles in every grocery store, vending machine, and sports venue. Coca-Cola may also bring to mind shiny red delivery trucks—one of which was driven by Coca-Cola's former CEO Muhtar Kent in his first job at the company. Muhtar's climb from truck driver to CEO was chronicled in Chapter 1, which shared his story of becoming inspired by his daughter, Selin, to create pipelines for women into leadership positions at Coca-Cola.

What most of us probably don't think about when we see a Coke bottle is the vast chain of farmers, suppliers, small retailers, recyclers, and artisans that support Coca-Cola across 207 countries. Once Muhtar had a daughter, however, he started considering the role of women in all of those entrepreneurial positions. Having seen the benefits of women leaders inside his company, he contemplated Coca-Cola's larger reach, which meant both a larger responsibility and a larger opportunity. Muhtar felt an obligation to the communities where Coca-Cola does business, and he wanted them to thrive. He also thought more about the world he wanted for his daughter. He wasn't satisfied with just running a more equitable company. What Muhtar wanted for his daughter—and for our next generation of girls—was a world "where the benefits of diversity are fully appreciated."

It didn't take long for Muhtar to realize that women aren't just an untapped resource of entrepreneurial potential, but that women are the key to global sustainability. Women earners invest about ninety percent of their income back into their local economies and their children's health and education. If women could contribute their full potential to the global economy, the world's GDP would rise by an estimated twenty-eight trillion dollars. "Empower women," says Muhtar, "and you recharge the world." Coca-Cola's massive supply chain offered the perfect opportunity to test that theory, which prompted him to launch the "5by20 initiative." The goal of 5by20 is to support five million women entrepreneurs around the world by the year 2020.

Muhtar's team is tackling this challenge in many creative ways. His company supports women entrepreneurs by providing mentors, financial services, small business loans, and legal advice. His team also offers women business skills training, including accounting, merchandising, marketing, and customer service. Some projects just require a small investment in technology to boost women's small businesses. In India, Coca-Cola provided solar-powered coolers for women shop owners. This allowed the women to carry more products and triple their income. In Mali, Muhtar's team dug a well in a rural village so that women wouldn't have to spend eight hours each day fetching fresh water. The women used their freed-up time to start a local catering business.

Muhtar's 5by20 initiative also set up a network of micro-distribution centers for Coca-Cola products in Africa. The centers are located in areas of Kenya, Tanzania, Ethiopia, and Mozambique that don't have infrastructure to support Coca-Cola's massive delivery trucks. The program helps women entrepreneurs become Coca-Cola distributors, often using pushcarts or bicycles. Rosemary Njeri is one of nearly 1,000 African women who run a distribution center. Her business is in Nairobi, where she's a hands-on and loyal boss who employs sixteen people.

Muhtar is most excited by what he calls the "multiplier effect." Rosemary has used her business earnings to educate her three children and invest in real estate. Two of her salespeople have built their own homes from the money they've earned at Rosemary's center. "We've seen, time and again," says Muhtar, "that as women rise in their communities—the communities themselves rise to new heights of prosperity and health."

Muhtar's program also focuses on environmental sustainability. One of his projects supports female artisans who transform recycled Coca-Cola products into jewelry, handbags, iPad covers, and home decorations. Coca-Cola donates used plastic and glass bottles, aluminum cans, packaging materials, and even outdated labels. The women get business skills training and product development advice from a professional designer. Coca-Cola also helps market the women's handicrafts. The company has sold nearly $220,000 of the women's merchandise from its online and US stores alone.

The women artisans in Coca-Cola's 5by20 program are proud to support their families with the income they earn from their crafts. They come from diverse countries, including Mexico, Brazil, Kenya, and the Philippines. Sandy Chimalhuacán, an artisan in Mexico City, says that the program has given her financial stability. "In my childhood," she explains, "I spent most of my life in the landfills." The women are also helping their local environments. Each handbag uses about fifty old Coca-Cola bottles, which is fifty fewer bottles on the streets.

Muhtar's investment in female entrepreneurship is part of a global trend. One out of every eleven working-age women around the world is involved in an entrepreneurial endeavor, and more women are joining this rising tide each year. The number of working women who are entrepreneurs has reached nearly twenty percent in Thailand, fourteen percent in India, twelve percent in Argentina, and ten percent in Mexico.

As of 2016, Coca-Cola had empowered more than 1.75 million women entrepreneurs around the globe.

Muhtar has some final words of advice for dads of daughters who share the privilege of being in leadership roles. "I would encourage any men who may think they don't have a real and abiding stake in women's empowerment to consider the kind of world they want for their female relatives, friends and colleagues," says Muhtar. "Men, don't we want the women and girls we know and respect to have every opportunity to learn, grow and succeed? If your answer is yes, we should make our voices heard in advocating for women's equality and economic empowerment."

The Start-Up Squad

Ever since Brian Weisfeld bought ninety-five pounds of gummy bears in elementary school and hired his friends to sell them for a profit, he's had the entrepreneurial spirit. As a teenager, he sorted baseball cards to earn money to buy more baseball cards. He created and sold mixtapes (which turned out not to be a great long-term business platform). He babysat. He hawked nuts and dried fruit. He worked at a ski shop. And he sold a lot more gummy bears. Along the way, he learned about marketing, selling, and branding, which served him well when he helped build several billion-dollar companies, including IMAX Corporation and Coupons.com. But it wasn't until he watched one of his two daughters try her hand at entrepreneurship that he became inspired to launch his most important venture.

When Brian's oldest daughter was eight, she proudly donned her official Girl Scout vest and marched down their driveway to sell her first batch of Girl Scout cookies. Brian saw a strong-willed girl who was full of enthusiasm—but who didn't know the first thing about selling her products. Brian later watched her struggle running a charity bake sale with a friend—her passion again outpacing her skillset. He started looking for children's books that teach girls entrepreneurial skills, but he came up empty-handed. Yet it wasn't until after his daughter asked him to read another *Rainbow Fairies* book—from a series of over 200 books that all share essentially the same storyline—that Brian finally had his "light bulb" moment.

That's when Brian decided to launch The Startup Squad, an initiative dedicated to inspiring girls to develop an entrepreneurial mindset. He imagined creating a community of like-minded girls through books, toys, games, workshops, and resources that teach basic business skills, along with the grit to try, fail, and start again.

Brian launched The Startup Squad with a book series to empower girls to think like entrepreneurs. His first challenge was a big one: Brian's a businessman, not a writer. So he spent several years hashing out his first book draft. This was much more daunting than Brian expected. "The hardest and most humbling years of my entire career," says Brian. At one point, he gave his manuscript to some eleven-year-old girls as test-readers, and one girl pointed out a grammatical error that he made 127 times. The first literary agent he met told him that if he was her friend, she'd tell him not to waste his time any longer.

That just fueled Brian's own entrepreneurial fire. He went back to basics to learn more about the genre he wanted to write by studying books targeted for 3rd to 6th grade girls. "You would not believe the looks I get on an airplane when I pull out a copy of *The Cupcake Diaries* and a highlighter," says Brian. He eventually made the savvy business decision to team up with a professional writer, Nicole Kear, and the first book in *The Startup Squad* series hit the shelves in 2019.

The first book chronicles a girl's attempt to launch a lemonade stand with her friends for a school competition. Resa discovers that it's harder to make money than she expects, and she learns some crucial business lessons along the way. The most important lesson is working as a team by nurturing the unique skills of each of her business partners. She discovers that her friend Harriet, the fashion-obsessed class clown, is a natural salesperson. Her friend Amelia's fixation with details makes her a great financial manager. And her friend Didi has a knack for problem-solving.

Each book in *The Startup Squad* series has three parts. The inspirational part—"described as *The Baby-Sitters Club* meets *Lean In*"—tells a fun story about girls tackling an entrepreneurial challenge. The informational part translates the story into business lessons, like highlighting marketing tips or suggesting how to choose a prime sales location. The aspirational part shares the profile of a real-life successful girl entrepreneur—or as Brian says, a "girlpreneur."

The Startup Squad website has resources for supporting girls' entrepreneurial journeys. Girls can find activity kits and business tip sheets on marketing, selling, merchandising, and customer care. There are recommendations for other kids' books that highlight girls in entrepreneurial roles. And there are dozens of profiles of girlpreneurs who have launched businesses selling toys, crafts, stuffed animals, clothing, accessories, backpacks, body products, candles, pet care, and even dog treats. It's hard not to be inspired by stories of fierce young girls who've turned their passions into profits.

When Brian is asked why he focused on *girl* entrepreneurs, he gives two reasons. "First of all, I did it for my daughters," he says. "This is something I wanted them to have and it didn't exist, so I had to create it myself." The other reason is because of the workplace inequality that he sees every day. He wants to empower girls to believe in their abilities and chase their dreams with tenacity. "Because not every girl wants to be a princess," Brian explains. "Some want to run the castle. Design the moat. Or break the glass slipper and open a company with better footwear."

How Dads Can Get Started

If you're a dad who wants to support female entrepreneurs, you can begin by nurturing your own daughter's entrepreneurial spirit. The Startup Squad website is the perfect starting place. You can follow the Girls Mean Business Blog for advice, and you can read and submit stories of girlpreneurs. The next time your daughter says she's bored or asks for money, you can also send her to the "Fun Business Ideas" link (with articles like "8 Ways for Kids to Make Money this Winter Break"), which might nudge her down an entrepreneurial path.

In addition to The Startup Squad activity kits and business tip sheets, there are an increasing number of children's books that highlight entrepreneurial girls.

One must-have is Rana DiOrio and Emma D. Dryden's *What Does It Mean to Be an Entrepreneur?* Other great options include Coco Simon's *Cracks in the Cone*, Jen Malone and Gail Nall's *You're Invited*, Laura Schaefer's *The Teashop Girls*, and Ann M. Martin's *The Baby-Sitters Club* series.

You can also send your daughters to a girls' entrepreneur camp. Girls can meet start-up leaders and learn about writing a business plan, pitching an idea, branding, marketing, advertising, basic accounting, financial literacy, and e-commerce. Some excellent options include Camp BizSmart, Bizzy Girls, Active.com's SPARK Business Academy, the SheEO Academy, Camp Girl Boss, the Business Girl Camp, and the Alexa Café.

Dads of daughters who have business expertise have even more direct opportunities to support women entrepreneurs. One way to share knowledge is by volunteering with SCORE, which provides free education for budding entrepreneurs. Through mentoring, workshops, and online courses, SCORE has supported more than eleven million entrepreneurs over the past fifty years. SCORE has over 10,000 volunteers who serve as mentors, consultants, and instructors. In 2018, SCORE mentors helped create more than 32,000 new small businesses in the US, many of which are run by women.

Another opportunity for dads with investment, finance, or other business expertise is to volunteer with Astia, a non-profit that creates a pipeline between women entrepreneurs and venture capitalists. Astia begins by evaluating high-potential, women-run start-ups. It then provides resources, training, and advice to women entrepreneurs who have promising ventures to prepare them for investor presentations. Astia links the top ventures with a pool of investors, so women can make their pitches to those who matter most. Dads of daughters can volunteer as screeners to evaluate women-run ventures in the Astia pipeline or serve as advisors to women entrepreneurs in the Astia program.

Every time you get to know a woman entrepreneur, you can also connect her with The Startup Squad to share her story with our next generation of girls. One of the key parts of The Startup Squad initiative is linking girls with entrepreneurial women to empower girls to imagine themselves creating products, launching businesses, and running companies. On The Startup Squad's website, the profile of twelve-year-old Sara Robinson, the founder and CEO of the handmade crafts start-up "Sara Sews," is alongside the profile of Anne Wojcicki, the co-founder and CEO of the genetic testing company 23andMe. Anne's story starts just like many of the girls who read the website—picking lemons from her neighbor's tree as a first-grader and selling them door-to-door. Anne's advice to aspiring girlpreneurs is simple: "If there's something that seems really wacky and you want to do it, do it."

CHAPTER 11

Taking an Encore

Having grown up as the first generation to expect the world to continually improve, Baby Boomers are flooding the retirement ranks. Since 2011, 10,000 Americans have turned sixty-five every day. One in four Americans will soon be over sixty-five and will outnumber those under fifteen by 2030. Many of these individuals have twenty to thirty years of productive post-retirement life, and they're asking themselves, "What's next?" For many of the more than seventy-six million Boomers, the answer is finding ways to improve the world for our next generations.

While Boomers have been called the "Me Generation" for their conspicuous consumerism, they're also among the most generous and socially active generations. From Vietnam War protests to civil rights marches, Boomers helped launch the disability rights, gay rights, and women's rights movements. With both experience and wealth, Boomers have a lot to offer, and they're seeking ways to have a positive impact through work, volunteerism, and philanthropy. A third of all Baby Boomers are planning to embark upon a post-retirement career, often in teaching, social service, and other public interest jobs. Boomer men are more likely to volunteer than men in any other age group. And nearly a third of multimillionaire Boomers in the US would prefer to pass on their wealth to charities than to their own children.

Boomers aren't the only ones seeking to make an impact. Many adults are making career shifts long before retirement to find greater meaning and satisfaction in their work. Unlike previous generations, adults now change careers an average of five to seven times. Each year, one to two million workers aged forty-five to sixty-five switch careers. These individuals are serving their communities in powerful ways, and they're also reaping the benefits of improved health, greater longevity, less stress, and increased happiness.

These social forces offer dads of daughters the opportunity to craft career encores that matter for our next generation of girls. For men who are looking for a career shift or a second-stage career—and who are also committed to advancing gender equality—there are many ways to invest your skills, experience, and passion to expand opportunities for girls. Three dads share their stories of taking the leap to build an encore career inspired by a desire to make the world better for their daughters.

ASSET India

Ray Umashankar couldn't help feeling emotional as he watched his daughter, Nita, perform her arangetram. This beautiful solo dance is a classical Indian dancer's debut performance after completing her training. It marks the dancer's transition from student to teacher. The word arangetram comes from India's Tamil language and means "climbing the stage." As Ray watched his daughter dance, he couldn't imagine the climb that Nita would inspire him to take on a global stage to empower girls in India. At that moment, he was just a proud dad supporting his daughter.

Ray had his first inkling that bigger things were in store when Nita asked if her friends and family could make donations instead of giving gifts for her performance. Nita raised $7,800 for a safe house for abused women and children. Although Nita and Ray didn't realize it at the time, that was the unofficial start of a father-daughter journey toward women's equality.

Ray immigrated to the US from India in 1968 when he was twenty-six. He came seeking medical care to save his younger child's life, but after several heart surgeries, his son lost his heroic battle. Ray was heartbroken, but he's always appreciated how his new country embraced his family at their darkest moment. Ray stayed in the US to study electrical engineering, and he soon welcomed Nita into his life. While she was growing up, Ray worked hard to become an engineer and become a Professor and Assistant Dean in the College of Engineering at the University of Arizona.

While Ray was building his career, Nita was also launching hers. After graduating from the University of Arizona in 2003 with degrees in biology and entrepreneurship, she was accepted to a PhD program in marketing strategy at the University of Texas. Although Nita was born in Tucson, she stayed connected to her family's Indian roots. She decided to put off her doctoral studies for a year to assist abused women and children in Bangalore. She was twenty-three years old and wanted some real-life experience. Nita asked her dad if he could use the money for a graduation gift to support her trip to India, and Ray readily agreed.

But when Ray heard Nita's next idea, he was more hesitant to jump on board. When Nita returned from her trip, she shared stories of women she'd met who had been forced into India's sex trade, and about how their children were outcast from society. Seven million women and girls in India are exploited in prostitution, sex trafficking, and slavery. In Mumbai alone, there are 100,000 women and girls who've been forced into prostitution, including 20,000 minors. Each day, 200 new women and girls are swept into India's sex trade. Recruiters often target families in poverty by tricking parents into selling their daughters with the promise of a new life, a well-paying job, or marriage to a wealthy man.

When Nita learned this, she felt compelled to act. She told her dad that she planned to return to India every six months to set up a program to support sex trafficking victims. Ray wasn't sure about this idea. "My wife and I were shocked," he said. "We were totally unprepared for something this radical from Nita." As a caring, sixty-four-year-old dad, Ray worried about his daughter's safety. He found himself imagining the dangers that Nita would face interfering with the pimps and brokers of India's sex trade. Ray told Nita that she needed a clearer plan.

Nita left for Austin to begin her PhD, but she kept hounding her dad about going back to India. So Ray gave her some research assignments, both to test her commitment and to determine if there was a safe way for her to get involved. His first assignment was for Nita to identify qualified NGOs that were already working with girls and women in India's sex trade. He wanted to understand which programs had worked, which had failed, and why. Nita returned a report to Ray within a month.

Ray and Nita learned that NGOs in India typically focused on teaching sex trafficking victims and their children nontechnical skills like sewing, selling vegetables, basket weaving, and bag making. Those trades paid under $12 per month—less than what girls earn in the sex trade. That's not a viable plan for helping girls move out of poverty and avoid the same exploitation as their mothers. A few nonprofits offered sex trafficking victims and their children more valuable computer literacy skills, but none were linked with potential employers, so their students had trouble translating new skills into jobs.

Ray and Nita decided that the best path for women and their daughters to escape the sex trade was through training in the informational technology skills that are in demand in India's growing high-tech market. Most importantly, they wanted to create a network of companies that would hire their graduates. Ray's initial idea was to raise funds for girls to attend existing computer training schools in India. But the school owners refused to admit students whose mothers were involved in the sex trade because of the fear and stigma surrounding HIV/AIDS. The owners told Ray that other parents would remove their kids from school if they discovered they were sharing a classroom with children of sex workers.

Ray was shocked but undaunted. It looked like the only option was to start their own educational program in India. At that point, there was no turning back. Together, Ray and Nita created the nonprofit ASSET India Foundation, which stands for Achieving Sustainable Social Equality through Technology. ASSET's goal is to provide marketable computer literacy training for rescued sex workers and their daughters.

Ray and Nita quickly learned that to succeed, they'd need to raise a whole lot of money. "You can have a dream," said Nita, "but if that dream isn't backed by resources, it goes nowhere." So Ray threw himself into fundraising. He had read Thomas Friedman's bestselling book *The World Is Flat* about the transition to global markets, and he contacted every CEO who's mentioned in the book. He spent many nights tracking down personal emails to make his pitch directly to CEOs. He stumbled onto the email address for the Chair of Silicon Labs after guessing at ten different word combinations—and his persistence paid off with a $10,000 donation.

One foundation president in Washington DC kept avoiding his fundraising requests. Ray had a wedding to attend in Virginia, so he called her and asked to meet. She told Ray that she didn't have time because she had to take her daughter to a piano lesson and run errands. "Great!" Ray replied. "I have a rental car. I can pick you up, and we'll run errands." Somewhere in between stops, he made his pitch for ASSET India and left with another $10,000 check.

After raising initial funds, Ray built partnerships with companies in India. He promised to provide well-trained students from ASSET, and the companies agreed to hire his students into entry-level tech jobs that paid $65 to $100 a month. Partners have included Aptech, Dell, Firstsource, IBM, Intel, Microsoft, and Tata Consultancy Services. Ray also connected with NGOs in India to hire local workers to become ASSET staff members, and he recruited local tech professionals for an advisory board to make sure that ASSET's curriculum matched the skills that companies needed.

Ray's work on ASSET India became all-consuming. It took over everything else in his life, including his passion for travel, mountain climbing, and watching his favorite sports team, the Redskins. He'd find himself getting bored at social events, so he'd hide in the bathroom to write down ideas for ASSET. In 2013, he resigned from the University of Arizona after thirty-three years to focus full-time on ASSET India. Ray enjoyed his time as a professor, but he never looked back. "Even as a youngster in India, I wondered about the purpose of my existence on this planet," said Ray. "Thanks to our daughter Nita, I have found that purpose."

With donated computer equipment, Ray set up centers in Bangalore, Delhi, Hyderabad, Kolkata, and Mumbai. To reach women and girls in rural areas, Ray sought help from the Rockefeller Foundation and InnoCentive Challenge. InnoCentive links non-profits with a global network of experts in science, engineering, technology, and business to support programs for vulnerable populations. The network helped Ray get a grant for a wireless network with solar-powered routers so he could expand virtual-based training beyond India's cities.

The ASSET India centers provide six- to nine-month training for girls and women aged fourteen to twenty-eight. The curriculum includes marketable technology skills like OfficeSuite software applications and data entry, as well as typing, accounting, and English transcription. "By training them in skills where there is a huge demand," explains Ray, "nobody cares what their background is." Through its programs, ASSET has diverted over 1,500 women and girls away from India's sex trade. While most ASSET graduates land jobs in data entry, document scanning and digitizing, inventory control, cash register operation, and retail sales, about fifteen percent go to college.

Ray and Nita have profoundly changed their students' lives. Vasanthy is one of their students, whose mother was forced into the sex trade in Chennai. When Vasanthy was sixteen, a recruiter offered her mom money so Vasanthy could be in a movie in Dubai. Vasanthy's mom thought the offer was real and was excited that her daughter had a chance for a decent future. But once Vasanthy arrived in Dubai, she was drugged and forced into prostitution. She finally escaped back to Chennai, where ASSET India took her under its wing. She now looks forward to following in the footsteps of other ASSET graduates, like Abhilasha, who's a medical representative for Toronto Pharmaceuticals in Delhi. Abhilasha earns $150 per month, and she's saving up to buy a scooter to drive to work.

Despite these successes, Ray knows that eradicating India's sex trade is a complex challenge, and job skills are only one piece of the puzzle. He's expanded the ASSET curriculum to include health education, HIV/AIDS prevention, and basic financial skills. Ray also learned that many Indian girls drop out of school because they don't have access to sanitary napkins. So ASSET partnered with the inventor of a low-cost sanitary napkin that's now being distributed to schools across India. ASSET also joined forces with Nobel Peace Prize winner Kailash Satyarthi to create a travelling education program that teaches girls and women in Indian villages how to protect themselves from human traffickers.

ASSET India has given hope not just to its students, but also to the girls' mothers who desperately want a better life for their daughters. Ray leads by example in supporting Nita through her challenges of juggling a career and motherhood. While Nita was helping her dad build ASSET India, she finished her PhD, become a business professor at Georgia State University, and had a child. Nita still sits on ASSET India's Executive Board and manages the curriculum and website. She also set up an internship program that gives American students work experience at ASSET centers.

When asked about his success, Ray is humble and introspective. He credits his age as an advantage because he's outlived his own fear of failure. He also thanks his daughter for her gift of inspiration. Ray recently brought the same determination that he applied to ASSET India to a personal challenge—climbing Mount Kilimanjaro after recovering from a shattered hip in a bike accident. "The thought of quitting crossed my mind several times," says Ray, "but the thought of Nita finishing her arangetram in spite of a severe knee injury kept me going."

Nita is incredibly proud of her dad. "At no age would he stop helping people with such vigor, such energy, such total commitment," she says. "It is an honor to work with him."

The Malala Fund

Ziauddin Yousafzai grew up in a remote part of Pakistan where the culture demanded that women wear burkas and never leave home without a male chaperone. Ziauddin loved his country, but he believed that women had rights and deserved an education. So he moved to Pakistan's Swat Valley and ran a school district that welcomed girls to attend. When the Taliban took over in 2007 and banned girls from schools,

Ziauddin's daily work became life-threatening, but he kept his classrooms open to girls despite the danger. One of those girls was his daughter Malala.

Malala became an outspoken advocate for girls' education in Pakistan. Using a pseudonym, she began blogging for the BBC about the Taliban threat and her fear that her school would be attacked for having girls. The Taliban figured out who Malala was after the *New York Times* featured her in a documentary. In retribution, the Taliban planned a cold-blooded assassination. In 2012, when Malala was just fifteen, a masked gunman boarded her school bus, asked for her by name, and shot her point-blank in the head. Miraculously, Malala survived. She and her family fled to the UK for medical treatment and protection. After a grueling recovery, Malala accepted the Nobel Peace Prize in 2014 and became the youngest-ever Nobel Prize laureate.

Although Ziauddin had been a long-time advocate of girls' education, Malala's courage pushed Ziauddin beyond his role as a school administrator to become a full-time global activist. "It strengthened my perspective about campaigning for girls' education," he explains. "It strengthened my belief in the truth." Ziauddin was named Pakistan's educational attaché, which let him work from Pakistan's consulate office in the UK. He was also appointed as the United Nations Special Advisor on Global Education. Ziauddin now spends his time speaking, educating, and fundraising around the world for girls' education. He thanks Malala for motivating him to become an advocate on a much bigger stage. "When she was a child, I was a leader and she was following me," says Ziauddin. "Now she's the leader and I follow her."

Ziauddin and his daughter co-founded the Malala Fund, which partners with local organizations around the world to provide girls K-12 education. The task is enormously daunting. Globally, there are over 130 million girls who are not in school. Ziauddin focused first on regions where the most girls are missing an education, including Pakistan, Afghanistan, India, Nigeria, and countries that are housing Syrian refugees like Lebanon and Jordan. The work is challenging, but Malala helps Ziauddin persevere. "We learned from her how to be resilient in the most difficult times," he explains.

Ziauddin understands that education is life-changing for girls in many countries. When girls are educated, they are less likely to get married and become pregnant at a young age, more likely to get a job, and better equipped to become mothers. Educated moms have lower infant and maternal mortality rates and are more likely to have well-nourished and educated children. "Education is emancipation," says Ziauddin. "You give a girl an education and she will do the rest herself."

Particularly in a male-dominated society like Pakistan, it takes courageous men to change the culture. "Yes, Pakistan needs more girls like Malala," says British journalist Saima Mohsin. "But what Pakistan really needs right now is more men like Ziauddin Yousafzai."

Editor Eleanor Goldberg agrees. "The only way to successfully make education accessible to everyone," she says, "is by joining both female activists, like Malala, and progressive men, like her father, who are willing to stand up against those who oppose women."

Brigadier General to K-12 Leader

Gary Krahn is a product of the San Diego public school system. When he was a high school sophomore, his dad had a heart attack and his family struggled financially. Gary's mom starting working at a middle school cafeteria and Gary took an afterschool job to make ends meet. Although nobody in his family had gone to college, Gary set his sights on higher education. Several recruiters visited his high school from the US Military Academy at West Point, and Gary asked them about the tuition cost. When Gary learned that West Point has no tuition and actually pays its cadets a salary, he signed on the dotted line. It took him almost a year as a West Point freshman to fully understand that he'd joined the army.

Gary excelled at math and got an engineering degree at West Point. While serving as an Army Officer, he studied applied mathematics at the Naval Postgraduate School and earned his master's degree. For the next twenty years, he was a professor and the Head of the Mathematics Department at West Point. During much of that time, Gary didn't think about sex discrimination or gender equality, which never quite made it onto his radar screen. That changed when he had two daughters who both wanted to pursue engineering careers.

Gary's first turning point was when his oldest daughter, Carolyn, followed his path and become a West Point cadet. At that time, only eighteen percent of West Point students were women. It was the first time that Gary's daughter felt like a minority, and she shared her struggles with her dad. Her experiences of failure suddenly shifted from being just individual shortfalls to inadequately representing womankind. Whenever she fell short, it meant that "women shouldn't be here," and the pressure was often overwhelming.

Gary was interested in Carolyn's experience both because he cared deeply about his daughter and because he was a West Point leader. "That started us in a conversation," says Gary, "and that's how the journey really began."

"It's embarrassing to say," he admits, "but it was the first time I started thinking about what it's like to be a minority and what are my roles and responsibilities in dealing with that."

Carolyn graduated from West Point as a Blackhawk helicopter pilot. She flew combat missions during a thirteen-month tour of duty in Iraq, which gave her dad profound respect for her skills and tenacity. Carolyn eventually left the military, became an engineer, and took a job as a project manager at Apple. Seeing his daughter navigate the challenges of male-dominated arenas gave Gary a new outlook. "She helped me see the world beyond what I only see from my own eyes and experiences," he explains.

Gary's second turning point was when his younger daughter Kelly started college at William & Mary. Kelly was the only female majoring in computer science, and she had the same experience as her sister—losing the luxury of being an individual and suddenly representing all women. Nothing changed when Kelly graduated and started working at a tech company where she was the only female engineer. Kelly learned first-hand about the gender biases that flourish in male environments. "Any time there was a social event," recalls Gary, "they would turn to her to organize it, as though it was her job. It still drives her crazy."

Gary had another wake-up call when Kelly had her own two daughters, Reese and Avery, and she faced the reality of being both a computer scientist and a mom. "I'd been leading organizations for forty years with over a hundred people in them," Gary reveals, "and I always thought that if someone can't be at work or you can't find care for your children, that's your problem." That thinking changed when he watched the extreme anxiety his daughter had from what he'd assumed was a mundane task of finding reliable childcare. "I have a whole new perspective," says Gary, who now manages his employees' work/family conflicts more compassionately. "Having daughters has provided me insights to become a better leader to those I serve."

Gary wondered how to apply his new perspective to better support women. Fortuitously, he was asked to help launch a new university in Kabul, Afghanistan. He fretted over developing the curriculum and hiring faculty members, but he quickly realized that those were the easy parts. The hard part was filling his seats with qualified students. As Gary met with administrators of K-12 schools throughout Afghanistan, he found that they didn't share the university's aspirations to train children—boys *and girls*—with the skills needed for college. Even with the hardest-working and most well-intentioned team, instilling values, mindsets, and work ethics at the college level was too late. "I realized that I'd spent twenty years in higher education," explains Gary, "but really the habits of heart and habits of mind are created at an earlier age."

Gary started studying K-12 education in the US, and he made some striking observations. In higher education, where he'd spent several decades, he was a mathematician first and a teacher second. But in K-12 education, he found the opposite—teachers were educators first and their disciplines were less important. "That reversal was exciting for me," says Gary, whose experiences with his daughters had made him think more about education as a human endeavor.

At the same time, Gary learned that gender biases exerted themselves in both overt and subtle ways in K-12 education to reduce girls' self-esteem, achievement, and future opportunities. From kindergarten through high school, teachers pay more attention to boys and interact less with girls. Boys dominate classroom discussions and get more feedback than girls—both criticism and praise. In educational materials, men show up more frequently and are depicted more positively than women. In commonly-used history books, men are mentioned over nine times more than women, and men outnumber women in named illustrations by nearly six-to-one. A high school diploma also means something different for boys and girls. Male high school graduates earn an average of fifteen percent more than girls with the same education.

For all of these reasons, rethinking K-12 education to be a more empowering place for girls became Gary's new passion. After twenty-nine years on active duty, including twenty years as a West Point professor, Gary left his post as Brigadier General and leapt into the K-12 world. Gary is now the Head of School at the La Jolla Country Day School in California, where he's established himself as a visionary leader in progressive K-12 education. His school's founder, Louise Balmer, was a single mom of four kids, and one of her core ethics was preparing children to be become community leaders. That was a perfect foundation for Gary's ideas.

When Gary explains what's unique about his school, he always mentions that he's a dad of two daughters—and a granddad of two granddaughters—so he's learned how to see the world from a different perspective. He discovered from his daughters that the greatest learning comes from relationships, so his school's staff values each child as an individual. "We know our students, respect their individuality, and support and love them," Gary explains. By emphasizing individuality, Gary hopes to avoid the traps that his own daughters faced having to represent an entire gender or feeling constrained by sex-role stereotypes. "Our role and responsibility," says Gary, "is to find the right place for each one of our students so they can make a difference in the world. Can you think of anything more exciting than that?"

Gary also learned from his daughters the importance of role models, especially for girls in STEM. Gary brings community leaders to his school to build relationships with his students and help them envision themselves in different roles. "Our local community is filled with visionaries in the arts, sciences and engineering who are transforming what we know today to reshape the future and make a better place," explains Gary. "Being around people who are different, with different experiences, is the key to continued growth."

Creating lifelong learners is the overarching goal of Gary's curriculum, and it requires four attributes: a strong work ethic, moral character, willingness to challenge the status quo, and an appreciation of belonging to something greater than ourselves.

Gender diversity is a core component of this vision because preparing students to be global citizens requires the ability to embrace and learn from difference. Gary's school supports this commitment with social justice clubs that explore equality issues, including Spectrum, which works with the Gender and Sexuality Alliance for individuals with diverse sexual orientations and gender identities. Providing these opportunities for students to expand their perspectives also teaches leadership skills. "If you are the one in the room who can see the world through different lenses," says Gary, "you will be the leader in that room."

Because he connects diversity with leadership, Gary recruited like-minded staff members to serve with him as Diversity Advocates. These individuals pledge to celebrate cultural competency, promote empathy, dignity, and curiosity, and stretch the understanding of gender, sexuality, and personal identity.

These are just some of the ways that Gary ties his passion for K-12 education to insights from being the dad of daughters. But of all the insights that Gary gained from Carolyn and Kelly, one has been the most important. It's something that Harvard business professor John Kotter discovered after studying dozens of companies that tried to shift course to compete in global markets. What most distinguished the successful companies was whether their leaders attacked the problems with sufficient urgency. Professor Kotter documents how even the best-laid plans will founder on the rocks of complacency if leaders can't see *and feel* the need for change. Gary credits his daughters with giving him that critical leadership skill. "Having two daughters gave me a sense of urgency," says Gary, "and that's why I've been part of the change to move the world forward."

How Dads Can Get Started

Dads of daughters who are interested in building encore careers focused on empowering girls and women don't have to take the leap alone. Excellent resources are available to support transitions into meaningful second-stage careers. A good first stop is Marc Freedman's book, *Encore: Finding Work that Matters in the Second Half of Life*. This book offers stories and suggestions from "encore career pioneers" who re-booted their careers to address social issues.

The next step is charting a roadmap, which is the goal of Marci Alboher's book, *The Encore Career Handbook: How to Make a Living and a Difference in the Second Half of Life*. This book offers practical advice for making an encore career transition. The book includes a comprehensive guide to assessing skills and passions, identifying education or training needs, making a financial plan, evaluating volunteer opportunities, and using social media and networking to launch a new career path. Other valuable resources include John Tarnoff's *Boomer Reinvention: How to Create Your Dream Career over 50*, which provides career shift strategies, and Richard J. Leider and Alan M. Webber's *Life Reimagined: Discovering Your New Life Possibilities*, which offers exercises to explore new career directions.

Career coach Nancy Collamer also has a book about launching encore careers, *Second Act Careers: 50+ Ways to Profit from Your Passions During Semi-Retirement*. Nancy's organization, MyLifestyleCareer.com, offers an online course called "Design Your Second Act," with strategies, videos, and a step-by-step guide for planning encore careers. You can also take advantage of Nancy's free online workbook. *25 Questions to Help You Identify Your Ideal Second Act*. Dads of daughters who want to build an encore career can also find information about the challenges facing girls and women from the United Nations #HeForShe initiative. The #HeForShe website identifies a range of issues that dads of daughters could help tackle, including girls' education, women's health, gender-based violence, and workplace inequality.

For further support, networking, and financial backing, dads of daughters can check out Encore.org, which is dedicated to "advancing second acts for the greater good." Marc Freedman, Encore's founder and CEO, hopes to tap into the under-utilized talent of older individuals to address compelling social problems. "We need to create a new stage between the end of the middle years and the beginning of retirement and old age," he explains, "an encore stage of life characterized by purpose, contribution and commitment, particularly to the well-being of future generations."

Encore.org offers resources and networking for individuals looking for second-act careers to advance social justice. The Encore Fellowship program places experienced professionals into transitional positions with social-purpose organizations. Encore Fellows have provided over 1.7 million service hours to non-profits in over fifty cities nationwide.

The annual Gen2Gen Encore Prizes also offer financial support, coaching, and marketing for innovative programs created by individuals over age fifty to benefit future generations. In 2008, Encore selected

Ray Umashankar as its prize recipient for his work with ASSET India. "What ASSET does," explained Encore's Prize Director, Jim Emmerson, "is nothing short of offering someone a completely new life." Jim was particularly impressed by Ray's collaboration with his daughter Nita. "A project connecting the two generations for whom social justice are so important was really powerful," said Jim.

If you're the dad of a daughter and you'd like to enrich your working life to advance equality, but you aren't ready to walk away from your day job, Encore.org hosts a platform to find volunteer opportunities for supporting girls. The Generation to Generation initiative has a website listing volunteer positions with girls' organizations around the country. The initiative has helped many dads of daughters jump into action by supporting a Girl Scouts troop, teaching a girls' computer class, running a girls' camp workshop, coaching a girls' track team with Girls on the Run, or becoming a mentor or tutor at a local girls' club.

Ray Umashankar, Ziauddin Yousafzai, and Gary Krahn can all attest to the satisfaction they've found from pushing themselves into new ventures in hopes of improving girls' futures. But straying from the beaten path can be daunting. In a recent survey, individuals who started new careers after age forty-seven were asked about their experiences. While they reported finding happiness and satisfaction, eighty-seven percent acknowledged that changing careers required courage. For dads who are contemplating an encore career or second-act endeavor, envisioning the world you want for your daughters can provide the courage—and the direction—to take the leap.

CHAPTER 12

Leveraging Political Power

Let's start with some good news. Multiple studies have found that when men have a daughter—particularly a firstborn daughter—they tend to become more supportive of antidiscrimination laws, equal pay policies, sexual harassment enforcement, and reproductive rights. One study found that men with first-born daughters are eleven percent more likely than men with first-born sons to support gender equality laws and policies.

Here's some more good news: this father-daughter effect is so powerful that it crosses political lines. Among Republican dads, those with first-born daughters were fifteen percent more likely than those with first-born sons to support gender equality initiatives, while the difference was nine percent for Democratic dads (who tended to start with stronger levels of support). Having a first-born daughter doesn't make dads more liberal in general. It doesn't affect men's attitudes on immigration or environmental protection, for example. And there's no similar mother-daughter effect. So there's something uniquely powerful about being the father of a daughter that specifically increases men's support for gender equality.

But here's the not-so-good news: supportive attitudes aren't enough by themselves to change laws and policies. Supportive attitudes alone don't get new federal, state, or local laws enacted to protect or expand women's rights. Supportive attitudes alone don't launch initiatives to enhance women's economic security or redirect government funding to programs that support women and girls. Only elected leaders, government officials, and public agencies can expand legal and public policy support for gender equality. So dads of daughters have an important role to play by leveraging political power on behalf of women and girls to achieve tangible results.

There are several ways that dads of daughters can exercise political power to advance equality. As elected leaders themselves, dads of daughters can connect their role as father with their role as representative and support laws and policies promoting girls and women. Of course, most men will never hold public office, but that doesn't mean there's no political power to wield. Dads can support candidates who will fight for policies that empower women such as paid family leave, equal pay enforcement, and access to healthcare and reproductive services. Dads can also pressure their elected representatives to advance pro-women initiatives.

Men can also get more women elected to public office. Momentum is building for women politicians with a record number of women candidates in 2018. Yet even with women's unprecedented success in the midterm elections, women remain under-represented at all levels of elected office. Women hold fewer than a quarter of Congressional seats—twenty-five of one-hundred Senators, and 102 of 435 members of the House of Representatives. Only nine state governors are women, and women make up only thirty percent of state legislators. In seven states, women fill less than sixteen percent of the legislative seats. This means that women are far less likely to be represented in legal and policy decisions. Dads of daughters can make a difference by casting their own votes, ensuring that more women exercise their right to vote, endorsing women candidates, and supporting organizations that groom women for public office.

If more men connected their father-daughter relationship with their ability to select, support, and lobby government leaders who can advance women's equality, we could amplify our voices and accelerate progress. An increasing number of dads of daughters are finding ways to do just that. By helping advance laws, policies, and funding decisions that expand equal opportunities and bolster women's health and economic security, these dads offer inspiring examples of how men can leverage their political power on their daughters' behalf.

Politicking like a Papa

When Barack Obama was sworn in as the forty-fourth President in 2009, he was surrounded by three strong female family members—his wife Michelle, his ten-year-old daughter Malia, and his seven-year-old daughter Sasha. That same week, President Obama wrote a letter to his daughters in *Parade* magazine sharing how they'd shaped his path toward what would become eight game-changing years in the White House.

Dear Malia and Sasha,

I know that you've both had a lot of fun these last two years on the campaign trail, going to picnics and parades and state fairs, eating all sorts of junk food your mother and I probably shouldn't have let you have. But I also know that it hasn't always been easy for you and Mom, and that as excited as you both are about that new puppy, it doesn't make up for all the time we've been apart. I know how much I've missed these past two years, and today I want to tell you a little more about why I decided to take our family on this journey.

When I was a young man, I thought life was all about me—about how I'd make my way in the world, become successful, and get the things I want. But then the two of you came into my world with all your curiosity and mischief and those smiles that never fail to fill my heart and light up my day. And suddenly, all my big plans for myself didn't seem so important anymore. I soon found that the greatest joy in my life was the joy I saw in yours. And I realized that my own life wouldn't count for much unless I was able to ensure that you had every opportunity for happiness and fulfillment in yours. In the end, girls, that's why I ran for President: because of what I want for you and for every child in this nation...

Love,
Dad

Malia and Sasha didn't just inspire their dad to seek the presidency, they also helped shape his White House agenda, making equal pay one of President Obama's signature initiatives. "I want to make sure my daughters are getting the same chances as men," he often said. "I don't want them paid less for doing the same job as some guy is doing." When he was elected, the gender wage gap sat at seventy-seven cents on the dollar, which accumulates to a massive loss of lifetime wealth for women. "I don't want that for Malia and Sasha," said President Obama. "I don't want that for your daughters... I want every child to grow up knowing that a woman's hard work is valued and rewarded just as much as any man's."

President Obama spent countless hours trying to enact the Paycheck Fairness Act (PFA), which would have made it easier for women to sue for pay discrimination by expanding pay transparency and increasing penalties for employer violations. Although he wasn't able to get the PFA through Congress, he did get support for a more modest bill, the Lilly Ledbetter Fair Pay Act, which was the first law he signed. The Ledbetter Act has made it easier for women to sue their employers for pay discrimination by getting rid of the law's prior time limit that required women to file suit within 180 days of the first unequal paycheck they received.

The old rule effectively closed the courthouse doors because it often takes years for women to discover that they're getting paid less than male colleagues. When they do, it's often hard for women to immediately file a lawsuit because that can put their jobs and incomes at risk. To address these issues, the Ledbetter Act treats each new paycheck that a woman receives with unfair pay as a new act of discrimination, which triggers a new 180-day time limit for taking legal action. This was a small but important step toward keeping employers accountable for unequal pay. President Obama also created the National Equal Pay Enforcement Task Force, which developed toolkits for employers to reduce pay disparities. "[O]ur journey to equality is not complete," said President Obama, "until...our daughters can earn a living equal to their efforts."

President Obama recognized that pay discrimination is only one piece of women's workplace inequality. Seeing the challenges that his wife faced as an attorney after having their daughters helped him understand the barriers to women's advancement. He didn't want women to feel forced to choose between being a good employee or being a good mom, and he found himself thinking ahead to when Malia and Sasha might have children. "I want to make sure that they're not having to quit their jobs, or in some other fashion be hampered because we don't have the kinds of policies in this country that support them," he explained. So he added workplace flexibility and paid family and sick leave to his agenda. He was appalled that the US is the only developed country in the world without a national law requiring paid parental or sick leave. "It's time do away with some of these workplace policies that belong in a 'Mad Men' episode," he said. "It's pretty clear that if men were having babies, we'd have different policies."

President Obama was also motivated by his daughters to become an outspoken defender of women's access to reproductive health services and medical care. "I want women to control their own health choices," said President Obama, "just like I want my daughters to have the same opportunities as your sons." This desire fueled President Obama's support for the Affordable Care Act (ACA), also known as Obamacare. One of the ACA's unheralded accomplishments is a provision ending discriminatory insurance pricing against women. Before the ACA, insurance companies routinely charged women more than men for health insurance. "It's just like the drycleaners. You send in a blouse, I send in a shirt—and they charge you twice as much," explained Obama. "But the same thing was happening in health insurance. And so we've banned that policy for everybody."

The ACA also provided over twenty million women access to free preventive health care, including mammograms, cervical cancer screenings, and contraception. More than a million young women gained access to health insurance under the ACA's rule requiring insurance companies to let children remain on their parents' plans until age twenty-six, and nearly two million women on Medicare received a much-needed fifty percent discount on medicine. "[E]very woman deserves to control her own health care choices," said President Obama, "not her boss, not her insurer, surely not Congress."

The challenges that low-income women have in accessing health care also highlighted for President Obama the impact of a stagnant minimum wage. He supported a bill to raise the federal minimum wage to $10.10 an hour, in part because most minimum wage earners are women, many of whom are their families' primary earners. To ensure that all policies like the minimum wage were being scrutinized for gender bias, President Obama established the White House Council on Women and Girls, which studied federal initiatives to determine how they impacted girls and women. The Council also coordinated federal agencies' efforts to advance women's economic security, including programs on health, education, and domestic violence.

Although the Trump Administration shuttered the Council in 2017, other Obama initiatives continue to bolster women. Under Obama's leadership, the Small Business Administration expanded loans and increased women-owned businesses by nearly thirty percent. His education reform initiative, "Race to the Top," dedicated over $4 billion to a grant competition to encourage state and local education innovations, particularly to support girls in STEM. The Obama Administration also increased Pell grants to help millions of women afford higher education. In 2015, President Obama and the First Lady created the "Let Girls Learn" initiative, which connects US agencies with the Peace Corps and the Millennium Challenge Corporation to increase girls' access to education globally.

By the time President Obama's second term was ending in 2016, Malia and Sasha had grown from little girls excited about their puppy to young women ready to take on the world. Malia was eighteen and heading to college, and Sasha was a fifteen-year-old high-schooler. Throughout his time in the White House, President Obama's daily highlight was asking his daughters about their day and learning about their hopes for the future. "That's what drives me every day when I step into the Oval Office," he said. "Every decision I make is all about making sure they and all our daughters and all our sons grow up in a country that gives them the chance to be anything they set their minds to; a country where more doors are open to them than were open to us."

In thinking about his daughters' future, President Obama also grew himself during his time in Office. He began with a sincere interest in ensuring equal opportunities for his daughters, but he ended as a full-fledged feminist. Near the end of his second term,

President Obama penned an emotional essay about what he'd learned, titled "This Is What a Feminist Looks Like." He shared his joy in watching his daughters "grow up into smart, funny, kind, wonderful young women," and he expressed optimism for their future. "[T]his is an extraordinary time to be a woman," he said. "The progress we've made in the past one hundred years, fifty years, and, yes, even the past eight years has made life significantly better for my daughters than it was for my grandmothers. And I say that not just as President but also as a feminist." In his farewell address to the nation on January 11, 2017, President Obama echoed these sentiments. "Malia and Sasha," he said, "of all that I've done in my life, I am most proud to be your dad."

While perhaps the most famous, President Obama isn't the only world leader who's both a dad and an unabashed feminist. Canadian Prime Minister Justin Trudeau—another father of a daughter—goes out of his way to self-identify as a feminist every opportunity he gets. Each time he does, it gets media attention, which shows him how much work needs to be done on gender equality. He vows to keep it up until everyone stops reacting. "[T]hat's where we want to get to," he explains. "If you're a progressive, you really should be a feminist because it's about equality, it's about respect, it's about making the best of the world that we have."

When Trudeau become Canada's Prime Minister in 2015 at age forty-three, he was the second youngest person ever to hold the office. He considered whether to seek such a demanding role while raising three young children—a daughter, Ella-Grace, and two sons, Xavier and Hadrien. But being a father made him even more invested in his country's future. "Now that I'm a dad, I look at my kids and I project forward to the world that I want to help create for them," he explains. "I'm in politics not in spite of the fact that I have kids, but because of the fact that I have kids."

Prime Minister Trudeau's hopes for his daughter shaped his agenda in significant ways. "For my daughter, Ella-Grace," he says, "I hope that she has every opportunity to succeed just as much as my sons." But he also knows that what's good for his daughter is good for his country. When women succeed, communities are more resilient, and the economy grows stronger. When women become leaders, it results in better decision-making. So the first thing he did after taking office was to appoint Canada's first-ever Cabinet with an equal number of women and men.

Prime Minister Trudeau is also one of the few world leaders who has openly acknowledged the link between gender and poverty. On the eve of International Women's Day in 2016, political leaders around the world received letters from the ONE Campaign. Co-founded by U2's Bono and supported by the Bill & Melinda Gates Foundation, the ONE Campaign seeks to eradicate world poverty. The Campaign's letters asked world leaders to address the disproportionate impact that poverty has on women and girls around the globe.

Prime Minister Trudeau responded immediately. "On behalf of the Government of Canada, I am writing you back to let you know that I wholeheartedly agree: poverty is sexist." He acknowledged that girls and women are less likely to get an education, more likely to face health risks, and much more likely to be impoverished. "I accept your challenge to lead," he said. As a first step, Canada contributed $785 million to the Global Fund to treat and prevent HIV/AIDS, malaria, and tuberculosis, which disproportionately affect girls and women. "But no one leader can make this happen alone," said Trudeau. "[W]e need other leaders around the world to step up, too."

These sentiments are shared by the Mayor of London Sadiq Khan. Mayor Khan had been a long-time social activist as a lawyer and a Parliament member representing the Labour Party. But he started focusing on gender equality when he thought about the city he wanted for his daughters. "My daughters are both teenagers now," said Kahn after becoming Mayor, "and they are growing up in London at a time when men still get paid nearly 12 percent more than women in this city, and while there are still too few female role models at the highest levels in public life. This simply isn't good enough."

Mayor Khan began by attacking the role model deficit and selecting women for over half of his Deputy Mayors and two-thirds of his Business Advisory Board. Under Kahn's leadership, London selected its first women Commissioners of the Police and Fire Brigades. Mayor Kahn also trained city department managers to use gender-blind hiring by requiring "no name" application forms.

He then took aim at the gender pay gap by launching a pay audit at London's City Hall, the transportation agency, and the police and fire departments. Based on the results, Kahn requested a plan to increase part-time and flexible work options and provide mentoring and career support for women. "[A]ll of us need to stand in solidarity with our mothers, sisters, daughters and friends to say that discrimination, in all shapes and forms, will not be tolerated," he says. "When we achieve true equality, we all benefit."

While their daughters inspired them to prioritize gender equality, being a women's advocate was a relatively comfortable fit within the political parties that President Obama, Prime Minister Trudeau, and Mayor Kahn represented. Being the dad of a daughter, however, can motivate men across the political spectrum to pay more attention to women's rights. Florida Governor Rick Scott is an example. Governor Scott is a conservative Republican who made millions as a business leader in the healthcare and pharmaceutical industries. In the 1990s, he partnered with George W. Bush to buy the Texas Rangers professional baseball team. He's definitely not someone who's described as a feminist.

As governor, Scott strengthened the death penalty and expanded Florida's "stand-your-ground" law, which protects individuals who use force instead of retreating in the face of perceived threats. In 2011, Governor Scott signed a law targeting welfare recipients that required mandatory drug screenings to participate in the federal Temporary Assistance for Needy Families program—a law that courts later struck down as unconstitutional. Recently, Scott signed a bill allowing any Florida resident to challenge teaching materials in public schools, which opponents say is designed to censor discussion about global warming, evolution, and LGBTQ rights.

So when a bill expanding the rights of sexual assault and rape victims was headed to Governor Scott's desk in 2016, many thought that his signature was a long-shot. The law was designed to speed up the forensic testing of rape kits, which contain DNA and other evidence that medical personnel collect while treating sexual assault victims. Rape kits evidence is often crucial for identifying and prosecuting perpetrators of rape and sexual assault. At the time, Florida had an astounding backlog of over 13,000 rape kits waiting to be tested—some that were decades old. The bill that needed Scott's signature would require local law enforcement agencies to submit rape kits for testing within thirty days of the initial report of a sexual assault. All kits would be submitted to a statewide crime lab, which must complete testing within 120 days.

Governor Scott not only signed the bill into law, but he held a press conference to advocate for women who've endured sexual assault. Rick Scott, it turns out, is the dad of two adult daughters, Allison and Jordan. He began his press conference by sharing a personal story about a frightening incident one of his daughters faced while she was a college freshman. Scott got a phone call from her one morning saying, "something very bad happened to me last night." Someone had put a date rape drug in her drink, landing her in the hospital. "Fortunately, she was not raped," recounted Governor Scott, but it was a scary moment.

The perpetrator was never caught, and Governor Scott vowed that his state would do more to protect sexual assault victims. To ensure the new law's success, his first state budget increased funding to the state crime lab. After speaking emotionally about his daughter's experience, he praised the bill's bipartisan support. "This legislation will provide thousands of women with a renewed sense of safety and closure as they heal from the horrific crime of rape," he said.

While Governor Scott illustrates how political leaders can support women by signing new laws, executive officials lack authority to get new laws written in the first place. For that, we need committed legislators who draft, propose, garner support, and vote for new bills to advance women's equality in education, employment, and reproductive rights. Dads of daughters have also been making progress for women in this important lawmaking role.

Yale University Economics Professor Ebonya Washington studied the legislative voting records of members of the US House of Representatives over a four-year period. She found that male legislators with at least one daughter had a more pro-women voting record on bills involving women's rights than male legislators without daughters. This father-daughter effect showed up on a range of bills involving equality, safety, economic security, education, and health. The largest effect was on bills addressing women's reproductive rights.

This effect existed for both Republican and Democratic fathers. While Republican male legislators generally had less liberal voting records on bills involving women's issues than Democratic male legislators, both shifted their voting records in a pro-women direction when they had at least one daughter. In this arena, the more daughters the better, as each additional daughter was linked to an even more pro-women voting record. For women legislators—who generally begin with a more feminist voting record on bills involving women's rights—having a daughter had no effect. This is probably because women legislators have shaped their positions on women's rights before they have kids.

Legislators can advance women's rights not only by casting their votes on pending bills, but also through the bills they draft and initiate. Dads of daughters sometimes become surprising sponsors of bills that support women, even when it means breaking from their party line. Pete Domenici, a six-term Republican Senator from New Mexico, was one of these unlikely sponsors who became a leading advocate for mental health care funding.

Senator Domenici served in Congress for thirty-six years from 1973 to 2009, marking the longest tenure in New Mexico's history. Known as a deficit hawk who was nicknamed "Mr. Fiscal," Domenici built his reputation on the Budget, Appropriations, and Energy and Natural Resources Committees. He was a proponent of nuclear power and oil drilling in the Arctic and marine waters, earning him a "Worst in the Senate" award from the Republicans for Environmental Protection. As a social conservative, he opposed abortion and same-sex marriage, and he supported three-strikes mandatory criminal sentencing, school vouchers, small government, and big tax cuts. He was also an ardent duck and quail hunter who resisted gun control. Funding for mental health care and insurance coverage for mental illness were not remotely near Senator Domenici's legislative radar screen.

That changed when his daughter, Clare, began struggling during her freshman year of college. Clare was Domenici's fourth child of eight, and one of six daughters. She was a gifted athlete who played high school tennis, baseball, and basketball. But during her first year of college, Clare's behavior changed dramatically. She lost her energy. Her thinking became fuzzy. She suffered from anxiety, and she was unable to make even simple decisions. "She was all out of whack," said Domenici.

His wife, Nancy, went to check on Clare and brought her home from college. "That's when things got really out of hand," Domenici recalls. "Her temperament totally changed. She became angry, mean. Throwing things at mirrors. Cussing, swearing. Crying, shrinking into a shell, taking to her bed." It was a frightening time of uncertainty. "[T]hat started two novice parents down the strange path of having to believe something we didn't want to believe," said Senator Domenici. "And to really believe it, to acknowledge that Clare was mentally ill, took a long time."

Clare was eventually diagnosed with atypical schizophrenia. Seeking a support network, Senator Domenici and his wife attended meetings at the National Alliance on Mental Illness (NAMI). They heard stories from other families who were coping with loved ones with mental illness—"stories of families going broke, splitting up, and mentally ill children ending up on the streets, in jail, or dead." As a parent, the stories were heartbreaking. As a Senator, the stories made him realize that mental illness wasn't getting the government support it needed.

Without his daughter's experience, Senator Domenici acknowledges that it would have been highly improbable for him to have become a mental health advocate. "I don't believe the subject ever would have come up," he admits. But once he delved into the issues, he couldn't stop.

Senator Domenici discovered that insurance companies treated mental illness far worse than physical illness. When Clare was diagnosed, many insurance plans set lifetime limits for treating mental illness as low as $125,000, while setting no limit or a much higher limit of around $1 million for treating physical illness. Most insurance plans also covered fewer doctor visits and imposed higher co-payments and deductibles for mental health care. Domenici also discovered how little federal money was being spent on research for mental illness, particularly brain diseases, and he made the connection between mental illness and homelessness.

Senator Domenici built a bipartisan coalition of legislators—all of whom had been touched by mental illness in some way—to enact the Mental Health Parity Act of 1996. The Act was modest, but an important first step. It required insurance companies to set equal annual and lifetime dollar limits for mental and physical conditions. For the next decade, Senator Domenici worked tirelessly to achieve true insurance parity for mental illness. While he'd come to think of this as a civil rights issue, employers and insurers lobbied against his efforts, branding his proposed legislation as burdensome government regulation. But Senator Domenici never gave up, and in the meantime, he increased federal funding for brain disease research, as well as housing and education programs for individuals with mental illness.

More than a dozen years after Senator Domenici began his quest, and on the eve of his retirement, Congress finally enacted a full mental health parity requirement in 2008. The law requires insurance companies to treat mental and physical illness the same in all respects, including co-payments, deductibles, and covered health care visits. Although the law only applies to employer-provided insurance plans at large companies, around 113 million Americans benefitted from the change. "Senator Domenici became a hero for us," says NAMI's Director Michael Fitzpatrick.

While it may be frustrating to realize that a personal experience like having a daughter with mental illness can play such a fortuitous role in developing federal legislation, the NAMI advocates are happy to embrace all supporters, regardless of their source of inspiration. "You'd be surprised how often legislation is directly informed by our lives," says Michigan Democratic House Representative Lynn Rivers. "In the field of mental health, I think it's possible that nothing at all would have been done by Congress if it weren't for legislators like Domenici who were galvanized by personal experience."

Senator Domenici's legacy will have lasting benefits for women, who experience mental illness at much higher rates than men. Women are hit particularly hard with depression, anxiety, and PTSD. Although Domenici's initial inspiration came from his daughter, his impact will be felt by millions of Americans, many of whom paid tribute when Domenici passed away at age eighty-five in 2017. At his memorial service, Kathy Finch, the President of NAMI's Albuquerque office, thanked Senator Domenici for "caring for the rest of America as if we were your family, too."

While Senator Domenici shows how legislators can advance women's rights, lawmakers ultimately derive power from voters. As voters, citizens can select lawmakers and hold them accountable when they seek re-election. They can also make change more directly through ballot initiatives and referenda. Nobody appreciates this power more than the President of America Votes, Greg Speed. America Votes is an organization that coordinates national and state progressive advocacy groups and election campaigns. While Greg has been a long-time influential voice on voting rights, his passion took on a new dimension when he became the dad of a daughter, whom he proudly described as "strong-willed," even at age three.

"Being a father has taught me the enormous importance of our daughters in making our progressive goals for women a reality," Greg explains:

> *Each day I am with my daughter, I have a growing understanding and appreciation of a point my allies in the women's movement emphasize all the time: women's issues are family issues, too, and are very much in the interest of men—however slow many of us have been to realize it. The fights for equal pay, reproductive freedom and access to women's health care directly benefit women and families—meaning fathers, husbands, male partners and sons also benefit from pro-women policies.*

Greg's daughter also helped him realize that conversations about the economy must focus on women. Although women are the sole or primary earners in forty percent of American households with children under age eighteen, women make up sixty-two percent of minimum-wage and sub-minimum wage earners. A single mom with two kids who earns $10 or less per hour will fall below the poverty line if she misses just four days of work in a month. Women also earn less than men for the same work at virtually every income level, which hits low-wage women workers the hardest. Closing the gender pay gap would not only boost the economy by three to four percent, it would cut in half the number of working women and families who live in poverty.

In thinking about his daughter's future, Greg figured out that women's equality is the lynchpin to economic growth and stability. This added fuel to his fight for passing laws to raise the minimum wage, provide paid family and sick leave, expand healthcare, and close the gender pay gap. His daughter also reminded him of the untapped power of women voters. Unmarried women in particular are a reliable progressive voting bloc, but they're less likely than other groups to cast their votes.

Greg wanted to get more women wielding their electorate power, so he prioritized support for new laws, initiatives, and campaigns focusing on women's economic security—both to empower women and to get them interested in showing up at the ballot box. To achieve these goals, America Votes partners with organizations like EMILY's List, Planned Parenthood, NARAL Pro-Choice America, and Women's Voices Women Vote Action Fund, which help women connect their voting power with their families' wellbeing. "[T]hat is work both women and men should support," says Greg.

Greg also serves on the board of American Women, a research organization that educates policy makers about social issues impacting women and families. The goal is to amplify women's voices in policy debates. American Women recently partnered with other organizations to write a guidebook for advocacy groups to engage more women in the political process. The guidebook, *Economic Security for Women and Families: A Conversation Guide*, is available free online.

Because women are among those most likely to benefit from progressive policies, but they're also among the least likely to vote, the guidebook explains how women can become politically active to benefit their families. It explains how to sign online petitions, register to vote, leverage social media, contact elected officials, and endorse candidates who support an economic agenda for women. The same advice applies for male allies, including dads of daughters.

"[W]e must be sure our daughters—and our sons—grow up with an understanding of gender inequality in today's world and how voting (or not voting) will make the difference," says Greg. "Thinking of my daughter 20 years from now, it is utterly implausible (and somewhat comical) to think that she would accept anything less than her full and equal share in matters of great importance to her—be it equal pay, work benefits, or dessert. And while I hope she chooses to be an active progressive in her parents' mold, it's most important to me that she understands that casting her vote is one of the most powerful things she can do to influence the policies that impact her life."

How Dads Can Get Started

As dads of daughters, the easiest way to leverage your political power to advance women's equality is to thoughtfully exercise your right to vote—in every election, for candidates at every level, and for every initiative and referendum on the ballot. It's particularly important not to sit out state and local elections. That's where the vast majority of new laws and policies affecting women are being adopted, and the results have been mixed. While some states are leading the way in expanding paid parental leave, others are adding draconian restrictions to women's access to reproductive health services. Dads of daughters can't afford to sit on the sidelines.

Dads of daughters can also become leaders in getting other men to exercise their votes for pro-women candidates. Begin by identifying candidates who support policies for economically empowering women, such as paid family and medical leave, paid sick days, raising the minimum wage, and increasing enforcement of sexual harassment and equal pay laws. Share what you've learned with other men and encourage them to vote. When you do, it's OK to mention your motivation as the dad of a daughter. Although invoking one's "dad of a daughter" status sometimes gets a bad rap because *all* men have a stake in gender equality, research finds that it's an effective way to get some men to listen when other men advocate for women's rights.

Highlighting how a particular candidate's agenda will benefit our next generation of girls also increases the likelihood that other dads of daughters will vote, particularly for women. Dads of daughters are generally more likely than other men to support female candidates. In the 2016 election, for example, dads with a firstborn daughter were ten percent more likely to support Hillary Clinton than dads with a firstborn son, even after controlling for partisanship, ideology, education, age, religiosity, income, employment status, marital status, evaluations of the economy, and racial attitudes. The support from dads of daughters, however, is even greater when candidates explicitly highlight daughters in their messaging.

In one study, researchers randomly gave dads three different descriptions of the same fictitious female candidate. A control group got a description that simply said: "Molly Smith is running to become the first woman to represent Minnesota's 10th District." A second group got a description that also said: "She supports policies that would help increase the participation of women in careers in science, technology, engineering, and mathematics (STEM)." A third group got a description that included this additional statement: "She has said of her candidacy, 'This campaign is about making sure there are no ceilings, no limits on any of us, and to ensure that our daughters will forever know that there is no barrier to who they are or what they can be in the United States of America.'" The men were asked to imagine that they lived in Smith's district and to rate their likelihood of voting for her.

Overall, dads of first-born daughters were more likely to support Smith than dads of first-born sons. But the level of support from dads of daughters was significantly higher in the third scenario. Compared to the control group, dads of daughters were nine percent more likely to support Smith when the campaign mentioned women in STEM, and they were twenty-five percent more likely to support Smith when the campaign specifically mentioned daughters. Although none of the descriptions included a partisan affiliation, the increased support was primarily from Democratic dads. While daughter-specific messaging had a big impact on dads of daughters, it also had a small but positive effect on dads with first-born sons. Men in that group were seven percent more likely to support Smith in the pro-daughter scenario than in the control condition, which means that the message may have broad appeal.

Dads of daughters can also follow Greg Speed's lead and encourage women to vote for pro-women candidates and initiatives. Start by reading *Economic Security for*

Women and Families: A Conversation Guide, which is available from the American Women website. This guide offers practical advice for engaging women voters—particularly unmarried women who tend to have low voter-turnout—by emphasizing links between policy initiatives and women's economic wellbeing. Men can also support organizations that register and mobilize women voters, such as the Women's Voices Women Vote Action Fund.

Dads of daughters can also support organizations that recruit, train, mentor, and support women candidates for public office. These include the Women's Campaign Fund, the National Women's Political Caucus, EMILY's List, the National Federation of Republican Women, and Running Start.

One outstanding nonpartisan organization is She Should Run, which offers programs to launch women candidates. Dads of daughters can join the group's #250KBY2030 campaign, which seeks to get 250,000 women running for public office by 2030. Men can also nominate a female friend or colleague as a potential political candidate through the website's "Ask a Woman to Run" initiative. The organization will send your nominee a pledge certificate with an invitation to run for office, along with access to the organization's resources. This includes the She Should Run Incubator, which is a training program for women interested in public office. Nominating women to consider public office is a critical step to expanding women's representation. When women run for office, they're elected at the same rate as men. But far fewer women than men run for office, largely because women aren't recruited to run as frequently as men.

Dads can also begin building political power closer to home by inspiring daughters to become politically active. The IGNITE organization focuses on reaching girls and young women to create a pipeline of future candidates. IGNITE has a K-12 curriculum available to schools, as well as college chapters, conferences, and a network of women in elected office. Dads who want to fuel daughters' political aspirations and build their leadership skills should check out IGNITE's "Empower Your Daughter" initiative. This initiative provides free toolkits, preteen and teen discussion guides, and infographics for dads to engage their daughters in public service activities and build their political ambitions.

For dads with younger daughters who aren't quite ready to launch a campaign, consider using story time to get girls imagining themselves as political powerhouses. Check out Andrea's Beaty's children's book, *Sophia Valdez, Future Prez*, which chronicles a young girl's decision to become a community activist. Or grab a copy of Kelly DiPuccio's *Grace for President*, in which young Grace becomes outraged when her teacher shows her class a poster of the US Presidents. "Where are the girls?," she asks angrily. Her teacher agrees that it's time for change and encourages Grace to run for school president. These books not only offer a much-needed break from fairies and princesses, but they'll also leave you feeling great about getting your daughters to dream about running the world someday.

CHAPTER 13

Misusing Father-Daughter Power

In 2016, two House Representatives, Duncan Hunter and Ryan Zinke—both dads of daughters—introduced a bill called, the "Draft America's Daughters Act," or "the DAD Act" for short. If the bill became law, it would expand military draft registration to include women. Currently, the US military is a voluntary service, but all men must register with the Selective Service within thirty days of their eighteenth birthday. There hasn't been a military draft since the Vietnam War era, but the debate over draft registration was re-ignited after President Obama expanded women's access to military combat roles. The bill's two sponsors adamantly opposed that step. In fact, neither Hunter nor Zinke supported their own proposed law. By explicitly mentioning daughters in the bill's title, they hoped to make a gender-neutral draft registration so emotionally tinged that it would halt women's progress in the military.

This illustrates a potential misuse of father-daughter power: strategically invoking the relationship to resist or roll-back equal opportunities for women. Representative Hunter has two daughters, Elizabeth and Sarah, and Representative Zinke has one daughter, Jennifer. So both men understood the resonance of the father-daughter relationship. Together, they decided to use daughters as a weapon when they believed women were overstepping their bounds.

Their opposition began in 2013, when Defense Secretary Leon Panetta rescinded the rule barring women from military combat units. Two years later, Defense Secretary Ash Carter announced that women could compete under gender-neutral standards for *all* combat positions, including elite special forces. Although many military leaders supported the move, Hunter and Zinke vehemently resisted the change.

Zinke, a former Navy SEAL, spoke out about the perceived risks of women in combat, even though his own daughter was a soldier. "I know women play an invaluable role in war," said Zinke, who described his daughter as "a damn good Navy diver." But he believed that allowing women into combat and special forces was "reckless and dangerous." Hunter, a former Marine Major who served in Iraq and Afghanistan, also thought that women shouldn't be allowed in infantry and special operations roles.

In February 2016, Army Chief of Staff General Mark Milley, Marine Corps Commandant Robert Neller, and other top military brass reported to the Senate Armed Services Committee. They told the Committee that once women were eligible for combat roles, they should also be required to register for the draft. President Obama supported that view, even though it would apply to his daughters, Malia and Sasha. But for Hunter and Zinke, that suggestion was the last straw. It prompted them to tactically invoke the father-daughter relationship in an attempt to stem the tide.

When introducing the Draft America's Daughters Act—with the hope of actually halting expansion of the draft for women—Hunter described vivid images of daughters being forced into hand-to-hand combat with armed men in foxholes. "The idea that eighteen-to-twenty-year-old women could be drafted, filling positions tasked with finding and destroying the enemy, sometimes in quarters so close that fighting is reduced to the use of hands, knives and even helmets is surely unsettling," said Hunter. "The draft is there to get more people to rip the enemies' throats out and kill them." He urged Americans to think about whether they "truly want to send their daughters...into harm's way."

Hunter and Zinke are conservative Republicans, who in no way supported their own bill. Hunter opposes same-sex marriage, abortion, funding for family planning, and even some forms of contraception. He voted against the Lilly Ledbetter Fair Pay Act, which expanded women's right to sue for pay discrimination. He voted against renewing the Violence Against Women Act, which funds prosecutions for sexual assault. And he voted against enforcing anti-gay hate crimes. Zinke, who became President Trump's Secretary of Interior in 2017, is also known for his anti-abortion views. (Hunter has since been indicted on charges of conspiracy, wire fraud, and campaign finance violations, and Zinke stepped down from his Secretary position in the wake of investigations for alleged ethics violations.)

Despite their obvious ulterior motives, once they framed the issue of a gender-neutral draft registration as a threat to the sanctity of daughters, several other Republican men joined the bandwagon. House Representative Pete Sessions characterized the idea as "coercing America's daughters," and Senator Mike Lee said he didn't want to see "my fifteen-year-old daughter drafted into the military."

Senator Ted Cruz—a presidential candidate at the time—called a gender-neutral draft registration "nuts." "[T]he idea that we would draft our daughters to forcibly bring them into the military and put them in close combat is wrong," he said. "It is immoral and if I'm president, we ain't doing it. I'm the father of two little girls. I love those girls with all of my heart. They are capable of doing anything in their heart's desire, but the idea that their government would forcibly put them in a foxhole with a 220-pound psychopath trying to kill them doesn't make any sense at all."

Retired Army General William Boykin, who was President George W. Bush's Deputy Undersecretary of Defense for Intelligence, also opposed a gender-neutral draft registration. Boykin is the VP of a conservative organization that lobbies against abortion, LGBTQ rights, and same-sex marriage. After hearing Ted Cruz's comments, he launched a petition called "Don't Draft Our Daughters," asking all presidential candidates to reject a gender-neutral draft registration. Cris Dosev, a combat veteran who was a Republican Congressional candidate at the time, swiftly fell in line. "My wife and I have three sons and five daughters," he explained. "One [son] is a 1st Lieutenant in a Marine infantry unit. His brothers are prepared to serve. But let me be clear: Law or no law, our daughters will not sign up for Selective Service."

These responses reveal that Hunter and Zinke's invocation of the father-daughter relationship tapped into some deeply-held instincts. But in the end, their strategy backfired. Influential Congresswomen—both Democratic and Republican—promptly spoke up in favor of the proposed bill, despite its provocative title, pushing back against antiquated female protectionism.

"I actually think if we want equality in this country, if we want women to be treated precisely like men are treated and that they should not be discriminated against," said Democratic House Representative Jackie Speier, "we should be willing to support a universal conscription." Republican House Representative Martha McSally agreed. McSally is a retired Air Force fighter pilot, and she reminded her colleagues that there are many noncombat positions during wartime—for both women and men—so draftees aren't all sent to foxholes.

The Draft America's Daughters Act ended up passing by a vote of thirty-two to thirty in the House Armed Services Committee—even with two "no" votes by its sponsors, Hunter and Zinke. After the vote, the headline in Zinke's home state Montana newspaper read: "Ryan Zinke Gets Schooled as his Sexist Stunt Amendment Passes." A universal draft provision also passed in the Senate's version of the National Defense Authorization Act in 2016 with support from Republican Senator John McCain, a decorated veteran with a daughter-in-law who's an Air Force captain.

The provision was ultimately omitted from the final compromise bill, but it got very close to becoming law. Experts predict that it's only a matter of time. "I think the change is inevitable," says military policy analyst Nora Bensahel from the American University's School of International Service. "[N]ow that you have women allowed to serve in any position in the military, there is no logical basis to say women should not be drafted." The last time a challenge reached the Supreme Court was in the 1981. In *Rostker v. Goldberg*, the Court ruled in a 6-3 decision that a male-only draft registration didn't violate the Constitution's Equal Protection Clause because only men were eligible for combat roles. Now that all military roles are open to women, the Court's rationale for upholding the male-only draft no longer exists. So new challenges to the draft registration are pending in court.

Although Representatives Hunter and Zinke invoked their daughters as a way to halt women's progress in the military, other dads of daughters have advocated for women's military opportunities. Chris Marvin is a retired Army officer who flew Black Hawk helicopters and was wounded in the Afghanistan war. As a Fellow at the Truman National Security Project, Chris supports a gender-neutral draft registration. "As a combat veteran and the father of two young daughters," says Chris, "I embrace the expansion of Selective Service. In Afghanistan and Iraq, women played integral roles on the front lines as members of cultural support teams. High-ranking female officers already hold leadership positions in all branches of the military. It is clear that more gender equality improves our national defense."

Other military dads have also been paving the way for women in military careers. Retired Brigadier General Harold Dunwoody was a veteran of World War II, the Korean conflict, and the Vietnam War. His older daughter, Susan, became the Army's third female helicopter pilot. One of his proudest moments was the day his younger daughter, Ann, moved up the military hierarchy to outrank him. Ann became the first female four-star general in US history. At the time, her dad was eighty-nine years old. He was overjoyed to see his daughter break through the brass ceiling, and he hoped that more women would follow.

Invoking daughters to resist women's progress is just one potential misuse of the father-daughter relationship. Another is when fathers disingenuously use their daughters as props or signals to indicate purported concern for women's rights. Sociologists call this "performative allyship," and some politicians are experts at it. Using daughters as props can help male politicians project a pro-woman image, mitigate a sexist reputation, mask inactivity on women's equality, or deflect criticism about anti-women policies.

This appears to be a major role that Ivanka Trump has played for her dad, President Donald Trump, whose misogynist reputation is well-known. Well before his campaign, he publicly referred to various women as "fat pigs," "dogs," "slobs," and "disgusting animals." He was accused of inappropriate behavior while hosting the Miss Universe pageant, and there are multiple allegations about his lewd conduct toward women during his stint on the reality TV show *The Apprentice*. To date, at least twenty-four women have accused Trump of sexual misconduct.

Trump's belittling comments about women continued during his campaign. He called Democratic presidential nominee Hillary Clinton a "nasty woman," insulted Republican candidate Carly Fiorina's appearance, and crudely described reporter Megyn Kelly as having "blood coming out of her eyes, blood coming out of her wherever." His reputation for demeaning and harassing women was reinforced during his campaign with the release of a 2005 taped conversation with *Access Hollywood's* host Billy Bush. In the tape, Trump used vulgar language to brag about grabbing women by their genitals. "[W]hen you're a star," he said, "[y]ou can do anything."

Trump's sexist comments have also targeted his own wives, and even his daughter, Ivanka. He's repeatedly expressed the view that men should be breadwinners and women should be homemakers and childcare providers. He says that he divorced his first wife, Ivana, because she spent too much time on her career. "Putting a wife to work is a very dangerous thing," he said. "[W]hen I come home and dinner's not ready, I go through the roof." In describing his current marriage to Melania, Trump says: "I'll supply funds and she'll take care of the kids." He proudly admits that he didn't change his children's diapers, nor has he done "anything to take care of them," because that would have been "the husband act[ing] like the wife." He has publicly referred to his daughter, Ivanka, as "hot," "voluptuous," and as having "a very nice figure." He told Howard Stern during a radio broadcast that Stern could refer to Ivanka as "a piece of ass."

Not surprisingly, this posed a challenge for Trump during his presidential campaign. At one point, an ABC News/*Washington Post* survey reported that seventy-seven percent of women viewed Trump unfavorably. Some Republicans actually invoked their father-daughter relationship to justify opposing their own party's candidate. When the *Access Hollywood* tape was discovered, several male Republicans withdrew their support for his candidacy, citing their daughters among the reasons for their defection. "It's not pleasant for me to renounce the nominee of my party," said Senator John McCain. "I have daughters, I have friends, I have so many wonderful people on my staff, they cannot be degraded and demeaned in that fashion."

Trump's presidential campaign enlisted Trump's daughter, Ivanka, to shore up her father's image.

Ivanka was an executive VP in the Trump Organization at the time. During the campaign, she spoke about Trump's commitment to women in his company. In one interview, she even described her dad as "a feminist." She also spoke about affordable childcare and paid maternity leave to deflect focus from Trump's promises to dismantle the Affordable Care Act, upon which so many women depend.

When the Trump campaign rolled out its initial childcare and family leave proposal, it was roundly criticized as both sexist and deficient. According to the Tax Policy Center, the proposal would do virtually nothing for low-income families, who would earn an average childcare benefit of $10 per year. TV host John Oliver joked that the only childcare the plan would pay for was a Master Lock for a child's door. The plan also included short, partially-paid leave for married women who give birth—excluding unmarried women, fathers, adoptive parents, same-sex partners, and workers who take care of family members other than newborns. In response to withering criticism, Ivanka made a campaign appearance describing the proposal as "incredibly comprehensive," "very innovative," and "a bold and fresh solution."

Ivanka's attempt to counterbalance her father's anti-women policies was rewarded with a speaking role at the Republican National Convention. During her speech, she promised that her dad "will fight for equal pay for equal work, and I will fight for this too right alongside him." Her attempts to deflect focus from Trump's misogyny and convince voters that she could have a moderating effect on his behavior were at times quite explicit. "Judge his values by those he's instilled in his children," she said.

To some extent, Ivanka's campaign presence was successful in masking Trump's sexism. Cornell Psychology Professor Peggy Drexler explained that when Ivanka was stumping for her dad, she was effectively positioned as his conscience—"the bright, reasonable, poised (and female) counter to his wild card, off-the-cuff, often openly misogynistic ways." But once she was in the White House—with the official title of Assistant to the President, a West Wing office, and security clearance—frustration has grown. Many are calling out her apparently symbolic role as cover for Trump's anti-women policies, which are being made by the most male-dominated cabinet since President Ronald Reagan's.

President Trump actually orchestrates "drop-by's" from Ivanka during high-profile meetings and media interviews to shift difficult conversations off-topic or place himself in a more favorable light. On one occasion, Ivanka was brought into the Oval Office in the middle of a tense meeting between Trump and congressional leaders about the debt ceiling and disaster relief funding. Ivanka interrupted the meeting to talk about a potential child tax credit. On another occasion, Trump was being interviewed by the *New York Times*. Just as he was answering a challenging question, Ivanka "popped in" to say hello with her daughter, Arabella. This allowed Trump to halt his response mid-sentence. "'Hi baby, how are you?'" he said, as his granddaughter entered the room.

"Just wanted to come say 'hi,'" said Ivanka, who used a similar line to interrupt her dad's interview with the *Wall Street Journal* later that month.

The so-called "Ivanka drop-by" has become such a pattern that it's been dubbed "Trump's Not-So-Secret Meeting Trick." Trump also uses Ivanka during public events. While giving a tax reform speech in North Dakota, Trump interrupted himself to pull Ivanka out of the audience. "By the way, Ivanka Trump? Everyone loves Ivanka Trump," he said, partway through his speech. "Come on, should I bring Ivanka up?" After Ivanka came onstage and made a few remarks, Trump told the crowd that she had requested to come on the trip. He said that she'd asked him, "Daddy, can I go with you?" and he had said, "yes, you can."

Despite these staged appearances, Ivanka has nudged her father's administration in a few small ways on women's equality, like pledging $50 million for the World Bank's Global Women's Fund and getting a very modest paid family leave provision into Trump's first budget proposal. Ivanka also seemed instrumental in getting Trump to sign two largely symbolic bills regarding women in STEM. The Promoting Women in Entrepreneurship Act encourages the National Science Foundation to support women in its entrepreneurial programs, and the INSPIRE Women Act directs NASA to help girls and women pursue aerospace careers.

Many commentators have criticized these steps, however, not just as incredibly minimal, but as strategic window dressing to cover up the massive steps that Trump has taken to roll-back women's rights, opportunities, and health and economic security. The pledge to the Global Women's Fund, for example, was dwarfed by sweeping budget cuts that the Trump Administration wanted to make to global women's health initiatives. Despite the inclusion of a modest family leave plan, Trump's first proposed budget was described as "one of the most anti-woman in years."

Trump's initial budget proposal would have cut a total of $2.2 billion in global health spending, much of which protects vulnerable women. The proposal sought to eliminate our country's current investment of $607.5 million per year in family planning support, including $524 million annually for USAID, which provides women in poor countries access to contraceptives and essential reproductive healthcare. Trump also announced that he would withhold $32.5 million that was earmarked for the United Nations Population Fund, which supports family planning and maternal health. Trump's desired cuts to aid for family planning services were estimated to result in twenty-six million fewer women and couples receiving services each year, as well as 3.3 million more abortions, eight million more unintended pregnancies, and 15,000 more maternal deaths.

One of the first things Trump did as President was to sign the Global Gag Rule. This rule cuts off all US foreign aid to organizations that inform women where they can get safe and legal reproductive health procedures. There's no evidence that the Global Gag Rule reduces the number of abortions, but it does increase the number of *unsafe* abortions, as well as limiting access to family planning resources and maternal and child healthcare. It also makes it more difficult for women to get contraception because organizations that violate the rule also lose their contraceptive supplies.

Domestically, Trump's first budget proposal sought to slash funding for women's health care and programs that support poor pregnant women and low-income mothers. The proposal included a $1.4 trillion cut to

Medicaid and the Children's Health Insurance Program, a $193 billion cut in food stamps, and $272 billion cuts to other programs for poor Americans, including children's after-school programs and support for domestic violence victims. For the first time in history, the budget singled out a health care provider by name, attempting to bar Planned Parenthood from Medicaid and other federally funded health programs for breast and cervical cancer screening, maternal and child health, infertility, Zika and HIV prevention, sexually transmitted diseases, and support for sexual assault victims and violence prevention. Women were particularly devastated by the proposed cuts to Medicaid, which provides health care for one in five women of reproductive age and covers nearly half of all childbirths in the country.

In addition to proposed budget cuts, President Trump has also restricted women's access to health care and reproductive services in other ways. In 2017, he largely eliminated the contraceptive mandate from the Affordable Care Act. The ACA had required employers to provide full insurance coverage for contraception, which enabled fifty-five million women to access contraception with no out-of-pocket costs. Nine out of ten women of reproductive age use some form of contraception during their life, often as medical treatment for conditions like endometriosis. Under Trump's rule, many employers can now opt out of the contraceptive mandate, which means that many low-wage women will lose access to affordable contraception. Dr. Haywood Brown, the President of the American Congress of Obstetricians and Gynecologists, fears that the new rule will increase unintended pregnancies, increase maternal mortality, and undermine the health and economic stability of women and their families.

President Trump also shuttered the White House Council for Women and Girls, which President Obama established in 2009 to monitor how federal initiatives affect women and girls. That made it easier for Trump to revoke President Obama's Fair Pay and Safe Workplaces executive order, which required companies with federal contracts to follow laws addressing parental leave, sex discrimination, sexual harassment, and equal pay. Yet the day before Trump signed his revocation order, Ivanka announced on Twitter that she would represent the Administration at a women's empowerment summit in Berlin.

President Trump's actions make it hard to take him seriously when he tweets that his daughter is "always pushing me to do the right thing!" The gap between Ivanka's rhetoric about her dad's support for women and Trump's conduct has generated enormous backlash. Ivanka has been charged by many critics with using "fake feminism" to deflect the harm that Trump is inflicting on women and girls. Ivanka got her first taste of this reaction when she received hisses after describing her father as a women's advocate during a G20 summit in Berlin. "Ivanka taking an interest in women's issues is fine," says writer Jessica Valenti, "but using them to cover for her father's rank bigotry is reprehensible."

Saturday Night Live took aim at Ivanka's perceived hypocrisy in a comedy sketch starring actress Scarlett Johansson as Ivanka. Scarlett's Ivanka sweeps through the room in a sparkly gown, turning heads while gliding glamorously through a fancy party. The scene is a mock ad for a pretend product: a high-end perfume with the not-so-subtle name, Complicit. The ad ends with the product's tagline: "Complicit: the fragrance for the woman who could stop all of this, but won't."

While President Trump may be the most prominent example of misusing the father-daughter relationship to undermine women's equality, politicians aren't the only ones to garner backlash for disingenuously invoking their daughters. Actor Matt Damon learned this lesson after news of the Harvey Weinstein scandal broke. In 2017, the *New York Times* and *The New Yorker* detailed allegations of Weinstein sexually assaulting women for over three decades. Damon joined other celebrities to publicly denounce Weinstein's conduct. "[E]ven before I was famous, I didn't abide by this kind of behavior," said Damon. "But now, as the father of four daughters, this is the kind of sexual predation that keeps me up at night." Twitter erupted with criticism of Damon for invoking his daughters in this way. Damon had allegedly helped quash a negative story about Weinstein's conduct in the past, which many thought had enabled Weinstein's wrongdoing. So when Damon invoked his daughters to distance himself from Weinstein, the move was viewed as hypocritical and self-serving. It felt insulting both to women and to women's genuine male allies.

Supreme Court Justice Brett Kavanaugh faced similar condemnation when his status as a dad of two daughters was invoked during his confirmation process. With an appellate court voting record that undermined women's reproductive rights and access to contraception—and while facing a serious allegation of prior sexual misconduct—highlighting stories about coaching his daughters' sports teams did not go over well.

These examples provide a cautionary note about how *not* to use father-daughter power—and about the importance of aligning words with actions. But these examples are the exception rather than the norm. As the stories in the rest of this book reveal, we are surrounded by men who have been truly inspired by their daughters to become advocates for gender equality. While having a daughter isn't the only way that men become women's allies, there's something about the relationship that has motivated many men to become supporters, advocates, and leaders in the fight for women's rights. Hopefully, their stories will inspire other dads of daughters to learn, grow, and get involved in the important work of advancing gender equality as well.

CONCLUSION

Leading for Our Daughters

There's no better gauge of social trends than Super Bowl commercials. In 2017, luxury automaker Audi of America's Super Bowl ad offered a hopeful one-minute glimpse into the potential future of gender equality. The scene followed a young girl's intense competition in a co-ed go-cart race. With each turn, bump, and skid, we hear the thoughts of the girl's father narrating her downhill dash to the finish line. He's proud, excited, and troubled. As he watches his daughter compete, he wonders how he's going to explain gender inequality to her as she gets older.

> *What do I tell my daughter? Do I tell her that her grandpa's worth more than her grandma? That her dad is worth more than her mom? Do I tell her that despite her education, her drive, her skills, her intelligence, she will automatically be valued as less than every man she ever meets?*

As the father runs to meet his daughter at the finish line to congratulate her for winning the race, his thoughts strike a more optimistic note. "Or maybe," he thinks, "I'll be able to tell her something different."

As the girl and her father drive away from the race in their shiny new Audi, the scene fades to a simple message: "Audi of America is committed to equal pay for equal work. Progress is for everyone."

This ad wasn't just an effective bit of marketing (although it did make me more likely to buy an Audi). It was also a not-so-subtle call to men to get involved in gender equality efforts. "To make good on the narrator's wish to be able to tell his daughter something different," says gender strategist Jeffery Halter, "fathers need to actively address and resolve workplace inequities for her—and all children."

Inviting men to join the fight for women's rights recently found a global platform at the United Nations with actress-turned-activist Emma Watson leading the charge. Having learned a thing or two about saving the world during her ten-year stint playing Hermione Granger in the *Harry Potter* movie series, Emma has become an influential voice for gender equality. She's earned this reputation not by organizing women, but by engaging men. In 2014, she was appointed as a Goodwill Ambassador to the United Nations where she helped launch the global UN Women campaign known as #HeForShe. In her kick-off speech, Emma shared her hope that men and women could partner in a global solidarity movement to advance gender equality. "Men," said Emma, "I would like to take this opportunity to extend your formal invitation. Gender equality is your issue, too."

While thousands of men rallied to Emma's call, many fathers of daughters lead the way by becoming outspoken supporters of #HeForShe. "I've been stunned," says Emma, "by the number of men in my life that have contacted me since my speech to tell me to keep going and that they want to make sure their daughter will still be alive in a world where women have parity, economically and politically." Ban Ki-moon, the UN's former Secretary-General, applauded the efforts of "fathers who want to raise empowered daughters" for supporting the #HeForShe initiative.

One of those fathers of daughters is Sébastien Bazin, the CEO of Accor, a global hotel group that runs 3,800 hotels across ninety-two countries. Another is Jes Staley, the CEO of Barclays, a global banking company. Another is Paul Boyle, the former President and Vice-Chancellor of the University of Leicester in England. Sébastien, Jes, and Paul were all inspired by their daughters to join #HeForShe and publicly establish goals for increasing women in leadership positions in their organizations. "As a leader, as a husband, and as a father," says Jes, "I believe that enabling true gender equality is a responsibility we all share."

Thankfully, you don't have to have to run a company to become a male ally and make a difference. As the stories and strategies in *Dads for Daughters* illustrate, all men have opportunities to support girls and women, with actions both big and small. If you're ready to get started, take a moment to join the 2.1 million other men who have signed the online #HeForShe Pledge to make your commitment official. The Pledge is a simple affirmation: "I am one of millions who believe that everyone is born free and equal. I will take action against: Gender Bias, Discrimination and Violence to bring the benefits of equality to us all."

Fathers around the globe are responding to this call to action with open hearts, open minds, and a passion fueled by their hopes for their daughters' future. As women's allies, fathers of daughters are stepping up to advance gender equality as business leaders, teachers, coaches, lawyers, judges, politicians, engineers, soldiers, athletes, and of course, in their most important role as dads. While this book applauds the extraordinary efforts by some of these dedicated dads of daughters, their biggest success will come when their efforts no longer strike us as extraordinary. Each time a daughter's father speaks up for equal pay, supports women's advancement, challenges gender stereotypes, or calls out sexual harassment, we take a step toward solidifying men's role in creating a gender-equitable world. In anticipation of a time when all men become partners in the fight for women's rights, *Dads for Daughters* celebrates the progress that's being made by members of the global Dadfly Army who battle each day to accelerate women's march toward equality.

Men and boys have much to gain by this progress as well. Advances in gender equality fuel financial gains for companies, increased health and stability for communities, and economic growth for nations. Advancing gender equality also frees up men and boys to chart their own paths as fathers, partners, and friends. As Emma Watson explained when launching #HeForShe: "I want men to take up this mantle so that their daughters, sisters, and mothers can be free from prejudice, but also so that their sons have permission to be vulnerable and human too, reclaim those parts of themselves they abandoned, and in doing so, be a more true and complete version of themselves."

Being committed to advancing gender equality begins at home with engaged parenting, including modeling the behavior that you'd like your daughters to expect and your sons to emulate. A study of fifty-three fathers who were highly involved in their daughters' lives found a range of positive ripple effects. The dads promoted gender equality by taking parental leave, sharing childcare and housework, selecting non-gendered toys and activities, using gender-neutral language, and modeling healthy relationships with women. As a result, their sons had a better understanding of how to build respectful and equitable relationships, and *all* of their kids grew up with a stronger commitment to shared parenting. That's a terrific way to build a foundation for a more equitable future while also enjoying time with your kids.

Becoming a male ally will also make you feel good about yourself and where we're headed. Research finds that fathers of daughters are happier and live longer than other parents, which means that the benefits of the father-daughter relationship go both ways. Writer and father John Gerzema shared the joy he felt from working with the UN Foundation's Girl Up Campaign, which empowers girls to become community leaders, advocates, and activists. After John spoke at the annual Girl Up Leadership Summit in Washington, DC, he was re-energized. "Spend two days with tween girls and you feel really good about our future," he said. John's daughter, Nina, was the youngest delegate at the conference, where she got inspired to start a Girl Up club at her school. When her dad peeked at her notebook from the conference on the train ride home, he couldn't stop smiling. In the margin, she had written: "girls can do anything."

Of course, the data in this book and the lessons from #MeToo remind us of how far we still need to travel to achieve an equitable world. To reach that goal, we need more men partnering with women to support gender equality in our homes, communities, workplaces, and governments. Each small step matters, and we are stronger working together than apart. So to all dads of daughters, this is your invitation to become dads *for* daughters. This is your invitation to become allies, advocates, and supporters for gender equality. This is your invitation to join women—and each other—to help create a better future for all of our daughters to rise.

Acknowledgments

Most of all, I want to thank daughters, Jordan and Alex, for the powerful influence they've had on both their dad and me. They've taught us to dream bigger, love deeper, and approach the world with more empathy. I am thankful for the support of my husband Richard who helped spark the idea for this book. I've also learned from my father Terry and my brothers, Michael and Patrick, who are also fathers of daughters.

I am immensely grateful to my phenomenal agent David Fugate of Launchbooks Literary Agency. As the dad of a daughter himself, David supported this project from the beginning. This book would not have gotten over the finish line without him.

Thanks are also due to the individuals who generously made time to share their journeys with me, including Jeffery Tobias Halter, Greg Helmstetter, Jason Kilar, Gary Krahn, Anthony Onesto, Qusi Alquarqaz, and Robin Workman. I also received incredible support, feedback, and encouragement from my friends and writing comrades Rachel Arnow-Richman, Camille Gear Rich, Tristin Green, Orly Lobel, Leticia Saucedo, and Deborah Widiss. I am also grateful to the University of San Francisco School of Law and for Lee Ryan's exceptional research support.

Notes

Introduction: Calling Dads of Daughters to Step Up for Gender Equality

Charlotte Alter, "11 Surprising Facts about Women and Poverty from the Shriver Report," *Time*, January 13, 2014.

Charlotte Andersen, "Fathers Have an Even Greater Influence on Daughters Than You May Realize," *Redbook*, August 22, 2017.

Kerstin Aumann, et al., The New Male Mystique, Families and Work Institute (2011).

Emily Bazelon, "The Place of Women on the Court," *New York Times Magazine*, July 7, 2009.

Allie Bidwell, "Women More Likely to Graduate College, But Still Earn Less than Men," *US News & World Report*, October 31, 2014.

Mireia Borrell-Porta, et al., "The 'Mighty Girl' Effect: Does Parenting Daughters Alter Attitudes Towards Gender Norms?," *Oxford Economic Papers*, no. 71 (2019): 25–46.

Tarana Burke, "#MeToo Was Started for Black and Brown Women and Girls. They're Still Being Ignored.," *Washington Post*, November 9, 2017.

Catalyst, First Step: Engaging Men (2012).

Center for American Women and Politics, Women in Congress 2017.

Nicola Davis, "Being a Father to School-Aged Daughter 'Makes Men Less Sexist,'" *The Guardian*, December 14, 2018.

Mark DeWolf, "12 Stats about Working Women," US Department of Labor Blog, March 1, 2017.

Barbara Ellen, "There's Nothing Like a Daughter to Make Dad See the World Differently," *The Guardian*, December 15, 2018.

Lídia Farré, "The Role of Men for Gender Equality (2011)," Background Paper for the World Development Report 2012.

Nolan Feeney, "Women Are Now More Likely to Have a College Degree than Men," *Time*, October 7, 2015.

Rebecca Fernandez, "John Gerzema: Co-Creator of the Athena Doctrine," johngerzema.com, June 20, 2013.

Emily Fitzgibbons Shafer and Neil Malhotra, "The Effect of a Child's Sex on Support for Traditional Gender Roles," *Social Forces*, no. 90 (2011): 209–222.

John Gerzema, Interview by Rebecca Fernandez, June 20, 2013.

John Gerzema, "The Future of Civil Rights Must Be Gender Equality," *CBS News*, July 11, 2014.

Sarah Jane Glynn, "Breadwinning Mothers are Increasingly the U.S. Norm," *Center for American Progress*, December 19, 2016.

Adam Grant, "Why So Many Men Don't Stand Up for Their Female Colleagues," *The Atlantic*, April 29, 2014.

Kathleen Mullan Harris, et al., "Paternal Involvement with Adolescents in Intact Families: The Influence of Fathers over the Life Course," *Demography*, no. 35 (May 1998): 201–216.

Institute for Women's Policy Research, Toward Our Children's Keeper (2015).

Nick Ismail, "Men vs. Women: CEOs in the Fortune 1000," *Information Age*, April 4, 2017.

Sarah Knapton, "The Mighty Girl Effect: Why Fathering a Daughter Protects Men Against Sexism," *The Telegraph*, December 14, 2018.

Michael E. Lamb, *The Role of the Father in Child Development* (2010).

Jamie Lawson, "5 Ways Fathers Influence Their Daughters," *LDS Living*, June 12, 2012.

LeanIn.org, "#MentorHer, Key Findings," https://LeanIn.org/sexual-harassment-backlash-survey-results/ (2019).

"Male Chief Executives with Daughters are More Likely to Champion Gender Diversity," *Business Day*, June 15, 2016.

Meg Meeker, *Strong Fathers, Strong Daughters: 10 Secrets Every Father Should Know* (2007).

Dominique Mosbergen, "At America's Largest Companies, Just 7 Percent of CEOs are Women," *The Huffington Post*, September 8, 2016.

National Partnership for Women and Families, Fact Sheet: America's Women and the Wage Gap (2018).

National Women's Law Center Fact Sheet, Women in the Judiciary: Still a Long Way to Go (2016).

National Women's Law Center, NWLC Resources on Poverty, Income, and Health Insurance in 2016 (2017).

Linda Nielsen, "How Dads Affect Their Daughters into Adulthood," *Institute for Family Studies*, June 3, 2014.

Andrew J. Oswald and Nattavudh Powdthavee, "Daughters and Left-Wing Voting," *The Review of Economics and Statistics*, no. 92 (2010): 213–27.

Danielle Paquette, "The Disturbing Differences in What Men Want in their Wives and their Daughters," *Washington Post*, April 27, 2015.

Plan International, "Dads Say They Want Equality for Girls this Father's Day," August 31, 2017.

Jeanine Prime and Corinne A. Moss-Racusin, "Engaging Men in Gender Initiatives: What Change Agents Need To Know," *Catalyst* (2009).

Jeanine Prime, et al., "Engaging Men in Gender Initiatives: Stacking the Deck for Success," *Catalyst* (2009).

Rebecca K. Ratner and Dale T. Miller, "The Norm of Self-Interest and Its Effects on Social Action," *Journal of Personality and Social Psychology*, no. 81 (2001): 5–13.

Sheryl Sandberg, *Lean In: Women, Work, and the Will to Lead* (2013).

Anna Sarkadi, et al., "Fathers' Involvement and Children's Developmental Outcomes: A Systematic Review of Longitudinal Studies," *Acta Paediatrica*, no. 97 (2008): 153–58.

The American Association of University Women, The Simple Truth about the Gender Pay Gap (2018).

The Shriver Report Snapshot: An Insight Into the 21st Century Man (2015).

The World Bank, World Development Report 2012: Gender Equality and Development (2011).

Rebecca L. Warner, "Does the Sex of Your Children Matter? Support for Feminism among Women and Men in the United States and Canada," *Journal of Marriage and the Family,* no. 53 (1991): 1051–56.

Rebecca L. Warner and Brent S. Steel, "Child Rearing as a Mechanism for Social Change: The Relationship of Child Gender to Parents' Commitment to Gender Equity," *Gender and Society*, no. 13 (1999): 503–17.

2020 Women on Boards, Gender Diversity Index Key Findings (2017).

Chapter 1: Building Pipelines to the Top

Charlotte Alter, "Coca-Cola Muhtar Kent: 'You Have to Be a Feminist,'" *Time*, November 20, 2015.

Tim Appelo, "The Aftermath of Hulu CEO's Bad Boy Memo," *The Hollywood Reporter*, February 18, 2011.

Stephen Bear, et al., "The Impact of Board Diversity and Gender Composition on Corporate Social Responsibility and Firm Reputation, *Journal of Business Ethics*, no. 97 (2010): 207–21.

Richard Bernardi, et al., "Does Female Representation on Boards of Directors Associate with the 'Most Ethical Companies' List?," *Corporate Reputation Review*, no. 12 (2009): 270–80.

Susan Bloch, "How to Succeed in Business: The Power of Daughters," *The Huffington Post*, July 3, 2013.

Susan Bloch, "Why We Need More Women in the Boardroom," *Huffington Post*, March 22, 2013.

Greg Bluestein, "Kasim Reed, Muhtar Kent were on Hillary Clinton's List of Potential VP Candidates," AJC.com, October 18, 2016.

Trudy Bourgeois, "Lessons from Muhtar Kent," *The Huffington Post*, August 6, 2013.

Katherine Bowers, "Men as Allies," *Working Mother*, February 17, 2016.

Nancy M. Carter and Harvey M. Wagner, "The Bottom Line: Corporate Performance and Women's Representation on Boards (2004-2008)," *Catalyst* (2011).

Claire Cohen, "Just Who are the 7 Women Bosses of the FTSE 100?," *The Telegraph*, September 20, 2016.

Credit Suisse, "Gender Diversity and Corporate Performance," July 31, 2012.

Cristina Díaz-García, et al., "Gender Diversity within R&D Teams: Its Impact on Radicalness of Innovation," *Innovation: Organization and Management*, no. 15, (2013): 149–60.

Diversity Lab, "44 Firms Pilot Mansfield Rule to Boost Diversity in Leadership Ranks," http://www.diversitylab.com/pilot-projects/mansfield-rule/.

Josh Dzieza, "Coke CEO: Promoting Women Is Good Business," *The Daily Beast*, March 9, 2012.

Janice Ellig and Carolyn Carter, "Achieving Gender Parity on Boards," *Directors & Boards*, 2019.

Gail Golden, "Men with Daughters are Fighting for Workplace Equality—Here's What it Means for Women," Code Like a Girl, June 20, 2016.

Shannon Gupta, "This Silicon Valley Exec Has Dedicated Her Career to Empowering Women. Has It Worked?," *CNN*, June 25, 2018.

Jeffery Tobias Halter, *Why Women: The Leadership Imperative to Advancing Women and Engaging Men* (2015).

Helen Weaver Heartman, "How the Coca-Cola Company Is Encouraging Women in Leadership," *Coke Solutions*, April 28, 2015.

Nick Ismail, "Men vs Women: CEOs in the Fortune 1000," *Information Age*, April 4, 2017.

Lois Joy, "Advancing Women Leaders: The Connection Between Women Board Directors and Women Corporate Officers," *Catalyst*, July 15, 2008.

Lois Joy, et al., "The Bottom Line: Corporate Performance and Women's Representation on Boards," *Catalyst*, October 15, 2007.

Muhtar Kent, "Q&A: Coca-Cola Chief Muhtar Kent," *Financial Times*, January 23, 2013.

Muhtar Kent, "This Century Goes to the Women," *The Huffington Post*, October 13, 2010.

Muhtar Kent, "Why I'm a Feminist," *Coca-Cola Journey*, March 7, 2017.

Muhtar Kent and James Quincey, "Letters from Muhtar Kent & James Quincey," *Coca-Cola Journey*, April 26, 2017.

Selin Kent, https://www.selinkent.com/pages/about-1.

Jason Kilar, Interview by Michelle Travis, September 20, 2017.

Jason Kilar, 2015 Commencement Address, UNC-Chapel Hill, May 10, 2015, https://www.youtube.com/watch?v=zLbP7WUGiB.

Jillian Kramer, "Coca-Cola CEO Muhtar Kent Says: 'You Have to Be a Feminist,'" *Glamour*, November 20, 2015.

Heather Landy, "These CEOs Made John Podesta's Purported List of Possible Running Mates for Hillary Clinton," *Quartz*, October 18, 2016.

Lean In and McKinsey & Company, Women in the Workplace (2018).

"Male Chief Executives with Daughters are More Likely to Champion Gender Diversity," *Business Day*, June 15, 2016.

Ellen McGirt, "How Lawyers are Working to Change Their Industry's Diversity Problem," *Fortune*, August 30, 2017.

Dr. Isabel Metz and Carol T. Kulik, "Champions of Change: Why Do Some CEOs Champion Gender Diversity?," *Gender, Diversity and Indigeneity*, no.4 (2016): 1–17.

Morgan Stanley, "Why it Pays to Invest in Gender Diversity," May 11, 2016.

Dominique Mosbergen, "At America's Largest Companies, Just 7 Percent of CEOs are Women," *The Huffington Post*, September 7, 2016.

Jay Moye, "Muhtar Kent Reflects on his Coca-Cola Journey and Legacy as Company's 15th Chief Executive," *Coca-Cola Journey*, May 1, 2017.

Jay Moye, "'Women Enable Success', Coke's Muhtar Kent Tells Execs," *Coca-Cola Journey*, August 1, 2013.

National Association of Convenience Stores, "The Success of Female Leaders," July 26, 2013.

Fred Paglia, Video, March 21, 2013, https://www.youtube.com/watch?v=5Iwwkh5sdcc.

Sheryl Sandberg, "Women Are Leaning In—But They Face Pushback," *Wall Street Journal*, September 27, 2016.

Nina Strochlic, "CEO Dads Want Their Daughters in the Boardroom," *The Daily Beast*, June 25, 2013.

Siri Terjesen and Val Singh, "Female Presence on Corporate Boards: A Multi-Country Study of Environmental Context," *Journal of Business Ethics*, no. 83 (2008): 55–63.

Ruth Umoh, "The Last All-Male Board on the S&P 500 Just Added a Female Member," *Forbes*, July 25, 2019.

Amy Wenk, "The Daughter of Coke CEO Muhtar Kent is Going after the Big (Read: $34B) Business of Jewelry," Bizwomen.com, November 9, 2015.

Arthur Yamamoto, "Diversity the Hard Way," Medium.com, June 13, 2018.

2016 Top Corporations for Women's Business Enterprises Award Recipients, WBENC.

2020 Women on Boards, Gender Diversity Index Key Findings (2017).

Chapter 2: Making Workplaces Work for Women

A Current Glance at Women in the Law, ABA—Commission on Women in the Profession, January 2017.

Barbara Annis and John Gray, *Work with Me: The 8 Blind Spots Between Men and Women in Business* (2013).

Adam Bain, Twitter post, @adambain, June 18, 2015, https://twitter.com/adambain/status/611613930020974592.

Subha Barry, "Working Mother's Subha Barry: 6 Ways Men Can Help Women Advance in the Workplace," *NBC News*, June 14, 2019.

Kristen Bellstrom, "You Won't Believe How Many Women in Tech Say They've Faced Sexual Harassment," *Fortune*, January 11, 2016.

Katrin Bennhold, "Another Side of #MeToo: Male Managers Fearful of Mentoring Women," *New York Times*, January 27, 2019.

Nicholas Bloom, "To Raise Productivity, Let More Employees Work from Home," *Harvard Business Review* (2014).

Mira Brancu, "A New Perspective on Mentorship in the Post-#MeToo Era," *Psychology Today*, August 11, 2019.

Kristen V. Brown, "Silicon Valley's Invisible Champion of Women," *Splinter*, August 13, 2015.

Maressa Brown, "When Dads Have Flexible Time Off to Help, New Moms Are Less Stressed and Sick," *Working Mother*, June 4, 2019.

Janet Burns, "Fenwick Study Tracks 20 Years of Gender Diversity at Top SV, S&P Firms," *Forbes*, March 10, 2017.

Sarah Green Carmichael, "When Men Mentor Women (Interview of David Smith and Brad Johnson)," *Harvard Business Review*, October 23, 2018.

Julie Carpenter, "The Crucial Role Male Mentors Can Play in the #MeToo Era," *CNN*, February 15, 2018.

Nancy Carter and Christine Silva, "Mentoring: Necessary but Insufficient for Advancement," *Catalyst*, 2010.

Champions for Change, Flexible Workplaces Toolkit, https://www.championsforchange.nz/what-we-do/promote-inclusion/flexible-workplaces-toolkit/.

Henrik Cronqvist and Frank Yu, "Shaped by Their Daughters: Executives, Female Socialization, and Corporate Social Responsibility," *Journal of Financial Economics*, no. 126 (2017): 543–62.

Jessica Deahl, "Countries around the World Beat the U.S. on Paid Parental Leave," *NPR*, October 6, 2016.

Deloitte, Parental Leave Survey (2016).

Richard Dickson, Interview by Michelle Travis, September 10, 2017.

Genevieve Douglas, "Men Just Dipping Toes in Expanding Sea of Paid Parental Leave," *Bloomberg Law*, December 21, 2018.

"Fenwick & West and Chairman Gordon Davidson Separately Honored by SCCBA for Commitment to Diversity," Press Release, December 18, 2016.

Gail Golden, "Men with Daughters are Fighting for Workplace Equality—Here's What it Means for Women," Code Like a Girl, June 20, 2016.

"Gordon Davidson Earns Watermark 'Man Who Gets It' Award," Press Release, November 14, 2016.

Gretchen Gavett, "Brave Men Take Paternity Leave," *Harvard Business Review*, July 7, 2014.

Erin Griffith, "Leadership Lessons from CEO Coach Bill Campbell," *Fortune*, July 13, 2016.

Prachi Gupta, "Men at Davos Discover New, Creative Excuse to Justify Excluding Women in the Workplace," *JEZEBEL*, January 28, 2019.

Sylvia Ann Hewlett, et al., "The Sponsor Effect: Breaking Through the Last Glass Ceiling," *Harvard Business Review Research Report*, January 12, 2011.

"Introducing the 2017 Women Leaders in Tech Law," *The Recorder*, July 28, 2017.

International Labour Organization, Maternity and Paternity at Work (2014).

W. Brad Johnson and David Smith, *Athena Rising: How and Why Men Should Mentor Women* (2018).

Shellie Karabell, "Daughters and Leadership: Influencing the CEO," *Forbes*, August 3, 2015.

Erica Keswin, "Intentional Flexibility Keeps Women in the Workforce," *Forbes*, January 30, 2018.

Julie Kratz, *One: How Male Allies Support Women for Gender Equality* (2017).

LeanIn.org, "#MentorHer," https://LeanIn.org/sexual-harassment-backlash-survey-results/.

Sharon Lerner, "The Real War on Families: Why the U.S. Needs Paid Leave Now," *In These Times*, August 18, 2015.

Josh Levs, *All In: How Our Work-First Culture Fails Dads, Families, and Businesses—And How We Can Fix It Together* (2015).

Joanne Lipman, *That's What She Said: What Men Need to Know (And Women Need to Tell Them) About Working Together* (2018).

Mindi Lowy, "Men Must Take an Active Role in Closing the Gender Gap in Corporate Leadership," *Fast Company*, July 19, 2019.

Fiona Macaulay, "The Surprising Benefits When Men Mentor Women," Inc.com, April 10, 2019.

"Male Chief Executives with Daughters are More Likely to Champion Gender Diversity," *Business Day*, June 15, 2016.

Heather Marcoux, "The 'Motherhood Penalty' Costs Working Moms

$16,000 a Year," *Motherly*, March 25, 2019.

John Markoff, "Bill Campbell, Coach of Silicon Valley Stars, Dies at 75," *Business Day*, April 18, 2016.

Nicola Middlemiss, "Why Professional Mentorships are a Problem for Many Young Women," LinkedIn, February 16, 2017.

Claire Cain Miller, "Paternity Leave: The Rewards and the Remaining Stigma," *New York Times*, November 7, 2014.

New Agency Partners, Flexible Workplaces HR Toolkit, https://newagencypartners.com/wp-content/uploads/2018/08/HR-Toolkit-Flexible-Offices.pdf.

Sara O'Brien and Laurie Segall, "Money, Power & Sexual Harassment," *CNN*, 2017.

Alexis Ohanian, "Paternity Leave Was Crucial After the Birth of My Child, and Every Father Deserves it," *New York Times*, August 12, 2019.

Lara O'Reilly, "Twitter COO Adam Bain: Companies that Focus on Gender Inclusion in the Workforce Perform Better," *Business Insider*, January 22, 2016.

Jeanine Prime and Corinne A. Moss-Racusin, "Engaging Men in Gender Initiatives: What Change Agents Need to Know," *Catalyst*, May 4, 2009.

Belle Rose Ragins and John L. Cotton, "Mentor Functions and Outcomes: A Comparison of Men and Women in Formal and Informal Mentoring Relationships," *Journal of Applied Psychology*, no. 84 (1999): 529-550.

Belle Rose Ragins and Kathy E. Kram, *The Handbook of Mentoring at Work: Theory, Research, and Practice* (2008).

Natalie Robehmed, "Amid #MeToo Backlash, Lean In's Sheryl Sandberg Launches #MentorHer Campaign," *Forbes*, February 6, 2018.

Laurie A. Rudman and Kris Mescher, "Penalizing Men Who Request a Family Leave," *Journal of Social Issues*, no. 69 (2013): 322-40.

Sheryl Sandberg, *Lean In: Women, Work, and the Will to Lead* (2013).

Sheryl Sandberg, "The Number of Men Who Are Uncomfortable Mentoring Women is Growing," *Fortune*, May 17, 2019.

Gené Teare, "In 2017, Only 17% of Startups Have a Female Founder," *TechCrunch*, April 19, 2017.

The Bar Association of San Francisco, No Glass Ceiling, https://www.sfbar.org/jdc/diversity/diversity-programs/no-glass-ceiling.aspx.

Meghan Tribe, "Study Shows Gender Diversity Varies Widely Across Practice Areas," *The American Lawyer*, April 17, 2017.

UN Women, "UN Women's HeForShe Impact CEOs from Fortune 500 Companies Reveal Gender Data," January 22, 2016.

John Veihmeyer and Lynne Doughtie, KPMG Women's Leadership Survey (2015).

Werk, "The Future is Flexible: The Importance of Flexibility in the Modern Workplace," 2019.

"What Moms Choose: The Working Mother Report," *Working Mother*, September 30, 2011.

"Workplace Loyalties Change, But the Value of Mentoring Doesn't," Wharton School of Business (podcast), May 16, 2007.

Eric Young, "Gordon Davidson Ends 18-Year Run at Fenwick & West LLP," *San Francisco Business Times*, May 3, 2013.

2018 Employee Benefits: The Evolution of Benefits, Society for Human Resource Management (2018).

Chapter 3: Welcoming Girls into STEM

Qusi Alquarqaz, "A Father's Perspective About Daughters and Engineering: Why this Parent Thinks the Field is a Great Place to Work," *The Institute*, April 7, 2016.

Catherine Ashcraft, et al., "Male Advocates and Allies: Promoting Gender Diversity in Technology Workplaces," National Center for Women and Informational Technology (2013): 1-68.

Kristen Bellstrom, "You Won't Believe How Many Women in Tech Say They've Faced Sexual Harassment," *Fortune*, January 11, 2016.

Catalyst, "Women in Science, Technology, Engineering, and Mathematics (STEM)," December 9, 2016.

Soraya Chemaly, "The Problem with a Technology Revolution Designed Primarily for Men," *Quartz*, March 16, 2016.

Kelly Couturier, "Harassment in the Tech Industry: Voices Grow on Social Media," *New York Times*, July 3, 2017.

Lauren Davidson, "Just One Percent of Parents Want Their Daughters to Be Engineers," *The Telegraph*, December 15, 2014.

Cristina Díaz-García, et al., "Gender Diversity within R&D Teams: Its Impact on Radicalness of Innovation," *Innovation: Organization and Management*, no. 15 (2013): 149-60.

Elephant in the Valley, Survey, https://www.elephantinthevalley.com/.

Ben Fischer, "The Women Software Engineers of Tomorrow Need a Hero Today—Even if it's a Cartoon," *Bizwomen*, March 13, 2014.

GoldiBlox, https://www.goldieblox.com/pages/about.

Greg Helmstetter, "A Gift to My Daughter," Code Like a Girl, June 25, 2017.

Greg Helmstetter, Interview by Michelle Travis, August 2, 2017.

Karen Horting, "What Role Do Men Play in Creating Diversity in the Workplace?," *Forbes*, November 1, 2017.

Kristin Houser, "The Tech Industry's Gender Problem Isn't Just Hurting Women," *Futurism*, January 31, 2018.

Sheelah Kolhatkar, "The Tech Industry's Gender Discrimination Problem," *The New Yorker*, November 20, 2017.

Sam Levin, "Sexism, Racism and Bullying are Driving People Out of Tech, US Study Finds," *The Guardian*, April 27, 2017.

Sam Levin, "Startup Workers See Sexual Harassment on 'Breathtaking' Scale in Silicon Valley," *The Guardian*, March 1, 2017.

Beau Lewis, "An Apology to My Future Daughter," GoldiBlox, October 28, 2013.

Marie McCausland, "It's So Damn Hard to Be a Mom in STEM and This New Attrition Stat Proves It," *Working Mother*, February 25, 2019.

Million Women Mentors, https://www.millionwomenmentors.com/about.

National Girls Collaborative Project, Statistics: State of Women and Girls in STEM (2016).

National Science Board, Science and Engineering Indicators (2016).

Anthony Onesto, "Can a Cartoon Character Change the Tech World?," TEDxYouth@Hewitt, February 24, 2017.

Anthony Onesto, Interview by Michelle Travis, August 8, 2017.

Anthony Onesto, "Interview with Anthony Onesto, Ella the Engineer—Pilot Episode, The Debrief with David Ushery," *Indiegogo* (2014).

Lara O'Reilly, "Twitter COO Adam Bain: Companies that Focus on Gender Inclusion in the Workforce Perform Better," *Business Insider*, January 22, 2016.

Emily Peck, "The Stats on Women in Tech are Actually Getting Worse," *The Huffington Post*, March 27, 2015.

Margot Peppers, "Meet Ella the Engineer! Father-of-Three Creates Female Software-Coding Cartoon to Get Young Girls Interested in Tech Careers," *Daily Mail*, March 11, 2014.

Michael Rothman, "GoldiBlox Will Be First Small Business to Have Super Bowl Ad," *ABC News*, January 31, 2014.

Schools and Closing the Gender Gap Related to STEM, http://smhp.psych.ucla.edu/pdfdocs/gengap.pdf.

Edward Stein, "Program Planning Team," CoolTechGirls, http://www.cooltechgirls.org/Team.html.

"TV Show Ella the Engineer Encouraging Young Girls to Pursue the Engineering Path," *The MakeGood*, April 2, 2014.

Joan C. Williams, et al., "Double Jeopardy?: Gender Bias Against Women of Color in Science," *Center for WorkLife Law* (2014).

Chapter 4: Confronting Gender Bias

Mahzarin R. Banaji and Anthony G. Greenwald, *Blindspot: Hidden Biases of Good People* (2013).

Kristen Bellstrom, "You Won't Believe How Many Women in Tech Say They've Faced Sexual Harassment," *Fortune*, January 11, 2016.

Mireia Borrell-Porta, et al., "The 'Mighty Girl' Effect: Does Parenting Daughters Alter Attitudes Towards Gender Norms?," *Oxford Economic Papers*, no. 71 (2019): 25-46.

Michelle J. Budig, "The Fatherhood Bonus and the Motherhood Penalty: Parenthood and the Gender Gap in Pay," *Third Way* (2014).

Patrick A. Coleman, "Fight the Wage Gap: Stop Paying Kids for Chores," *Fatherly*, August 9, 2018.

Shelley J. Correll, et al., "Getting a Job: Is There a Motherhood Penalty?," *American Journal of Sociology*, no. 112 (2007): 1297-1339.

Dads4Daighters, http://dads4daughters.com/.

Elephant in the Valley, Survey, https://www.elephantinthevally.com/.

Clarissa Farr—Our Sixth Ambassador, Look Fabulous Forever, Video, May 19, 2017, https://www.lookfabulousforever.com/blog/clarissa-farr-our-sixth-ambassador/.

Clarissa Farr, Dads4Daughters, March 13, 2017, https://www.linkedin.com/pulse/dads4daughters-clarissa-farr.

#FlipItToTestIt, https://flipittotestit.com/.

Michelle Fox, "The 'Motherhood Penalty' Is Real, and it Costs Women $16,000 a Year in Lost Wages," cnbc.com, March 25, 2019.

"Girls' Schools Encourage Fathers to Take 'Unconscious Bias' Test to Mark the First National Dads4Daughters Day," *GSA News*, March 13, 2017.

Imogen Groome, "Would You Prefer a Male Boss? Dads4Daughters Day Test Reveals if You're Comfortable with Gender Equality," *Metro*,

March 15, 2017.

Madeline E. Heilman and Julie J. Chen, "Same Behavior, Different Consequences: Reactions to Men's and Women's Altruistic Citizenship Behaviors," *Journal of Applied Psychology*, no. 90 (2005): 431-41.

LeanIn.org, "50 Ways to Fight Bias," https://LeanIn.org/50-ways-to-fight-gender-bias.

Joanne Lipman, *That's What She Said: What Men Need to Know (And Women Need to Tell Them) About Working Together* (2018).

Claire Cain Miller, "A 'Generationally Perpetuated' Pattern: Daughters Do More Chores," *New York Times*, August 8, 2018.

Claire Cain Miller, "The Motherhood Penalty vs. the Fatherhood Bonus," *New York Times*, September 6, 2014.

Anna Pujol-Mazzini, "Fathers in London's Bank District Urged to Test Sex Bias to Help Daughters," *Reuters*, March 13, 2017.

Brian A. Nosek, et al., "Pervasiveness and Correlates of Implicit Attitudes and Stereotypes," *European Review of Social Psychology*, no. 18 (2007): 36-88.

Karen Pressner, "Are You Biased? I Am.," TEDxBasel, https://flipittotestit.com/#6251ad66-0d51-4f07-942.d-67c92e7c38c4.

Kieran Snyder, "How to Get Ahead as a Woman in Tech: Interrupt Men," *Slate*, July 23, 2014.

Kieran Snyder, "The Abrasiveness Trap: High-Achieving Men and Women Are Described Differently in Reviews," *Fortune*, August 26, 2014.

Split Second Research, "Take the Dads4Daughters Test," https://splitsecondresearch.co.uk/2017/03/09/take-the-dads-for-daughters-test/.

Rhea F. Steinpreis, et al., "The Impact of Gender on the Review of Curricula Vitae of Job Applicants and Tenure Candidates: A National Empirical Study," *Sex Roles*, no. 41 (1999): 509-28.

Take the Dads4Daughters Test, http://dads4daughters.uk/what-is-dads4daughters/.

Take the Pledge, http://dads4daughters.com/take-pledge/.

"UBS Goes to the Headmistress," Finews.com, March 16, 2017.

Joan Williams and Rachel Dempsey, *What Works for Women at Work: Four Patterns Working Women Need to Know* (2018).

Mark Wilson, Aviva plc, @avivaplc, March 15, 2017, https://twitter.com/avivaplc/status/842026521325907968.

Worklife Law, "Bias Interrupters," https://biasinterrupters.org/bias-at-work/.

Chapter 5: Rethinking Masculinity

A CALL TO MEN, http://www.acalltomen.org/about-us/our-vision/.

Nancy Armour, "NFL Draft Shows Teams Still Don't Care about Domestic Abuse," *USA Today*, May 2, 2017.

Sarah Barshop, "15 NFL Players Arrested for Violence Against Women in the Last Two Years," *Sports Illustrated*, September 11, 2014.

Ines Bebea and Simone Sebastian, "For Battered NFL Wives, a Message from the Cops and the League: Keep Quiet," *Washington Post*, October 17, 2014.

Tarana Burke, "#MeToo Was Started for Black and Brown Women and Girls. They're Still Being Ignored.," *Washington Post*, November 9, 2017.

M.L. Carr and Peter Harvey, "The Ray Rice Teachable Moment: Coaching Boys into Men," *The Huffington Post*, August 8, 2014.

Stephen L. Carter, "Commentary: The NFL Has a Serious Violence Problem," *Chicago Tribune*, May 2, 2017.

Susan Chira, "Numbers Hint at Why #MeToo Took Off: The Sheer Number Who Can Say Me Too," *New York Times*, February 21, 2018.

Coaching Boys into Men, http://www.futureswithoutviolence.org/engaging-men/coaching-boys-into-men/.

Coaching Boys into Men, An Evidence-Based Dating Violence Prevention Program (2016).

Coaching Boys Into Men, Video, http://www.coachescorner.org/.

Scott Davis, "Fathers and Daughters, A CALL TO MEN," Out of the Man Box, October 24, 2017.

"Davis Participates in 'It's On Us' Rally with VP Biden at University of Illinois," Press Release, April 23, 2015.

Department of Justice, Office of Justice Programs, Bureau of Justice Statistics, National Crime Victimization Survey, 2010-2016 (2017).

Domestic Violence Statistics, https://domesticviolencestatistics.org/ (2019).

Domestic Violence Statistics and Facts, safehorizon, https://www.safehorizon.org/ (2019).

Emily Dreyfuss, "In Praise of Dadfluencers," *Wired*, June 16, 2019.

Charlotte Edmond, "Justin Trudeau Wants To Raise His Sons as

Feminists. New Research Backs Him Up," *World Economic Forum*, September 18, 2017.

Julia Fair, "Joe Biden Lady Gaga Team Up Again, Saying 'It's On Us' to Stand Up Against Sexual Assault," *USA Today*, October 26, 2017.

Chai R. Feldblum and Victoria A. Lipnic, "Select Task Force on the Study of Harassment in the Workplace," EEOC (2016).

Doug Flutie, Boys Into Men, http://www.coachescorner.org/healthy-relationships-advocates/.

Futures Without Violence, https://www.futureswithoutviolence.org/engaging-men/.

Margaret Gardiner, "Why Women Don't Report Sexual Harassment," *The Huffington Post*, July 22, 2017.

Emma Gray, "Justin Trudeau: I'll Keep Saying I'm a Feminist Until There's No Reaction," *The Huffington Post*, March 25, 2016.

Mark Greene, *Remaking Manhood: Stories from the Front Lines of Change* (2016).

Mark Greene, *The Little #MeToo Book for Men* (2018).

Barbara Bradley Hagerty, "An Epidemic of Disbelief," *The Atlantic*, July 22, 2019.

International Center for Research on Women, Leveraging Education to End Female Genital Mutilation/Cutting Worldwide (2016).

It's On Us, Take the Pledge, https://shop.itsonus.org/pages/about-us.

Paul Kivel, *Men's Work: How to Stop the Violence that Tears Our Lives Apart* (1998).

Hannah Lang, "Biden, Lady Gaga Release Sexual Assault Awareness PSA," *CNN*, October 26, 2017.

Juliet Macur, "NFL Shows it Doesn't Really Care about Domestic Violence," *New York Times*, October 21, 2016.

Allison McCann, "The NFL's Uneven History of Punishing Domestic Violence," *FiveThirtyEight*, August 28, 2014.

Claire Cain Miller, "How to Raise a Feminist Son," *New York Times*, June 2, 2017.

Kenza Moller, "This New Statistic about Sexual Assault Is So Important after #MeToo," *Romper*, January 2, 2018.

NFL Dads Dedicated to Daughters (2010).

Anna North, "Measuring #MeToo: More than 80 Percent of Women Have Been Sexually Harassed or Assaulted," *Vox*, February 21, 2018.

Stephanie Petit, "Sexual Harassment and Assault Movement Tweeted over 500,000 Times as Celebs Share Stories," *People*, October 16, 2017.

Mary Pilon, "Inside the NFL's Domestic Violence Punishment Problem," *Bleacher Report*, January 31, 2017.

Plan International, "Female Genital Mutilation," January 19, 2018.

Plan International, "Men Speak Out Against Female Genital Mutilation," February 4, 2016.

Plan International, "5 Feminist Fathers from around the World," June 12, 2017.

Elizabeth Plank, "Interview of Prime Minister Justin Trudeau," Vox Video 2016ish, March 25, 2016.

Tony Porter, *Breaking Out of the "Man Box": The Next Generation of Manhood* (2016).

Tony Porter, TEDWomen 2010, https://www.ted.com/speakers/tony_porter.

Nadja Sayej, "Interview, Alyssa Milano on the MeToo Movement: We're Not Going to Stand for It Anymore," *The Guardian*, December 1, 2017.

Jared Yates Sexton, *The Man They Wanted Me to Be: Toxic Masculinity and a Crisis of Our Own Making* (2019).

Michael David Smith, "NFL Frequently Flouts Its Own Six-Game Suspension Domestic Violence Policy," *NBC Sports*, August 11, 2017.

The Criminal Justice System: Statistics: The Vast Majority of Perpetrators Will Not Go to Jail or Prison, RAINN, 2019.

The Facts Behind the #MeToo Movement: A National Study on Sexual Harassment and Assault, February 2018.

The National Domestic Violence Hotline, https://www.thehotline.org/ (2019).

The National Intimate Partner and Sexual Violence Survey: 2010-2012 State Report, Centers for Disease Control and Prevention, April 2017.

"There are 44 NFL Players Who Have Been Accused of Sexual of Physical Assault," *Broadly*, December 8, 2015.

Claire Zillman, "A New Poll on Sexual Harassment Suggests Why 'Me Too' Went So Insanely Viral," *Fortune*, October 17, 2017.

Chapter 6: Being More Than Just a Sports Fan

Lindsey Adler, "52 NBA Players Who Make More Money than Every Player in the WNBA Combined," *BuzzFeed*, May 19, 2014.

Ella Alexander, "Andy Murray Reminds Everyone that Female Tennis Players Aren't Invisible in Clip," *Harper's Bazaar*, July 13, 2017.

Kent Babb, "Gregg Popovich Has Found the Opponent of his Life: President Trump," *Washington Post*, February 17, 2017.

"Becky Hammon, Spurs Claim Las Vegas Summer League Title," *ESPN*, July 21, 2015.

"Becky Hammon to be First Female Head Coach in Summer League," *ESPN*, July 3, 2015.

Becky's Story, Video, http://LeanIn.org/together/men.

Kathryn Bertine, ASO (Amateur Sports Organization): Allow Female Professional Cycling Teams to Race the Tour de France, Change.org.

Karen Blumenthal, *Let Me Play: The Story of Title IX—The Law that Changed the Future of Girls in America* (2005).

Danny Boyle, "Andy Murray's Wife Kim Gives Birth to their Second Daughter," *The Telegraph*, November 8, 2017.

Justin Brown, "A Family Who Cries 'Foul,'" *Christian Science Monitor*, October 24, 2001.

Scott Cacciola, "Emboldened N.B.A. Coaches Rip Donald J. Trump's Rhetoric," *New York Times*, November 12, 2016.

Hadley Catalano, "What Do Sports Teach Women for Business?," *The Glass Hammer* (2014).

Brooke de Lench, "Sports Benefit Girls in Many Ways," *Moms Team*, May 23, 2014.

Herb Dempsey, A Simple Exercise in Gender Equity: A Summary of One Parent's Concerns with the Practices of a Local School District, http://teachertech.rice.edu/Participants/mborrow/////GenderEquity/father.html.

Herb Dempsey, Interview by Lorraine Berry, "Testing Title IX: Herb Dempsey Explains Why Even the Nicest Parents File Complaints," *Athletic Search* (2000).

Ernst & Young, Women Athletes Business Network: Perspectives on Sports and Teams (2013).

Kate Fagan, "Becky Hammon was Born to Coach," *ESPN*, August 5, 2014.

Feminist Majority Foundation, Winning Title IX Cases (2014).

Go Out and Play: Youth Sports in America, Women's Sports Foundation (2008).

Tom Goldman, "40 Years On, Title IX Still Shapes Female Athletes," *NPR*, June 22, 2012.

Lizzy Goodman, "The Best Women's Soccer Team in the World Fights for Equal Pay," *New York Times*, June 10, 2019.

Jenna Goudreau, "The Secret to Being a Power Woman: Play Team Sports," *Forbes*, October 12, 2011.

Sandra Hanson, "Young Women, Sports, and Science," *Theory Into Practice*, no. 46 (2007): 155-61.

Sandra L. Hanson and Rebecca S. Kraus, "Women, Sports, and Science: Do Female Athletes Have an Advantage?," *Sociology of Education*, no. 71 (1998): 93-110.

Zach Harper, "Greg Popovich's Daughter Gave Him a Pep Talk about the NBA Finals," *CBS*, September 20, 2013.

Buck Harvey, "At Last, Summer Ending for Popovich," *San Antonio Express News*, September 19, 2013.

Greg Jayne, "Title IX Brings Out the Gadflies," *The Columbian*, October 20, 2012.

Jeffery M. Jones, "As Industry Grows, Percentage of U.S. Sports Fans Steady," *Gallup*, June 17, 2015.

Mary Jo Kane, "Progress and Inequality: Women's Sports and the Gender Gap," CEHD Vision 2020, January 27, 2017.

Ken Knutson, "Pioneering Strokes: Champion Marathon Swimmer Pushed Boundaries as a Female in Male-Dominated Sport," *The Hinsdalean*, July 26, 2012.

Rebecca Leung, "The Battle Over Title IX: Male Athletes Suing the Change the Law," *60 Minutes*, June 27, 2003.

Kayla Lombardo, "Becky Hammon will be First Woman to Serve on All-Star Coaching Staff," *Sports Illustrated*, January 29, 2016.

Diana Lustig, "Supporting Girls' Sports Nationwide Brings Equal Opportunities to Play and Excel," *Women You Should Know*, September 18, 2014.

Jennifer Matt, "The Importance of Fathers in Sports Gender Equality," *The Huffington Post*, June 18, 2016.

Madalyn Mendoza and Melissa Rohlin, "Popovich Slams Trump's 'Childishness,' 'Gratuitous Fear-Mongering,' after Political Sports

Weekend," *SFGate*, September 25, 2017.

Lorenda Naylor, "Women's World Cup Winners: Four Star Performances Deserve Four Star Pay," *The Baltimore Sun*, July 25, 2019.

NCAA, Title IX Frequently Asked Questions, http://www.ncaa.org/about/resources/inclusion/title-ix-frequently-asked-questions.

Amy Nelson, "Serena Williams, A Woman's Work and the Silence of Men," *Forbes*, September 9, 2018.

"New Nationwide Research Finds: Successful Women Business Executives Don't Just Talk a Good Game...They Play(ed) One," *PR Newswire*, February 8, 2002.

Wendy Owen, "The Man Behind Thousands of Title IX Complaints, Herb Dempsey: Q&A," *The Oregonian*, April 21, 2014.

Bill Pennington, "High School Sports: Title IX Trickles Down to Girls of Generation Z," *New York Times*, June 29, 2004.

Rokas Laurinavicius, "Andy Murray Interrupts Reporter's Sexist Question to Stop Casual Sexism, and His Interview Goes Viral," *Bored Panda*, 2017.

Terrance F. Ross, "What Gender Inequality Looks Like in Collegiate Sports," *The Atlantic*, March 18, 2015.

David Sadker, et al., *Still Failing at Fairness: How Gender Bias Cheats Girls and Boys in School and What We Can Do about It* (2009).

Rebecca Savransky, "Spurs Coach Gregg Popovich Goes after 'Embarrassing' President Trump," *The Hill*, May 14, 2017.

"Thanks for the Dadflys," *Feminist Philosophers*, June 24, 2012.

The National Women's Law Center, Check It Out: Is the Playing Field Level for Women and Girls at Your School? (2000).

U.S Department of Education, Equity in Athletics Data Analysis, https://ope.ed.gov/athletics/#/.

US Department of Education, How to File a Discrimination Complaint with the Office for Civil Rights (2010), https://www2.ed.gov/about/offices/list/ocr/docs/howto.pdf.

"U.S. Women's Team Files Wage-Discrimination Action vs. U.S. Soccer," *ESPNW*, April 1, 2016.

Julie Van de Vyver, "Gender Inequality in Sports: Who Cares?," *GroupLab*, July 22, 2013.

Anya van Wagtendonk, "U.S. Women's Soccer Team Wins Its Fourth World Cup," *Vox*, July 7, 2019.

Kelly Wallace, "The Real March Madness: When Will Women's Teams

Get Equal Buzz?," *CNN*, March 14, 2016.

Alexander Wolff, "Father Figures: A Girl's Best Friend in the Fight for Playing Time was often her Dad," *Sports Illustrated Vault*, May 7, 2012.

Women's Sports Foundation, Awards, https://www.womenssportsfoundation.org/programs/awards/.

Women's Sports Foundation, Step by Step: A Practical Guide to Assessing and Achieving Gender Equity in School Sports, https://www.womenssportsfoundation.org/athletes/for-athletes/know-your-rights/parents/step-by-step/.

Alia Wong, "Where Girls are Missing Out on High-School Sports," *The Atlantic*, June 26, 2015.

Julie Zeilinger, "5 Inequalities Female Athletes Still Face, Even If They're World Champs," *Mic*, July 7, 2015.

Dave Zirin, "U.S. Women's Soccer Is More Popular Than Men's, But the Players Are Still Paid Less," *The Nation*, April 5, 2016.

Chapter 7: Engaging Other Men

Madeline Albright, Celebrating Inspiration Luncheon with the WNBA's All-Decade Team (2006).

Rania H. Anderson, *WE: Men, Women, and the Decisive Formula for Winning at Work* (2018).

Catherine Ashcraft and Wendy DuBow, "The Tricky (and Necessary) Business of Being a Male Advocate for Gender Equality," *Fast Company*, May 28, 2015.

Elizabeth Broderick, Interview by Jackie Frank, "Frankly Speaking with Elizabeth Broderick," *Marie Claire*, August 15, 2014.

Elizabeth Broderick, "In Defence of the Male Champions of Change," *Women's Agenda*, November 25, 2014.

Elizabeth Broderick, "Male Champions of Change—Engaging Male Leaders for Gender Equality," Australian Human Rights Commission, March 11, 2014.

Elizabeth Broderick, et al., "Championing Gender Equality in Australia," McKinsey & Company, February 2015.

Emily Brooks, "Elizabeth Broderick to Take Male Champions of Change Global in UN Senior Advisor Role," *The Huffington Post*, August 3, 2016.

Catalyst, First Step: Engaging Men (2012).

Tracy Clark-Flory, "Stephen Curry Is the Woke 'Father of Daughters,'" *Jezebel*, August 27, 2018.

Stephen Curry, "This is Personal," *The Players' Tribune*, August 26, 2018.

Nancy Eisenberg, "Empathy-Related Responding and Prosocial Behaviour," in *Empathy and Fairness* (2007).

Nancy Eisenberg and Paul A. Miller, "The Relation of Empathy to Prosocial and Related Behaviors," *Psychological Bulletin*, no. 101 (1987): 91-119.

Lídia Farré, The Role of Men for Gender Equality (2011), Background Paper for the World Development Report (2012).

Father of a Daughter Initiative, http://ywomen.biz/father-of-daughter-initiative/.

Lois P. Frankel, *Nice Girls Don't Get the Corner Office: 101 Unconscious Mistakes Women Make that Sabotage Their Careers* (2010).

Lois P. Frankel, *See Jane Lead: 99 Ways for Women to Take Charge at Work* (2009).

Adam Grant, "Why So Many Men Don't Stand Up for Their Female Colleagues," *The Atlantic*, April 29, 2014.

Jeffery Tobias Halter, "Celebrating the Legacy of a Male Feminist: Dave Goldberg," *YWomen*, May 5, 2015.

Jeffery Tobias Halter, "Instead of Expecting Women in Business to Lean In, We Need Men To Stand Up for Them," *New York Daily News*, April 28, 2016.

Jeffery Tobias Halter, Interview by Michelle Travis, June 27, 2017.

Jeffery Tobias Halter, TEDx Centennial Park Women, Atlanta, Georgia (2015).

Jeffery Tobias Halter, Walmart's International Women's Day (2015).

Jeffery Tobias Halter, *Why Women: The Leadership Imperative to Advancing Women and Engaging Men* (2015).

Sally Helgesen and Marshall Goldsmith, *How Women Rise: Break the 12 Habits Holding You Back from Your Next Raise, Promotion, or Job* (2018).

Pat Heim and Susan K. Golant, *Hardball for Women* (2005).

Lance Hodgson, "The United Group of Men Helping Increase Gender Diversity," *Mentorloop*, https://mentorloop.com/men-helping-increase-gender-diversity/.

Narelle Hooper, et al, *New Women, New Men, New Economy: How Creativity, Openness, Diversity and Equity are Driving Pro$perity Now* (2016).

Kate Jenkins, "Victoria's Male Champions of Change Tackle Gender

Equality in Workplace," *Herald Sun*, October 21, 2015.

W. Brad Johnson and David Smith, *Athena Rising: How and Why Men Should Mentor Women* (2018).

Michael Kaufman, *The Time Has Come: Why Men Must Join the Gender Equality Revolution* (2019).

Katty Kay and Claire Shipman, *The Confidence Code: The Science and Art of Self-Assurance—What Women Should Know* (2014).

Catherine Keenan, "Let's Talk about Sex," *the(sydney)magazine*, March 4, 2011.

Nassim Khadem, "Accounting 100: How Women are Slowly Climbing the Ladder," *Australian Financial Review*, October 23, 2013.

Michelle King, "Nigel Barker Shares How All Men Can Be Feminist Fathers," *Forbes*, June 11, 2018.

Julie Kratz, *One: How Male Allies Support Women for Gender Equality* (2017).

Sallie Krawcheck, *Own It: The Power of Women at Work* (2017).

Joanne Lipman, *That's What She Said: What Men and Women Need to Know (and Women Need To Tell Them) About Working Together* (2018).

Male Champions of Change, "A Message from Elizabeth Broderick," http://malechampionsofchange.com/message-from-elizabeth-broderick/.

Lee E. Miller and Jessica Miller, *A Woman's Guide to Successful Negotiating: How to Convince, Collaborate, and Create Your Way to Agreement* (2010).

Michael E. Morrell, *Empathy and Democracy: Feeling, Thinking, and Deliberation* (2010).

Andrew Nimmo, "Get: Going—Male Champions of Change," *Parlour*, April 11, 2015.

Nicole Buonocore Porter, "The Blame Game: How the Rhetoric of Choice Blames the Achievement Gap on Women," *Florida International University Law Review*, no. 8 (2013): 447-68.

Jeanine Prime and Corinne A. Moss-Racusin, "Engaging Men in Gender Initiatives: What Change Agents Need to Know," *Catalyst* (2009).

Jeanine Prime, et al., "Engaging Men in Gender Initiatives: Stacking the Deck for Success," *Catalyst* (2009).

Rebecca K. Ratner and Dale T. Miller, "The Norm of Self-Interest and Its Effects on Social Action," *Journal of Personality and Social Psychology*, no. 81 (2001): 5-16.

Selena Rezvani and Lois P. Frankel, *Pushback: How Smart Women Ask—and Stand Up—for What They Want* (2012).

Raz Robinson, "Steph Curry Speaks on How He Is Raising His Daughters To Be Empowered," *Fatherly*, August 27, 2018.

Sheryl Sandberg, *Lean In: Women, Work, and the Will to Lead* (2013).

Vicki Schultz, "Telling Stories about Women and Work: Judicial Interpretations of Sex Segregation in the Workplace in Title VII Cases Raising the Lack of Interest Argument," *Harvard Law Review*, no. 103 (1990): 1749-1843.

Anna Sheffer, "Stephen Curry Wrote an Essay about Why All Men Should Care about Women's Equality—Not Just 'Fathers of Daughters,'" *HelloGiggles*, August 27, 2018.

Debra Shigley, *The Go-Getter Girl's Guide: Get What You Want in Work and Life (and Look Great While You're at It)* (2009).

TEDx Centennial Park Women, http://TEDxcentennialparkwomen.com/about-us.

Avivah Wittenberg-Cox, "Is It Ok for a Bunch of Men To Lead a 'Women in the Workforce' Initiative?," *Harvard Business Review*, February 6, 2017.

YWomen Corporate Gender Consulting, http://ywomen.biz/.

Chapter 8: Flexing Empathy Muscles

Paul Anderson and Sara Konrath, "'Why Should We Care?'—What to Do About Declining Student Empathy," *The Chronicle of Higher Education*, July 31, 2011.

Emily Bazelon, "The Place of Women on the Court," *New York Times Magazine*, July 7, 2009.

Elizabeth Bernstein, "In Two-Career Marriages, Women Still Do More of the Work at Home," *The Wall Street Journal*, September 30, 2015.

Abigail Bessler, "Even Today, Women Still Do Most of the Housework and Childcare," *ThinkProgress*, June 18, 2014.

Joan Biskupic, "Family, Justices Remember Rehnquist," *USA Today*, October 3, 2005.

Joan Biskupic, "Ginsburg: Court Needs Another Woman," *USA Today*, October 5, 2009.

Christina L. Boyd, et al., "Untangling the Causal Effects of Sex on Judging, *American Journal of Political Science*, no. 54 (2010): 389-411.

Noel Brinkerhoff, "Having a Daughter Makes Judges More Sympathetic to Women's Issues," *All Gov*, June 18, 2014.

Steven G. Calabresi, "Obama's 'Redistribution' Constitution, *Wall Street Journal*, October 28, 2008, A17.

Thomas B. Colby, "In Defense of Judicial Empathy," *Minnesota Law Review*, no. 96 (2012): 1944-2015.

Cynthia L. Cooper, "Women Supreme Court Clerks Striving for 'Commonplace,'" *Perspectives*, no. 17 (2009): 18-22.

Damozel, "Supremes Don't Care if School Officials Strip Search Your Daughter to Look for Advil," *Buck Naked Politics*, April 22, 2009.

Mark H. Davis, *Empathy: A Social Psychological Approach* (1995).

Frédérique de Vignemont and Tania Singer, "The Empathic Brain: How, When and Why?," *Trends in Cognitive Science*, no. 10 (2006): 435-41.

Tanya Edwards, "3 Must-Watch Moments from Ruth Bader Ginsburg's Awesome Interview with Katie Couric," *Glamour*, August 1, 2014.

Nancy Eisenberg, "Empathy-Related Responding and Prosocial Behaviour," *Empathy and Fairness* (2007).

Nancy Eisenberg and Paul A. Miller, "The Relation of Empathy to Prosocial and Related Behaviors," *Psychological Bulletin*, no. 101 (1987): 91-119. *Empathy and Its Development* (1987).

Lisa Evans, "Why Men with Daughters May Be the Key To Closing the Gender Wage Gap," *Fast Company*, June 30, 2014.

Rebecca Fernandez, "John Gerzema: Co-Creator of the Athena Doctrine," johngerzema.com, June 20, 2013.

Kelli K. Garcia, "The Gender Bind: Men as Inauthentic Caregivers," *Duke J. Gender Law and Policy*, no. 20 (2012): 1-43.

Major Garrett, "Obama Pushes for 'Empathetic' Supreme Court Justices," *Fox News*, May 1, 2009.

Gretchen Gavett, "Brave Men Take Paternity Leave," *Harvard Business Review*, July 7, 2014.

John Gerzema, Interview by Rebecca Fernandez, June 20, 2013.

John Gerzema, "The Future of Civil Rights Must Be Gender Equality," *CBS News*, July 11, 2014.

Ruth Bader Ginsburg, Interview by Katie Couric, https://genius.com/Ruth-bader-ginsburg-couric-interview-with-ruth-bader-ginsberg-excerpts-annotated.

Adam N. Glynn and Maya Sen, "Identifying Judicial Empathy: Does Having Daughters Cause Judges to Rule for Women's Issues?,"

American Journal of Political Science, no. 59 (2015): 37-54.

Sarah Jane Glynn, "Breadwinning Mothers are Increasingly the U.S. Norm," Center for American Progress, December 19, 2016.

Robert Gould and Harold Sigall, "The Effects of Empathy and Outcome on Attribution: An Examination of the Divergent-Perspective Hypothesis," *Journal of Experimental Social Psychology*, no. 13 (1977): 480-91.

Linda Greenhouse, *Becoming Justice Blackmun: Harry Blackmun's Supreme Court Journey* (2005).

Linda Greenhouse, "Evolving Opinions: Heartfelt Words from the Rehnquist Court," *New York Times*, July 6, 2003.

Linda Greenhouse, "William H. Rehnquist, Chief Justice of Supreme Court, Is Dead at 80," *New York Times*, September 4, 2005.

Jeffery Tobias Halter, "Gender Conversation QuickStarters. Advancing Women in the Workplace One Conversation at a Time," *YWomen*, October 16, 2018.

Jeffery Tobias Halter, "Listen—Tips To Create Male Allies, Champions and Advocates," *The Huffington Post*, September 27, 2017.

Jeffery Tobias Halter, "The 4 Things Your Company Needs To Do To Advance Women," *The Huffington Post*, December 7, 2015.

Lynne N. Henderson, "Legality and Empathy," *Michigan Law Review*, no. 85 (1987): 1574-1653.

Linda Hirshman, *Sisters in Law: How Sandra Day O'Connor and Ruth Bader Ginsburg Went to the Supreme Court and Changed the World* (2015).

Kelley Holland, "Working Moms Still Take on Bulk of Household Chores," *CNBC*, April 28, 2015.

David L. Hudson, Jr., "Court Surprises with Family Leave Act Ruling," *A.B.A. J. E-Report*, May 30, 2003.

Arianna Huffington, Review of *The Athena Doctrine*, http://www.wiley.com/WileyCDA/WileyTitle/productCd-111845295X.html.

Dawn Johnsen, "Supreme Court Breakfast Table, Entry 18: Stanching the Avalanche of Bad Law," *Slate*, June 27, 2016.

Abby Johnston, "Six Attacks on Roe v. Wade in 2016—And Exactly How to Fight Back," *Bustle*, December 9, 2016.

Richard Just, "The Empathy War," *New Republic*, July 13, 2009.

Jesse Lee, "The President's Remarks on Justice Souter," May 1, 2009, https://obamawhitehouse.archives.gov/blog/2009/05/01/presidents-remarks-justice-souter.

Josh Levs, "Dads are Stepping Up in the Fight for Caregiver Rights," *Time*, May 17, 2016.

Josh Levs, "'Primary' Caregiver Benefits Sound Gender-Neutral but Aren't," *The Atlantic*, October 1, 2015.

Adam Liptak, "Another Factor Said to Sway Judges to Rule for Women's Rights: A Daughter," *New York Times*, June 16, 2014.

Dahlia Lithwick, "History's Justice: What Rehnquist Didn't Do," *Slate*, September 4, 2005.

Dahlia Lithwick, "Search Me: The Court is Neither Hot Nor Bothered by Strip Searches," *Slate*, April 21, 2009.

Dahlia Lithwick and Sonja West, "The Unsung Empathy of Justice Stevens," *Slate*, April 9, 2010.

Frank D. LoMonte, "Safford v. Redding Analysis: High Court Surprises with Some Support for Students' Constitutional Rights," *American Constitution Society*, June 25, 2009.

Amanda Marcotte, "Even When They Don't Have Jobs, Men Do Less Housework than Women," *Slate*, June 6, 2015.

Serena Mayeri, "Constitutional Choices: Legal Feminism and the Historical Dynamics of Change," *California Law Review*, no. 92 (2004): 755-839.

Memorandum from William H. Rehnquist, Assistant Attorney General, Office of Legal Counsel, DOJ, to Leonard Garment, Special Counsel to the President (1970), reprinted in *Legal Times*, Sept. 15, 1986.

Claire Cain Miller, "Paternity Leave: The Rewards and the Remaining Stigma," *New York Times*, November 7, 2014.

Bert S. Moore, "The Origins and Development of Empathy," *Motivation & Emotion*, no. 14 (1990): 75-80.

Michael E. Morrell, *Empathy and Democracy: Feeling, Thinking, and Deliberation* (2010).

Reldan Nadler, *Leading with Emotional Intelligence: Hands-On Strategies for Building Confident and Collaborative Star Performers* (2010).

National Partnership for Women & Families Fact Sheet, A Look at the U.S. Department of Labor's 2012 Family and Medical Leave Act Employee and Worksite Surveys, February 2013.

National Women's Law Center Fact Sheet, Women in the Judiciary: Still a Long Way to Go, October 2016.

Viveca Novak, "Justice Rehnquist, Secret Feminist?," *Time*, June 1, 2003.

Todd S. Purdum, "Eulogies for Rehnquist Recall a Man of Many Interests," *New York Times*, September 8, 2005.

Dennis T. Regan and Judith Totten, "Empathy and Attribution: Turning Observers into Actors," *Journal of Personality and Social Psychology*, no. 32 (1975): 1498-1510.

Jeffrey Rosen, "Rehnquist the Great? Even Liberals May Come to Regard William Rehnquist as one of the Most Successful Chief Justices of the Century," *The Atlantic*, April 2005.

Laurie A. Rudman and Kris Mescher, "Penalizing Men Who Request a Family Leave," *Journal of Social Issues*, no. 69 (2013): 322-40.

Charlie Savage, "A Judge's View of Judging is on the Record," *New York Times*, May 14, 2009.

Reva B. Siegel, "You've Come a Long Way, Baby: Rehnquist's New Approach to Pregnancy Discrimination in Hibbs," *Stanford Law Review*, no. 58 (2006): 1871-98.

Tania Singer, "The Neuronal Basis of Empathy and Fairness," in *Empathy and Fairness* (2007).

Statement of President Obama, Press Briefing by Press Secretary Robert Gibbs, May 1, 2009.

States with Most Government Employees: Total and Per Capita Rates, governing.com (2014).

Casey C. Sullivan, "Why Is There So Little Diversity Among SCOTUS Clerks?," *FindLaw*, September 16, 2015.

Gail Sullivan, "Study: Judges with Daughters Are More Likely To Rule in Favor of Women," *Washington Post*, June 17, 2014.

"Supreme Court Chief Justice Rehnquist Dies," *New York Times*, September 3, 2005.

Testimony of Judge Alito, Confirmation Hearing on the Nomination of Samuel A. Alito, Jr. to be an Associate Justice of the Supreme Court of the United States Before the S. Comm. On the Judiciary, 109th Cong. 333, January 9-13, 2006.

Transcript of Oral Arguments in Safford Unified School District v. Redding, April 21, 2009.

Shankar Vedantam, Interview by Steve Inskeep, "Research: Children of Judges May Influence Court Decisions," *NPR*, May 28, 2014.

Linda J. Wharton, "Roe at Thirty-Six and Beyond," *William and Mary Journal of Women and the Law*, no. 15 (2009): 469-534.

Martha C. White, "Male Caregivers Face Gender Bias at Work," *Today*, February 8, 2013.

Joan C. Williams, "Hibbs as a Federalism Case; Hibbs as a Maternal Wall Case," *University of Cincinnati Law Review*, no. 73 (2004): 365-98.

Joan C. Williams, "Keynote Address: Want Gender Equality? Die Childless at Thirty," *Women's Rights Law Reporter*, no. 27 (2006): 3-16.

Joan C. Williams, et al., "Law Firms as Defendants: Family Responsibilities Discrimination in Legal Workplaces," *Pepperdine Law Review*, no. 34 (2007): 393-416.

Robin Workman, Interview by Michelle Travis, July 18, 2017.

Chapter 9: Drinking the Daughter Water

Australia's Hidden Resource: The Economic Case for Increasing Female Participation, Goldman Sachs JBWere Research Report, November 26, 2009.

Linda Babcock and Sara Laschever, *Ask For It: How Women Can Use the Power of Negotiation to Get What They Really Want* (2008).

Linda Babcock and Sara Laschever, *Women Don't Ask: Negotiation and the Gender Divide* (2003).

Linda Babcock and Sara Laschever, *Women Don't Ask: The High Cost of Avoiding Negotiation—and Positive Strategies for Change* (2007).

Yolanda Beattie, "Something in the Water? In Australia, Male CEOs with Daughters Have Smaller Gender Pay Gaps in their Companies," *Womanthology*, December 17, 2014.

Gillian Berman, "Gender Pay Gap Likely Won't Go Away Until After You Retire: Study," *The Huffington Post*, September 23, 2013.

Hannah Riley Bowles and Kathleen L. McGinn, "*Untapped Potential in the Study of Negotiation and Gender Inequality in Organizations*," *The Academy of Management Annals*, no. 2 (2008): 99-132.

Jane Bruton, "Help Close the Gender Gap for the Sake of Your Sister, Mother and Daughter," *The Telegraph*, July 3, 2014.

Michelle J. Budig, "The Fatherhood Bonus and the Motherhood Penalty: Parenthood and the Gender Gap in Pay," *Third Way*, September 2, 2014.

Campaign Brief, 300 CEOs across OZ to Receive 'Daughter Water' in New Campaign for the WGEA via DDB Sydney, September 30, 2014.

Ana R. Cardoso and Rudolf Winter-Ebmer, "Female-Led Firms and Gender Wage Policies," *Industrial and Labor Relations Review* no.

64 (2010): 143-163.

Andrew Chamberlain, "How to Analyze Your Gender Pay Gap: An Employer's Guide," *Glassdoor*, April 4, 2017.

Cody Cook, et al., "The Gender Earnings Gap in the Gig Economy: Evidence from over a Million Rideshare Drivers," The CATO Institute, June 2018.

Michael S. Dahl, et al, "Fatherhood and Managerial Style: How a Male CEO's Children Affect the Wages of His Employees," *Administrative Science Quarterly*, no. 57 (2012): 1-25.

Michael S. Dahl, et al., "Like Daughter, Like Father: How Women's Wages Change When CEOs Have Daughters" (2012).

Daughter Water, WGEA, June 9, 2015, https://www.youtube.com/watch?v=BtIrKLh7Gz0.

Lydia DePillis, "Even in the Gig Economy Women Earn Less than Men," *CNN*, July 5, 2018.

Christine Elzer, "Wheeling, Dealing, and the Glass Ceiling: Why the Gender Difference in Salary Negotiation Is Not a 'Factor Other Than Sex' Under the Equal Pay Act," *Georgetown Journal of Gender and Law*, no. 10 (2009): 1-35.

EOC, Close the Gap, https://www.closethegap.org.uk/content/resources/prepare-your-daughter.pdf.

"Equal Pay Counts: What Companies Can Do," https://LeanIn.org/what-companies-can-do-about-equal-pay.

Lisa Evans, "Why Men with Daughters May Be the Key To Closing the Gender Wage Gap," *Fast Company*, June 30, 2014.

Anne Fisher, "Pay Transparency Can Keep People from Quitting," *Fortune*, October 15, 2015.

Sylvia Fuller and Lynn Prince Cooke, "Workplace Variation in Fatherhood Wage Premiums: Do Formalization and Performance Pay Matter?," *Work, Employment and Society*, no. 32 (2018): 768-88.

Beth Gaze, "Drinking 'Daughter Water' Won't Be Enough to Deliver Pay Equity," *The Conversation*, October 8, 2014.

Grazia Equal Pay Campaign To Get Section 78 of the Equality Act Enacted—Please Sign the Petition, *womensgrid*, June 13, 2014.

Jeffery Tobias Halter, "Instead of Expecting Women in Business To Lean In, We Need Men To Stand Up for Them," *New York Daily News*, April 28, 2016.

Institute for Women's Policy Research, Fact Sheet: The Gender Wage Gap: 2018 Earnings Differences by Race and Ethnicity (2019).

Deborah M. Kolb and Judith Williams, *The Shadow Negotiation: How Women Can Master the Hidden Agendas that Determine Bargaining Success* (2000).

Deborah M. Kolb, et al., *Her Place at the Table: A Women's Guide to Negotiating Five Key Challenges to Leadership Success* (2010).

KPMG, "She's Price(d)less: The Economics of the Gender Pay Gap, Update Report Prepared for Diversity Council Australia (DCA) and the Workplace Gender Equality Agency (WGEA)," October 2016.

LeanIn.org and McKinsey & Company, Women in the Workplace (2018).

Tanza Loudenback, "More Tech Companies Have Stopped Keeping Employee Salaries Secret—and They're Seeing Results," *Business Insider*, May 3, 2017.

Heather Marcoux, "The 'Motherhood Penalty' Costs Working Moms $16,000 a Year, *Motherly*, March 25, 2019.

Claire Cain Miller, "The Motherhood Penalty vs. the Fatherhood Bonus," *New York Times*, September 6, 2014.

Lee E. Miller and Jessica Miller, *A Woman's Guide to Successful Negotiating: How to Convince, Collaborate, and Create Your Way to Agreement* (2010).

National Partnership for Women and Families, The Lifetime Wage Gap, State by State (2018).

National Women's Law Center, Fact Sheet: Equal Pay for Mothers Is Critical for Families (2019).

Ben Penn, "Gender Pay Gap Won't Close Until 2058, IWPF Projects, as Democrats Push for Law," 181 *Daily Labor Reporter*, no. 181 (2013): A-12.

Kristina Peterson, "How a Male CEO's Kids Affect His Workers' Pay," *The Wall Street Journal*, January 4, 2013.

Nicole Buonocore Porter, "The Blame Game: How the Rhetoric of Choice Blames the Achievement Gap on Women," *Florida International University Law Review*, no. 8 (2013): 447-68.

Nicole Buonocore Porter and Jessica R. Vartanian, "Debunking the Market Myth in Pay Discrimination Cases," *Georgetown Journal of Gender and Law*, no. 12 (2011): 159-211.

Gowri Ramachandran, "Pay Transparency," *Pennsylvania State Law Review*, no. 116 (2012): 1043-79.

Sheryl Sandberg, *Lean In: Women, Work, and the Will to Lead* (2013).

Tracy Saunders, "5 Ways Men Can Help Close the Gender Pay Gap," The Good Men Project, May 10, 2018.

She Works Hard for the Money: Australian Women and the Gender Divide, AMP.NATSEM Income and Wealth Report (2009).

Christopher Shea, "Male CEOs with Daughters Treat Women Better," *The Wall Street Journal*, March 3, 2011.

Jessica K. Simon and Megan McDonald Way, "Why the Gap? Determinants of Self-Employment Earnings Differentials for Male and Female Millennials in the U.S.," *Journal of Family and Economic Issues*, no. 37 (2016): 297-312.

James Steinberg, "Like Daughter, Like Father," *Columbia Business School: Ideas at Work*, February 22, 2011.

The Paycheck Fairness Act, S. 84, 113TH CONG. (2013).

Michelle A. Travis, "Disabling the Gender Pay Gap: Lessons from the Social Model of Disability," *Denver University Law Review*, no. 91 (2014): 893-923.

Urban Dictionary, http://www.urbandictionary.com/define.php?term=daughter+water.

US Bureau of Labor Statistics, Contingent and Alternative Employment Arrangements, June 7, 2018.

US Bureau of Labor Statistics, Highlights of Women's Earnings in 2016 (2017).

Mikelann R. Valterra, *Why Women Earn Less: How to Make What You're Really Worth* (2004).

WGEA, "Analyzing Gender Pay Gaps," https://www.wgea.gov.au/topics/addressing-pay-equity/analysing-gender-pay-gaps.

"What If Bottled Water Could Help CEOs Conceive a Daughter? Australia's Workplace Gender Equality Agency Creates Fake Drink to Highlight Fairer Pay," *Ad Age*, April 2, 2015.

Workplace Gender Equality Agency, https://www.wgea.gov.au/.

"Workplace Gender Equality Agency to Send 'Daughter Water' to CEOs as Part of Pay Equity Campaign," news.com.au, September 29, 2014.

Nareen Young, "Gender Pay Inequality is Still Holding Australia Back," *The Drum*, October 15, 2013.

Chapter 10: Investing in Women Entrepreneurs

American Express, The 2017 State of Women-Owned Businesses Report (2017).

Astia, http://astia.org/.

Katie Benner, "A Backlash Builds Against Sexual Harassment in Silicon Valley," *New York Times*, July 3, 2017.

Katie Benner, "Women in Start-Up World Speak Up about Harassment," *New York Times*, July 4, 2017.

Katie Benner, "Women in Tech Speak Frankly on Culture of Harassment," *New York Times*, June 30, 2017.

Mark A. Ciavarella, et al., "The Big Five and Venture Survival: Is There a Linkage?," *Journal of Business Venturing*, no. 19 (2004): 465-483.

Coca-Cola Company, 2016 Sustainability Report, *Coca-Cola Journey*, August 17, 2017.

"Despite More Women, VCs Still Mostly White Men," *The Information*, December 14, 2016.

Michael Ewans and Richard R. Townsend, "Are Early Stage Investors Biased Against Women?," *Journal of Financial Economics* (2019).

Paul A. Gompers and Sophie Q. Wang, "And the Children Shall Lead: Gender Diversity and Performance in Venture Capital," *Harvard Business School Working Paper* (2017): 17-103.

Hilal Isler, "How To Support Women Entrepreneurs," *The Huffington Post*, December 6, 2017.

Beth Jenkins, et al., "The Coca-Cola Company's 5by20 Initiative: Empowering Women Entrepreneurs Across the Value Chain," *Harvard Kennedy School*, September 2013.

April Jordin, "Meet the 5by20 Artisans, Film Profiles Women Who Make Beautiful Items from Beverage Packaging," *Coca-Cola Journey*, October 12, 2015.

Philipp Koellinger, et al., "Seeing the World with Different Eyes: Gender Differences in Perceptions and the Propensity to Start a Business," *Tinbergen Institute* (2011).

Claire Cain Miller, "Why Women Don't See Themselves as Entrepreneurs," *New York Times*, June 9, 2017.

Sara O'Brien and Laurie Segall, "Money, Power & Sexual Harassment," *CNN*, 2017.

Maria Russo, "8 Organizations that Help Women Entrepreneurs Turn their Business Ideas into Reality," *The Culture-ist*, March 9, 2012.

Peter Schulz, "Introducing the Information's Future List," *The Information*, October 6, 2016.

SCORE, https://www.score.org/.

Lucinda Shen, "Venture Capital Firms with More Teenage Daughters Perform Better," *Fortune*, May 30, 2017.

Gené Teare, "In 2017, Only 17% of Startups Have a Female Founder," *TechCrunch*, April 19, 2017.

The Start-Up Squad, https://www.thestartupsquad.com/.

Sarah Thebaud, "Why are There so Few Women Entrepreneurs?," *Newsweek*, March 9, 2015.

Brian Weisfeld, "Kindling Inspiration from My Two Daughters," TEDxLAHS, April 19, 2019.

Eilene Zimmerman, "Only 2% of Women-Owned Businesses Break the $1 Million Mark—Here's How To Be One of Them," *Forbes*, April 1, 2015.

#5by20, *Coca-Cola Journey*, http://www.coca-colacompany.com/5by20.

Chapter 11: Taking an Encore

Marci Alboher, *The Encore Career Handbook: How to Make a Living and a Difference in the Second Half of Life* (2013).

American Institute for Economic Research, New Careers for Older Workers (2015).

ASSET India Foundation, https://assetindiafoundation.org.

Nancy Collamer, *Second-Act Careers* (2013).

Nancy Collamer, "25 Questions To Help You Identify Your Ideal Second Act," https://www.mylifestylecareer.com/.

Encore.org, https://encore.org/.

Marc Freedman, *Encore: Finding Work that Matters in the Second Half of Life* (2007).

Annie Gersh, "The Spark Behind the Flame: Malala's Father," *The Huffington Post*, June 18, 2014.

Eleanor Goldberg, "Malala Yousafzai's Dad at TED2014: 'I Am Known By My Daughter And Proud Of It,'" *The Huffington Post*, March 18, 2014.

Renee Schafer Horton, "UA Dean Helps Kids Break away from India's Sex Trade," *Tuscan Citizen*, December 3, 2008.

"Is There a Gender Bias in Education?," *Learning Liftoff*, May 11, 2006.

Abdul Hai Kakar, "The Wind Beneath Her Wings: A Look At The Family Behind Malala," Radio Free Europe/Radio Liberty, November 5, 2013.

John P. Kotter, "Leading Change: Why Transformation Efforts Fail," *Harvard Business Review,* no. 60 (1995).

Gary Krahn, Interview by Michelle Travis, May 31, 2017.

Gary Krahn, "Inspiring Greatness for a Better World," La Jolla Country Day School, Video, https://www.ljcds.org/page/about.

Gary W. Krahn, "Welcome from the Head of School," La Jolla Country Day School, https://www.ljcds.org/page/about.

Richard J. Leider, *Life Reimagined: Discovering Your New Life Possibilities* (2013).

LJCDS Diversity Statement and Diversity Advocates Commitment, La Jolla Country Day School, https://www.ljcds.org/page/about/diversity.

Matthew Lynch, "Boys, Girls and K-12 Classroom Gender Bias," *The Edvocate*, March 20, 2016.

Ashley Mackin-Solomon, "Meet Gary Krahn: New La Jolla Country Day School Chief to Focus on Grooming Leaders," *La Jolla Light*, August 25, 2015.

Saima Mohsin, "Malala's Father Brings Hope of a Brighter Future for Pakistan's Women," *CNN*, October 11, 2013.

David Neilsen, "Baby Boomers: All You Ever Needed to Know," HowStuffWorks.com, June 1, 1007.

Plan International, "One-on-One with Malala's Father, Ziauddin Yousafzai" (2016).

Myra Sadker and David Sadker, *Failing at Fairness: How America's Schools Cheat Girls* (1994).

Anthony Salcito, "Courage Finds a Voice: A Conversation with Malala's Father, Ziauddin Yousafzai," *Daily Edventures*, June 18, 2015.

Stanford Center on Longevity, Study of Cognitive Benefits of Volunteering—Santa Clara County Project (2013).

John Tarnoff, *Boomer Reinvention: How to Create Your Dream Career over 50* (2017).

"The Rediff Interview with Professor Ray Umashankar," *Rediff India Abroad*, January 2, 2009.

"The Rockefeller Foundation and InnoCentive Renew Partnership Linking Non-Profit Organizations to World-Class Scientific Thinkers," *InnoCentive*, June 23, 2009.

The World Bank, Girls' Education, September 25, 2017.

Ray Umashankar, "Inspiring Youth: The ASSET Foundation, The Weight of Silence: Invisible Children of India," June 6, 2011.

UNESCO, Education for All Global Monitoring Report, Girls' Education—The Facts (2013).

Steve Vernon, "Good News for Older Workers Seeking New Careers," *CBS MoneyWatch*, April 27, 2015.

Trevor Williams, "Tech Training Empowers Indian Trafficking Victims," *Global Atlantic*, July 15, 2013.

A. Wolfe, "The Father and Daughter Saving India's Women from Sex Slavery," *takepart*, March 12, 2015.

Ziauddin Yousafzai, "My Daughter, Malala," Video, http://www.ted.com/talks/ziauddin_yousafzai_my_daughter_malala/transcript?language=en.

Chapter 12: Leveraging Political Power

American Women, https://www.americanwomen.org/about.

Mireia Borrell-Porta, et al., "The 'Mighty Girl' Effect: Does Parenting Daughters Alter Attitudes Towards Gender Norms?," *Oxford Economic Papers*, no. 71 (2019): 25-46.

Dave Boyer, "Obama Pushes To Close Gender Pay Gap—Yet He Pays Women Less Than Men," *The Washington Times*, March 20, 2014.

A.G. Cancarski, "Rick Scott Ceremonially Signs Rape Kit Testing Bill," *Florida Politics*, April 21, 2016.

Center for American Women in Politics, Summary of Women Candidates (2018).

Samantha Cooney, "Justin Trudeau Perfectly Explains Why Men Should Fight for Gender Equality," *Motto*, September 23, 2016.

Jessica Deahl, "Countries Around the World Beat the U.S. on Paid Parental Leave," *NPR, All Things Considered*, October 6, 2016.

Andrew Denny, "Fathers Will Vote for Female Political Candidates under Certain Conditions According to New Study," *Inquisitr*, November 3, 2018.

Brogan Driscoll, "9 Men Fighting for Women's Rights and Gender Equality," *The Huffington Post*, March 28, 2017.

Economic Security for Women and Families, A Conversation Guide, https://www.americanwomen.org/body/EconSecurityToolkit_National.pdf.

Charlotte Edmond, "This is How You Should Raise Your Sons, According to Research—and Justin Trudeau," *World Economic Forum*, September 18, 2017.

Lizzy Francis, "Why Fathers of Daughters Vote for Gender Equality (and Other Men Don't)," *Fatherly*, November 6, 2018.

Lawrence Goodman, "How Will Dads Vote?," *BrandeisNOW*, November 6, 2018.

"Governor Scott Signs Legislation to Eliminate Rape Kit Testing Backlog," Press Release, March 23, 2016.

Emma Gray, "Justin Trudeau: I'll Keep Saying I'm a Feminist Until There's No Reaction," *The Huffington Post,* March 25, 2016.

Jill S. Greenlee, et al., "Helping to Break the Glass Ceiling? Fathers, First Daughters, and Presidential Vote Choice in 2016," *Political Behavior*, October 31, 2018.

Jody Heymann, et al., "Contagion Nation: A Comparison of Paid Sick Day Policies in 22 Countries," Center for Economics and Policy Research (2009).

Lauren Holter, "9 Women Were Elected Governor in the 2018 Elections—Matching the Previous Record," *Bustle*, November 7, 2018.

Susan Donaldson James, "Tragedy Fuels Mental Health Parity Bill," *ABC News*, October 9, 2008.

Sean Kilpatrick, "Justin Trudeau Says Anti-Abortion Candidates Can't Run as Liberals," *National Post*, May 7, 2014.

Let Girls Learn, https://letgirlslearn.gov/.

Stephen Miller, "Pete Domenici, New Mexico's Deficit-Hawk Senator, Dies at 85," *Bloomberg Politics*, September 13, 2017.

Christin L. Munsch, "Fathers as Leaders: How CEOs' Children Affect Employee Wages," The Clayman Institute for Gender Research, January 29, 2013.

Jessica Murphy, "Trudeau Gives Canada First Cabinet with Equal Number of Men and Women," *The Guardian*, November 4, 2015.

Barack Obama, "A Letter to My Daughters," *Parade*, January 18, 2009.

Barack Obama, "Glamour Exclusive: President Barack Obama Says, 'This Is What a Feminist Looks Like,'" *Glamour*, August 4, 2016.

Barack Obama, President at Campaign Event, Hyatt Regency, Denver, Colorado, May 23, 2012.

Barack Obama, Remarks by the President at the White House Forum on Women and the Economy, April 6, 2012.

Barack Obama, Remarks by the President on Equal Pay for Equal Work via Conference Call, June 4, 2012.

Barack Obama, Remarks by the President on Raising the Minimum Wage, East Room of the White House, Washington, D.C., April 20, 2014.

Barack Obama, Remarks by the President on the Minimum Wage, Valencia College, Orlando, Florida, March 20, 2014.

Barack Obama, Remarks by the President on the 50th Anniversary of the Equal Pay Act, June 10, 2013.

Barack Obama, Statement by the President on Equal Pay, June 20, 2010.

Mark Oswald, "Team was First for Sen. Domenici," *Albuquerque Journal*, September 16, 2017.

Andrew J. Oswald and Nattavudh Powdthavee, "Daughters and Left-Wing Voting," *The Review of Economics and Statistics*, no. 92 (2010): 213-27.

Tara Palmeri, "White House Council for Women and Girls Goes Dark Under Trump," *Politico*, June 30, 2017.

President Obama Farewell Address: Full Text, *CNN*, January 11, 2017.

Race to the Top, https://obamawhitehouse.archives.gov/issues/education/k-12/race-to-the-top.

Althia Raj, "Trudeau: Gender Inequality and Extreme Poverty are Indisputably Linked," *The Huffington Post*, August 25, 2016.

Rebecca K. Ratner and Dale T. Miller, "The Norm of Self-Interest and Its Effects on Social Action," *Journal of Personality and Social Psychology*, no. 81 (2001): 5-13.

Republicans for Environmental Protection, Congressional Scorecard 2006.

Madhuri Sathish, "Justin Trudeau's 7 Most Wonderfully Feminist Moments Will Make You Love the Canadian Leader Even More," *Bustle*, August 30, 2016.

Katherine Sellgren, "Raising Girls 'Changes Fathers' Views on Gender Stereotypes," *BBC News*, December 17, 2018.

Elizabeth A. Sharrow, et al., "Here's How Female Candidates Can Sway Fathers' Votes—If Their First Child Is a Daughter," *Washington Post*, November 3, 2018.

Elizabeth A. Sharrow, et al., "The First-Daughter Effect: The Impact of Fathering Daughters on Men's Preferences for Gender-Equality Policies," *Public Opinion Quarterly*, no. 82 (2018): 493-523.

She Should Run, https://www.sheshouldrun.org/.

Deborah Sontag, "When Politics is Personal," *New York Times*, September 15, 2002.

Greg Speed, "On Father's Day, Remember the Power of Our Daughters," *The Huffington Post*, June 12, 2015.

The White House Council on Women and Girls, https://obamawhitehouse.archives.gov/administration/eop/cwg.

Jill Treanor and Graeme Wearden, "Embrace Feminism to Improve Decision-Making Says Justin Trudeau," *The Guardian*, January 22, 2016.

Justin Trudeau, Remarks at the United Nations Women's Movement HeForShe Second Anniversary, video, http://motto.time.com/4505692/justin-trudeau-un-speech-feminism/.

Jeremy Wallace, "Daughter's Experience Motivates Florida Governor Rick Scott on Rape Kit Laws," *Bradenton Herald*, April 21, 2016.

Jeremy Wallace, "Governor Rick Scott Gets Personal in Calling Attention to Backlog of Untested Rape Kits," *Miami Herald*, April 21, 2016.

Rebecca L. Warner, "Does the Sex of Your Children Matter? Support for Feminism among Women and Men in the United States and Canada," *Journal of Marriage and the Family*, no. 53 (1991): 1051-56.

Rebecca L. Warner and Brent S. Steel, "Child Rearing as a Mechanism for Social Change: The Relationship of Child Gender to Parents' Commitment to Gender Equity," *Gender and Society* no. 13 (1999): 503-17.

Ebonya L. Washington, "Female Socialization: How Daughters Affect Their Legislator Fathers' Voting on Women's Issues," *American Economic Review*, no. 98 (2008): 311-32.

Women in State Legislatures for 2019, National Conference of State Legislators (NCSL), February 14, 2019.

World Health Organization, Gender and Women's Mental Health (2017).

Joel L. Young, "Women and Mental Illness," *Psychology Today*, April 22, 2015.

Chapter 13: Misusing Father-Daughter Power

Nurith Aizenman, "Trump's Proposed Budget Would Cut $2.2 Billion From Global Health Spending," *NPR*, May 25, 2017.

Michael Blood, "Feds: Rep. Duncan Hunter Paid for Affairs with Campaign Cash," *Associated Press*, June 25, 2019.

Dan Brooks, "With DAD Act, Commander Zinke Invades the Realm of Satire," *Combatblog.net*, February 18, 2016.

Troy Carter, "Zinke Introduces Bill Requiring Women to Enter Draft," *Bozeman Daily Chronicle*, February 4, 2016.

Morgan Chalfant, "GOP Senator to Introduce Legislation Barring Women from the Draft," *The Washington Free Beacon*, February 10, 2016.

Paola Chavez, et al., "A History of the Donald Trump-Megyn Kelly Feud," *ABC News*, October 26, 2016.

Complicit—*SNL*, March 12, 2017, https://www.youtube.com/watch?v=F7o4oMKbStE.

Karoun Demirjian, "Are Women Headed for the Draft? Support for the Idea Grows in Congress," *Washington Post*, April 28, 2016.

Jeremy Diamond, "Trump Issues Defiant Apology for Lewd Remarks—Then Goes on the Attack," *CNN*, October 8, 2016.

"Donald Trump Insults Rival Carly Fiorina's Appearance," September 10, 2015, https://www.youtube.com/watch?v=xKevXvC_Eik.

"Donald Trump's Cabinet is Complete. Here's the Full List.," *New York Times*, May 11, 2017.

Cris Dosev, "Viewpoint: Don't Draft Our Daughters," *Pensacola News Journal*, May 21, 2016.

Will Drabold, "Read Ivanka Trump's Speech at the Republican Convention," *Time*, July 21, 2016.

Peggy Drexler, "Ivanka Can't Have It Both Ways," *CNN*, September 16, 2017.

Peggy Drexler, "Ivanka: Key Player or Daddy's Little Girl?," *CNN*, September 7, 2017.

Ronan Farrow, "From Aggressive Overtures to Sexual Assault: Harvey Weinstein's Accusers Tell their Stories," *The New Yorker*, October 10, 2017.

Jill Filipovic, "Ivanka Trump Has a Lot To Learn," *CNN*, June 26, 2017.

Jill Filipovic, "Ivanka Trump's Dangerous Fake Feminism," *New York Times*, January 13, 2017.

Jill Filipovic, "Melania and Ivanka's Plastic Feminism Cover Up Trump's Misogyny," *CNN*, February 23, 2017.

Rachel Giese, "The Truth about Ivanka's Trumped-Up, Me-First Feminism," *Maclean's*, February 16, 2017.

Tara Golshan, "How a Too-Clever Attempt to Oppose Women in Combat Turned into a Bill Opening the Draft to Women," *Vox*, April 28, 2016.

Debbie Gregory, "Congressmen Introduce Bill To 'Draft Our Daughters,'" *Military Connection*, February 17, 2016.

Nicola Heath, "Men Shouldn't Have to Have Daughters to Treat Women Well," *Daily*, March 31, 2019.

Barbara Hollingsworth, "Conservative Leaders Oppose Call to Require Young Women to Register for Draft," CNSnews.com, February 9, 2016.

"How a New Ethics Investigation Fits into Ryan Zinke's Other Problems," *PBS*, October 19, 2018.

Duncan Hunter, "America Needs To Debate Impact of Drafting Women into Military," *Military Times*, February 9, 2016.

"Ivanka Trump Replies on Paid Family Leave," *The Wall Street Journal*, July 4, 2017.

Laura Jarrett and Maeve Reston, "Rep. Duncan Hunter and His Wife Indicted in Use of Campaign Funds for Personal Expenses," *CNN*, August 22, 2018.

Andrew Kaczynski and Megan Apper, "Donald Trump Thinks Men Who Change Diapers Are Acting 'Like the Wife,'" *BuzzFeed*, April 24, 2016.

Jodi Kantor and Rachel Abrams, "Gwyneth Paltrow, Angelina Jolie and Others Say Weinstein Harassed Them," *New York Times*, October 10, 2017.

Jodi Kantor and Megan Twohey, "Harvey Weinstein Paid Off Sexual Harassment Accusers for Decades," *New York Times*, October 5, 2017.

Betsy Klein, "Ivanka Trump Advocates for 'Investment' in Family Leave," *CNN*, July 5, 2017.

Betsy Klein, "Ivanka Trump Supports Ending Obama-Era Equal Pay Data Collection Rule," *CNN*, September 1, 2017.

Betsy Klein, "The 'Ivanka Drop-By': Trump's Not-So-Secret Meeting Trick," *CNN*, September 7, 2017.

Tom Kludt, "McCain: I 'Might Write in Lindsay Graham' for President," *CNN*, October 11, 2016.

Gregory Korte, "Ivanka Trump Praises Saudi Arabia's Progress on Women's Rights," *USA Today*, May 21, 2017.

Gregory Korte, "Trump Pledges $50 Million for Global Women's Fund," *USA Today*, July 8, 2017.

Ariane Lange and Jaimie Etkin, "Here are the Women who Harvey Weinstein has Allegedly Sexually Harassed or Assaulted," *BuzzFeed*, October 11, 2017.

Richard Lardner, "House Committee Votes to Require Women To Register for Draft," *Associated Press*, April 28, 2016.

Hannah Levintova, "In One Executive Order, Trump Revoked Years of Workplace Protections for Women," *Mother Jones*, April 5, 2017.

Stephanie McNeal, "People are Dragging Men Who Say They Care about Rape Culture Because They Have Daughters," *BuzzFeed*, October 11, 2017.

Dan Mangan, "GOP Health-Care Bill Could Cost Women $1,000 More Per Month For 'Maternity' Insurance Coverage—and Even More When They Have Kids," *CNBC*, May 25, 2017.

Chris Marvin, "Commentary: Draft Our Daughters," *Military Times*, December 27, 2015.

Alana Moceri, "Ivanka Trump Is an Anti-Feminist in Feminist Clothing," *The Huffington Post*, April 28, 2017.

Chris Moody, "Republican Women Organize to Support Clinton," *CNN*, July 3, 2016.

Michael Nedelman, et al., "Trump Administration Deals Major Blow to Obamacare Birth Control Mandate," *CNN*, October 6, 2017.

Jay Newton-Small, "Ivanka Trump Steals the Show," *Time*, July 21, 2016.

"Obama Backs Requiring Women To Register for the Draft," *The New York Post*, December 2, 2016.

Cortney O'Brien, "Retired General: 'Don't Draft Our Daughters,'" *Townhall*, February 11, 2016.

Inae Oh, "Clinton's Newest Ad Shows Girls Looking in the Mirror while Trump Mocks Women's Appearances," *Mother Jones*, September 23, 2016.

Tara Palmeri, "White House Council for Women and Girls Goes Dark Under Trump," *Politico*, June 30, 2017.

Emily Peck, "Ivanka's Maternity Leave Plan is a Cruel Joke," *The Huffington Post*, May 23, 2017.

Emily Peck, "Playing Up Brett Kavanaugh as a Good Dad to Girls Is Shameless," *The Huffington Post*, July 11, 2018.

Lucia Peters, "27 Women Share What They Wish Their Fathers Had Known About Raising Daughters," *Bustle*, March 15, 2018.

Don Pogreba, "Ryan Zinke Gets Schooled as his Sexist Stunt Amendment Passes," *The Montana Post*, April 28, 2016.

Catherine Rampell, "How Ivanka Trump Makes Money Off Faux Feminism," *Chicago Tribune*, September 5, 2017.

Ryan Reed, "Watch John Oliver Prove Ivanka Trump, Jared Kushner Aren't White House Heroes," *Rolling Stone*, April 24, 2017.

Eliza Relman, "The 24 Women Who Have Accused Trump of Sexual Misconduct," *Business Insider*, June 21, 2019.

Remarks of Ted Cruz at a Town Hall in Peterborough, New Hampshire, February 7, 2016.

Michelle Ruiz, "The Trump Administration is Making it Harder for Women to Get Birth Control: So Where's Ivanka Now?," *Vogue*, May 30, 2017.

Eugene Scott, "Obama Signs onto Women Registering for Selective Service," *CNN*, December 2, 2016.

Eugene Scott and Betsy Klein, "German Crowd Hisses, Boos at Ivanka When She Defends her Dad," *CNN*, April 25, 2017.

Galen Sherwin and Kate Meyer, "In Trump's 'Maternity Leave' Plan, The Devil—and the Stereoptypes—are in the Details," ACLU, March 3, 2017.

Angela Simaan, "Trump's Family Leave: An Empty Envelope for American Workers," *Today's Workplace*, June 8, 2017.

Steven J. Smith and Charlotte Sun, "Retired General Revels in Success of a Daughter Who Outranks Him," *The Ledger*, July 21, 2008.

Jennifer Steinhauer, "Senate Votes to Require Women to Register for the Draft," *New York Times*, June 14, 2016.

Sophie Tatum and Allie Malloy, "Trump: Ivanka Asked, 'Daddy, Can I Go with You?'," *CNN*, September 7, 2017.

Jane C. Timm, "Trump on Hot Mic: 'When You're a Star...You Can Do Anything' to Women," *NBC News*, October 7, 2016.

Bridget Todd, "Trump Budget to Women: We Don't Care about You, Planned Parenthood," May 24, 2017.

Donald J. Trump, @realDonaldTrump, February 8, 2017, https://twitter.com/realDonaldTrump/status/829356871848951809.

Ivanka Trump, @IvankaTrump, March 26, 2017, https://twitter.com/ivankatrump/status/846171853584580608?lang=en.

"Trump Calls Clinton a 'Nasty Woman' During Final Debate," *The Guardian*, 2016.

Jessica Valenti, "Ivanka Trump Using Feminism to Cover for her Father's Bigotry is Reprehensible," *The Guardian*, March 2, 2017.

Julie Watson, "Indicted Congressman's Wife Pleads Guilty to Corruption," *Associated Press*, June 13, 2019.

Adam Withnall, "Donald Trump's Unsettling Record of Comments about His Daughter Ivanka," *Independent*, October 10, 2016.

David Wright, "Trump in 1994: 'Putting a Wife to Work Is a Very Dangerous Thing,'" *CNN*, June 2, 2016.

Caitlin Yilek, "Ivanka Trump: My Dad is 'a Feminist,'" *The Hill*, July 3, 2016.

Conclusion: Leading for Our Daughters

"AccorHotels Chairman & CEO Champions HeForShe at Davos World Economic Forum," *Hospitality Net*, February 5, 2016.

"AccorHotels Partners HeForShe, a Solidarity Movement for Gender Equality," AccorHotels, October 7, 2015.

Charlotte Alter, "Meet 10 CEOs and University Leaders Working for Gender Equality," *Time*, May 5, 2015.

Barclay's, #HeForShe, https://www.home.barclays/news/2016/03/HeforShe.html.

Alexandra Bruell, "Audi's Super Bowl Ad on Gender Pay Gap Faces Criticism," *The Wall Street Journal*, February 2, 2017.

Rebecca Fernandez, "John Gerzema: Co-Creator of the Athena Doctrine," johngerzema.com, June 20, 2013.

John Gerzema, Annual Girl Up Summit, JohnGerezema.com.

John Gerzema, Interview by Rebecca Fernandez, June 20, 2013.

John Gerzema, "The Future of Civil Rights Must Be Gender Equality," *CBS News*, July 11, 2014.

Jeffery Tobias Halter, "It's Time for Dads to Step up for our Daughters, and Audi Is Showing the Way," *The Huffington Post*, February 7, 2017.

HeForShe, http://www.heforshe.org/en.

HeForShe, "Corporate IMPACT Champion Jes Staley," http://www.heforshe.org/en/impact/jes-staley.

HeForShe, "Corporate IMPACT Champion Sébastien Bazin," http://www.heforshe.org/en/impact/sebastien-bazin.

Grazyna Jasienska, et al., "Daughters Increase Longevity of Fathers, But Daughters and Sons Equally Reduce Longevity of Mothers," *American Journal of Human Biology*, no. 18 (2006): 422-25.

Michael Kaufman, "Bringing Men into the Heart of the Gender Equality Revolution," *apolitical*, February 15, 2019.

Michael Kaufman, *The Time Has Come: Why Men Must Join the Gender Equality Revolution* (2019).

Justin Lester, "In Support of HeForShe UN Women Solidarity Movement for Gender Equality," November 25, 2015.

Office of the Secretary General's Envoy on Youth, UN Women Launches Next Phase in "HeForShe" Campaign at Davos Forum, January 28, 2015.

Emma Watson, Transcript of Emma Watson's Speech on Gender Equality at the UN, *Thoughtco.*, September 20, 2014.

UN Women Goodwill Ambassador Emma Watson Calls Out to Men and Boys to Join HeForShe Campaign, September 20, 2014.

United Nations Entity for Gender Equality and the Empowerment of Women: UN Women's HeForShe IMPACT CEOs from Fortune 500 Companies Reveal Gender Data, January 22, 2016.

"Want to Be Happy? Have Two Daughters," *The Telegraph*, April 5, 2011.

About the Author

Michelle Travis is a law professor at the University of San Francisco School of Law, where she is the Co-Director of USF's Labor and Employment Law Program. She is an expert on employment discrimination law, gender stereotypes, and work/family policy. She teaches courses on employment law and civil litigation, and she has won multiple teaching awards. She has a JD from Stanford Law School and a BA in psychology from Cornell University.

Michelle grew up in Colorado and now lives in the Bay Area with her husband, two daughters, and pet chinchilla. She is a former collegiate gymnast, a novice ballerina, and an avid non-fiction reader. Michelle has also published an award-winning children's picture book, *My Mom Has Two Jobs*, which celebrates working moms.

Mango Publishing, established in 2014, publishes an eclectic list of books by diverse authors—both new and established voices—on topics ranging from business, personal growth, women's empowerment, LGBTQ studies, health, and spirituality to history, popular culture, time management, decluttering, lifestyle, mental wellness, aging, and sustainable living. We were recently named 2019's #1 fastest growing independent publisher by *Publishers Weekly*. Our success is driven by our main goal, which is to publish high quality books that will entertain readers as well as make a positive difference in their lives.

Our readers are our most important resource; we value your input, suggestions, and ideas. We'd love to hear from you—after all, we are publishing books for you!

Please stay in touch with us and follow us at:

Facebook: Mango Publishing

Twitter: @MangoPublishing

Instagram: @MangoPublishing

LinkedIn: Mango Publishing

Pinterest: Mango Publishing

Sign up for our newsletter at www.mango.bz and receive a free book!

Join us on Mango's journey to reinvent publishing, one book at a time.